# ROBERT I. SUTTON

# *WEIRD IDEAS THAT WORK*

**HOW TO BUILD A CREATIVE COMPANY**

FREE PRESS

*New York    London    Toronto    Sydney*

FREE PRESS
A Division of Simon & Schuster, Inc.
1230 Avenue of the Americas
New York, NY 10020

Copyright © 2002 Robert I. Sutton

First Free Press trade paperback edition May 2007

FREE PRESS and colophon are trademarks
of Simon & Schuster, Inc.

For information about special discounts for bulk purchases,
please contact Simon & Schuster Special Sales:
1-800-456-6798 or business@simonandschuster.com

DESIGNED BY LISA CHOVNICK

Manufactured in the United States of America

10   9   8   7   6   5   4   3   2   1

Library of Congress Cataloging-in-Publication Data is available.

ISBN-13: 978-0-7432-1212-0
ISBN-10:  0-7432-1212-6
ISBN-13: 978-0-7432-2788-9 (pbk)
ISBN-10: 0-7432-2788-3 (pbk)

*To Annette and Lewis Sutton, for teaching me the*

*hazards of comparing myself to others and for putting up with me*

*when I was an obnoxious teenager.*

# CONTENTS

# PART I

# WHY THE WEIRD IDEAS WORK

## CHAPTER 1

# Why These Ideas Work, but Seem Weird

To invent, you need a good imagination and a pile of junk.

—*Thomas Edison*

The question is not what you look at, but what you see.

—*Henry David Thoreau*

I realized that my competition was paper, not computers.[1]

—*Jeff Hawkins, describing the key insight that led his team to design the Palm Pilot*

I ADMIT IT. I call the novel ideas in this book "weird" to get your attention. After all, unexpected, even strange, management practices are more fun and memorable than bland old ideas. But there is another reason these ideas may seem counterintuitive: To innovate, companies must do things that clash with accepted management practices, with common but misguided beliefs about the right way to manage any kind of work. In company after company, managers act as if they can keep developing new products, services, and solutions by adhering to customary ways of managing people and making decisions. This happens even in companies where managers say that innovative work requires different practices than routine work. Yet these same managers continue to use methods that force people to see old things in old ways, expecting new and profitable ideas somehow to magically appear.

Last year, for example, I had a long conversation with an executive who wanted some ideas about sparking innovation in a multibillion dollar corporation in a mature industry. I can't reveal the company, but I can tell you it was a book publisher. Profits were falling, and so was the stock price. Wall Street analysts were complaining that the company wasn't innovative enough. This executive was exasperated because her company, especially the CEO, "hates taking risks," and she believed that other senior managers wouldn't back any program that might fail or distract people in the core businesses. She especially emphasized that any program that might further reduce quarterly profits would be unacceptable, even if it had long-term benefits. The CEO and other senior executives were convinced that the business practices they were using to do the company's routine work, the things they did to make money right now, could somehow generate profitable new products and business models.

These executives were dreaming an impossible dream. To build a company where innovation is a way of life, rather than a rare accident that can't be explained or replicated, people need to discard, and often reverse, their deeply ingrained beliefs about how to treat people and make decisions. They need to follow an entirely different kind of logic to design and manage their companies, even though it may lead them to do things that some people—especially people focused on making money *right now*—find to be counterintuitive, troubling, or even downright wrong.

Trying to spark innovation with methods that actually stifle it doesn't happen just in big, old companies. Entrepreneurs start new companies partly because they are purported to be more innovative, free from the pressures in established firms to follow ingrained precedents. Yet, after coaching start-ups for over 20 years, James Robbins finds that entrepreneurs can fall prey to ingrained habits just like managers in big firms. Long before it was a fad, Robbins was creating and managing new business incubators, including an Environmental Business Cluster in San Jose and in Wuhan, China, the Software Business Cluster in San Jose, the Panasonic Incubator in Santa Clara, and the Women's Technology Cluster in San Francisco  The software Business Cluster has been especially successful since it was started in 1994. It has nurtured more than 50 new companies, which have attracted over $300 million in funding .

Robbins coaches the entrepreneurs in these incubators to build companies that generate, rather than stifle, new ideas. A sign in his office—the only sign I saw—says: The definition of insanity is doing the same thing over and over and expecting a different result. He posts it because so many entrepreneurs suffer from this kind of insanity, which makes it impossible to do anything new. These people are not crazy when they do the same thing over and over again, *but* expect to get the *same* result. That is the right way to manage routine work, to make the future a perfect imitation of the past. But repeating the same old routines again and again in pursuit of innovation is pure insanity.

Practices that are well-suited for cashing in on old, proven ways can make innovation impossible. To thrive and survive in the long term, companies must keep inventing (or at least keep uncovering) new ways of thinking and acting.

## Organizing Principles for Routine versus Innovative Work

The difference between organizing for routine versus innovative work can be seen by contrasting "cast members" at Disney theme parks with the "Imagineers" at Disney Imagineering, the company's research and development facility in Burbank, California. The job titles are revealing metaphors for the two kinds of work. Cast members in theme parks follow well-defined scripts; Imagineers dream up wild ideas about new things that guests might experience. Whether they are dressed as Cinderella or Goofy, acting as guide on the Jungle Cruise, or sweeping the streets, precise guidelines are enforced to ensure that cast members stay "in role" when they are "on stage." This is Disney's routine work. In contrast, Disney Imagineering is a place where people are expected to keep trying different things, where creativity is the goal. As one former "Imagineer" put it: "You're encouraged to come up with all these great fantasies. Most of your ideas are never executed into reality. That is frustrating sometimes, but protecting the brand, creating compelling guest experiences, and telling great stories are important. The romance is still there. Where else are you asked to come up with wacky ideas for the next great ride for Disneyland!?"

Stanford's James March expresses this difference as: *exploiting* old ideas versus *exploring* new possibilities.[2,3] Exploiting old ideas means relying on past history, well-developed procedures, and proven technologies to do things that generate money *right now.* Exploiting old ideas happens when McDonald's makes and sells a Big Mac hamburger. Billions of Big Macs have been made in the past, so unless they ask for something special, customers expect all Big Macs to look and taste the same.

McDonald's goal is to use old knowledge to make the next Big Mac exactly the same as the last one.

March points out that, in the long run, no company can survive by relying only on established and proven actions. To make money later, companies need to try new things, to *"explore"* new possibilities. This means experimenting with new procedures, hiring new kinds of people, and inventing and testing new technologies.[4] New ideas need to be invented (or imported) to satisfy customer demands, to enter new markets, to gain an advantage over competitors, or at least to keep pace. McDonald's uses some of the cash from all those Big Macs to explore new possibilities. The question is not whether McDonald's or any other company should do exploration *or* exploitation. It is silly to argue about whether a company should do only one or the other; it's like arguing over which is more important for an automobile, the engine or the transmission, or which you need more, your heart or your brain. *Both* are necessary for moving forward. The real question is what proportion of the firm's time and money should be spent on which.

Like other companies that have performed well over the long haul, McDonald's experiments with new ideas. At their Core Innovation Center near Chicago, for example, they constantly try new products, new ways of cooking old products, new ways of queuing customers, and different ways of organizing work in their fully functioning kitchens. Similar labs generate and test ideas for new products in other countries where McDonald's establishments are located. At the moment, for example, McDonald's is experimenting with a technology for cooking their famous fries in about 65 seconds rather than the current 210 seconds. And experiments don't happen just in corporate labs; the Big Mac was invented and tested in 1967 by Jim Delligatti, who operated a dozen stores in Pittsburgh. Other experiments have also been successful, like the McHuevo (poached egg hamburger) in Uruguay, Vegetable McNuggets in India, and the "Made for You" innovation in the United States, where, instead of being kept warm until it is purchased, every sandwich is quickly assembled after it is ordered. But the majority fail, like the McLean hamburger in the United States and a cheese and pickle sandwich tested in Britain called the McPloughman's.[5]

My weird ideas spark innovation because each helps companies do at least one of three things: (1) *increase variance in available knowledge,* (2) *see old things in new ways,* and (3) *break from the past.* These are the three basic organizing principles for innovative work, but as the table shows,

TABLE 1 **Basic Organizing Principles:** *Exploitation vs. Exploration*

| Exploiting Old Ways: Organizing for Routine Work | Exploring New Ways: Organizing for Innovative Work |
|---|---|
| Drive out variance | Enhance variance |
| See old things in old ways | See old things in new ways |
| Replicate the past | Break from the past |
| Goal: Make money now | Goal: Make money later |

the opposite principles are right for routine work. This contrast is not only essential for understanding where I got my weird ideas and why they work, it is also essential for understanding why so many managers unwittingly use flawed practices that fail to spark innovation.

### Variance: "A Range of Differences"

Companies where people want to do things in proven ways are wise to drive out variation. This mostly means doing old things in time-tested ways. This is why total quality management experts emphasize that driving out errors, reducing costs, and increasing efficiency of existing products and services requires driving out variation in what people and machines do.[6] This is why Intel, which has dominated the semiconductor industry largely through its manufacturing prowess, uses a technique called "Copy Exactly." When Intel managers agree that something is a good idea, there is a religious fervor about implementing it in an identical way in every Intel factory throughout the world, down to the color that things are painted. It is also why General Electric's CEO Jack Welch has made a fetish out of "six sigma," the quality control regime that aims to reduce variance down to one error in every one million repeated processes.

Driving out variation makes sense when organizations do proven things in proven ways that still work. The exact steps for manufacturing a computer chip at Intel are known in great detail, as are the steps for flying an airplane, doing simple surgical procedures like hernia repairs, or operating a ride at Disneyland. Straying from proven ways is rarely a creative act in such cases; rather, it is a sign of poor training, lack of attention, incompetence, substance abuse, or stupidity. For example, the captain of Aeroflot Flight 593 who broke the rules by giving his children a flying lesson in midflight was stupid, not creative. He first let his daughter fly the plane, then he gave his son a chance. Unfortunately, this 15-year-old boy made an error with the yoke, the plane stalled, and went into a dive that his dad could not reverse. All 75 people on board were killed.[7] When people are flying an airplane or assembling a Toyota Camry, there are enormous advantages to following proven methods. Safety is one of them! Companies that use tried-and-true methods are not only usually safer, they do things faster, cheaper, and more consistently than those that rely on new and unproven knowledge.[8]

When innovation is the goal, however, organizations need variation in what people do, think about, and produce. What might be called errors and mutations in a system meant to do old things in old ways are the lifeblood of innovation. People need to constantly find and produce new ideas, which, like mutations in plants and animals, often fail to endure and spread. The notion that diversity, new combinations, and mutations of existing forms are required for creating new forms is, of course, inspired by Darwin's theory of evolution. The biologist Stephen Jay Gould explains why amplifying, rather than dampening, variation leads to excellence in social systems, not just biological systems.

> Excellence is a range of differences, not a spot. Each location on the range can be occupied by an excellent or an inadequate representative—and we must struggle for excellence at each one of these varied locations. In a society driven, often unconsciously, to impose a uniform mediocrity upon a former richness of excellences . . . an understanding and defense of full ranges as natural reality might help stem the tide and preserve the rich raw material of any evolving system: Variation itself.[9]

Hundreds of behavioral scientists have borrowed and modified Darwin's theory of evolution.[10] One of the most robust findings in this vast literature is that variance in people, knowledge, activities, and organizational structures is crucial to creativity and innovation. Research by Dean Keith Simonton shows that the success of individual geniuses like Mozart, Shakespeare, Picasso, Einstein, and Darwin himself, is best understood from an evolutionary perspective, where excellence results from "a range of differences." These famous creators generated a wider range of ideas and completed more products than their contemporaries. They didn't succeed at a higher rate than others. They simply *did more.* So they had both more successes and more failures.[11] There are renowned geniuses who defy this trend, but they usually have less impact than their more productive counterparts. The great artist Vermeer created fewer than 50 paintings in his lifetime, all in a similar style. He achieved a singular excellence that, despite the stunning beauty of his art, adds something less than Picasso's astonishing range and history-changing influence.

Research on groups and organizations suggests that variation is just as important to collective creativity. New ideas are generated when groups and organizations have people who act and think in diverse ways, express diverse opinions, are connected to diverse knowledge networks outside the organization, and store and constantly make use of diverse technical knowledge.[12] The belief that innovation depends on a broad palette of ideas was around long before academics started studying innovation. Thomas Edison remarked that inventors need "a pile of junk." His West Orange laboratory had a "well-stocked storeroom and a collection of apparatus and equipment left over from previous experiments" that included "machine tools, chemicals, electrical equipment, loads of supplies—not only lengths of steel and pipe, but rare and exotic materials such as seahorse teeth and cow hair." This "big scrap heap" provided the raw materials that Edison and his staff used to invent new things.[13]

An evolutionary perspective means that variation is essential because, to find a few ideas that work, you need to try a lot that don't. This is why scientific research mostly consists of trying things that fail. As Susan Greenfield, a renowned British neuroscientist, put it, "Safe is a word that goes much better with sex than science."[14] A similar philosophy helps explain the success of Capital One, which has been called the the most innovative credit-card company in the world. Just a few years ago, all credit cards were pretty much the same; you could have whatever you wanted as long it cost $20 per year and had an interest rate of 19.8 percent! Capital One has been the leader in offering thousands of different credit cards, with varying rates, and limits, which are targeted at people with different beliefs, hobbies, and affiliations: "They tinkered with credit lines, mileage awards, with the design of the cards, and with the color of the envelopes of their mailings. They tried different ways of retaining customers and pursuing deadbeats. Essentially they made Capital One an endless experiment." The company tried about 45,000 experiments in the year 2000, for example. Capital One has succeeded by targeting smaller and smaller audiences for these experiments, like a "platinum MasterCard for middle-income hikers who drive Saturn automobiles." Most of these ideas fail, but the constant experimentation with one variant after another, and constant learning, are big reasons why Capital One has over 30 million credit-card accounts.[15]

The story is the same in the toy business. Brendan Boyle is founder and head of Skyline, the toy design studio at IDEO, a product design firm in Palo Alto, California. Boyle provides compelling evidence that innovative companies need a wide range of ideas and that success requires a high failure rate. Boyle and his fellow designers keep careful track of the ideas they generate in brainstorming sessions and informal conversations, and that just pop into their heads. Skyline keeps close tabs on its ideas because it sells and licenses ideas for toys that are made, distributed, and marketed by big companies like Mattel and Fisher-Price. Boyle showed me a spreadsheet indicating that in 1998 Skyline (which had fewer than 10 employees) generated about 4,000 ideas for new toys. Of these 4,000 ideas, 230 were thought to be promising enough to develop into a nice drawing or working prototype. Of these 230, 12 were ultimately sold. This "yield" rate is only about one-third of 1 percent of total ideas and 5 percent of ideas that were thought to have potential. Boyle pointed out that the success rate is probably even worse than it looks because some toys that are bought never make it to market, and of those that do, only a small percentage reap large sales and profits.[16] As Boyle says, "You can't get any good new ideas without having a lot of dumb, lousy, and crazy ones. Nobody in my business is very good at guessing which are a waste of time and which will be the next Furby."[17]

Not all innovative businesses require—or can survive—such a high failure rate. Venture capital firms have lower, but still substantial, failure rates. Between 10 percent and 30 percent of the start-up firms that receive funds from top Silicon Valley venture capitalists yield big financial returns, and the majority fail.[18] The optimal failure rate depends on the industry and technology, but all innovative firms keep importing, remembering, and trying a wide range of new things; they reach a lot of dead ends, and keep learning from their successes and failures. Variation is a hallmark of companies that are continuously creative, that keep coming up with exciting new ideas, products, and services that leave competitors running back to the drawing board to copy them, or wondering, "Why didn't I think of that?"

Another way to get varied ideas is to work with diverse people. The BrainStore is an "idea factory" in Biel, Switzerland, using a network of teenagers to generate solutions to clients' problems. Cofounder Markus

Mettler says, "We're not looking for average ideas. We're looking for crazy ideas. We use kids to find those ideas, because they know how to talk without their thinking getting in the way." Mettler's cofounder, Nadja Schnetzler, adds that the company blends "the professionalism of experts with the unbridled enthusiasm of kids." They assign 17-year-olds to work on products and advertising campaigns for companies like Nestlé and the Swiss Railway. By mixing the ideas of experts and novices, of young and old people, this company increases the diversity of solutions that can be generated for clients.[19]

Any group can spark innovation by broadening "the range of differences." This first organizing principle is part of many quality programs, especially in brainstorming sessions and experiments used by quality-improvement teams.[20] Even when companies want new ideas about how to drive out variation in established processes like manufacturing cars and running hotels, they *increase variance* in the ideas generated, considered, and tested. Most work involves some blend of routine and innovative tasks; the weird ideas in this book are meant to help people, teams, and companies better understand the difference and do a better job of switching between the two kinds of work.

As I show in the next chapter, creative firms don't just have diverse knowledge, but they keep trying to find different uses for it and trying to combine it in new ways. That's one of the main reasons my 11½ weird ideas work; each of these counterintuitive practices brings a broader range of ideas into a company.

### *Vu ja de:* Seeing Old Things in New Ways

The second organizing principle is seeing the same old thing in new ways, or the *"vu ja de"* (pronounced "voo-zha-day") mentality. If *déjà vu* is the feeling that you have had an experience before even though it is brand new, then *vu ja de* is what happens when you feel and act as if an experience (or an object) is brand-new even if you have had it (or seen it) hundreds of times.

The *vu ja de* mentality is not always a good thing. It can be a disaster when, as the result of stress, confusion, poor training, or sheer incompetence, proven techniques are forgotten when the stakes are high. Organizational theorist Karl Weick uses the term *vu ja de* in this pejorative way.[21] He shows how a group of 19 experienced smoke jumpers (firefighters who parachute into remote areas) responded to the stress of a fast-moving fire in Mann Gulch, Montana, by forgetting what they knew. These skilled and experienced smoke jumpers were so distressed by their group's disorganization and the threat of death that they acted as if "I've never been here before, I have no idea where I am, and I have no idea who can help me."[22] Thirteen of them died. But Weick's example is a case where mostly routine work was needed, not innovation.

The very thing that can kill a smoke jumper, or an airplane pilot, can save a worker who needs to be innovative. The *vu ja de* mentality can breed learning and creativity. I first heard the term in the 1980s from Jeff Miller, who has won numerous sailing championships. Miller argued that great sailors have a *vu ja de* mentality where "the same old stuff seems brand new" because it enables "you to keep learning small lessons from every race" and it "keeps you excited about the sport." Jeff's funny and insightful comment made me realize that innovative people and companies have this same ability. They can keep looking at the same thing but keep changing which aspects they think about and which they ignore.

Miller also has a Ph.D. in biochemistry. Perhaps he is taking a cue from Nobel Prize–winning biochemist Albert Szent-Gyorgi, the first scientist to isolate Vitamin C, who said: "Discovery consists of looking at the same thing as everyone else and thinking something different."[23] Statistician Abraham Wald's research on where to put extra armor on warplanes during World War II is a wonderful example. The British and U.S. air forces were concerned because many of their planes were being shot down. They wanted to use more armor, but were not quite sure where to put it. Wald put a mark on every bullet hole in the airplanes that *returned from battle.* He found that two major sections of the fuselage—one between the wings and the other between the tails—had far fewer bullet holes. He decided to put the armor in these places, where he saw fewer, not more, holes. Why? Because it stood to reason that the planes were hit randomly. The planes he analyzed had not been shot down! So it was the holes he *wasn't seeing*—in the planes that *weren't returning*—that needed extra protection.

A similar kind of *vu ja de* mentality is seen in innovative high-technology firms. Bill Joy is Sun Microsystems' resident technical genius. Joy was one of the primary designers of the UNIX operating system and of some of the most crucial chip sets in Sun's microprocessors, and other advances that enabled the Internet to reach its current technical sophistication. Joy has been hailed as "the smartest man in Silicon Valley" (although he lives in Colorado!) and the "Edison of the Internet." He is famous for seeing technical problems in a different light than others, for his "late-night programming epiphanies, way-outside-of-the-box thinking, and uncanny technical clairvoyance." This goes back to his student days. Most students look for Ph.D. programs that have the best possible equipment, especially in technical fields like computer science. In contrast, Joy reports, "I went to Berkeley [rather than Caltech or Stanford] because it had the worst computer facilities of the three. I figured it would force me to be more ingenious."[24]

*Vu ja de* can also be a cultural characteristic of groups and companies. People can learn the *vu ja de* mentality; they don't have to be born with it. For example, although well past his 80th birthday, Ettore Sottsass remains one of the most famous and prolific of Italian designers. Sottsass rose to fame as an industrial designer for Italian firms, including Olivetti and Alessi, as well as a sculptor and photographer, and is a founding member of the Memphis Design Group. In 1980, he and several young designers formed Sottsass Associates in Milan, Italy. They have taken a radical approach to designing everything from an electronic telephone directory and a golf club and resort in China, to robots, the interior of an airport in Milan, televisions, telephones, prefabricated windows, and the interior of a New York City apartment. The hallmark of their philosophy is that, while most modern designs are meant to be bland and rational, to be functional without being noticed, the things we use and see in modern life should provoke strong feelings. Their view is that a strong reaction, even if it is negative, is far better than none at all, that it is better to feel alive than numb and lifeless.

Sottsass Associates uses unusual colors, shapes, and sizes to jar people out of the numbness of modern life. Sottsass teaches his colleagues to see things differently by using his own work as a source of inspiration, like the much-talked-about and commercially successful "Valentine" portable typewriter he designed for Olivetti in 1969, which was the color of bright red lipstick. Sottsass also gives explicit guidance, for example, by suggesting that his colleagues' designs "look stranger," by using colors and shapes that provoke discomfort rather than contentment.[25]

The *vu ja de* attitude is also evident at BrightHouse, an "ideation company" that charges clients like Coca-Cola, Hardee's, and Georgia Pacific $500,000 to $1,000,000 for a single idea. Founder Joey Reiman rejects the taken-for-granted assumption that doing things faster is always better. He brags that BrightHouse does "business at the speed of molasses." He emphasizes that you can't rush great ideas. "I tell our clients that we're the slowest company they'll ever meet—and that we're the most expensive." BrightHouse works on only one idea at a time, with everyone in the small company (about 20 people) devoting two to three months to creative approaches for the single client they are serving. Reiman developed this way of working after running a conventional advertising firm for many years, which led him to believe that most of the work done was so rushed and there were so many different clients to keep happy that creativity was stifled. BrightHouse has had impressive results. Reiman and his team helped the giant fragrance house Coty Inc. to create "ghost myst," the first perfume to embrace values and spirituality ("inner beauty" rather than physical beauty) as the focus of its market positioning. Ghost myst became the best-selling fragrance of 1995, and it launched a spirituality-in-beauty movement that many other fragrance and cosmetics companies have rushed to join. BrightHouse's competitive advantage is that they are a thoughtful tortoise in a world filled with speedy hares. When you move more slowly than everyone else, the same old things look different to you, and you can think about them in different ways.[26]

No matter how it is accomplished, the *vu ja de* mentality is the ability to keep shifting opinion and perception. It means shifting our focus from objects or patterns that are in the foreground to those in the background, between what psychologists call "figure" versus "ground." It means thinking of things that are usually assumed to be negative as positive, and vice versa. It can mean reversing assumptions about cause and effect, or what matters most versus least. It means not traveling through life on automatic pilot. Many of the weird ideas in this book are about how to make the *vu ja de* mentality a way of life in a company.

### Breaking from the Past

There is a lot of hype in the business press about the dangers of clinging to the past, and much of it is justified. But all the excitement about building better products and companies can make us forget that most new ideas are bad and most old ideas are good. After all, that is what Darwinism predicts. The death rate of new products and companies is dramatically higher than old ones. Dozens of new breakfast cereals fail every year, while Cheerios and Wheaties persist. Hundreds of new toys are introduced every year, yet most are flops. Even toys that are wildly popular for a while, like the Furby or Beanie Babies, fade from the scene, while Play-

Doh persists. If there was truth in advertising, the slogan "innovate or die" would be replaced with "innovate and die." Tried and true wins out over new and improved most of the time.

My aim is *not* to convince you to discard every routine your company uses and to devote all efforts to inventing new ways of thinking and acting. On the contrary; doing routine work with proven methods is the right thing to do most of the time. It is wise to manage much of the time as if the future will be a perfect imitation of the past. Hospitals want surgical residents to perform operations exactly like their experienced mentors. Airlines want new pilots to fly a 747 just like the experienced pilots who came before them. McDonald's wants each new trainee to make every Big Mac just as it has always been done.

Does this mean that you should stop trying to innovate? Not at all. The problem is that the world does change, new technologies are developed, competitors come up with superior products and services, and consumer preferences change. These are the times and places when innovation is crucial, when the ideas in this book can help you and your company. Many companies have made a lot of money by creating new and better futures. So, although it usually entails a high failure rate and a lot of resources, every company—or at least part of it—needs to keep trying to discard old ways and replace them with better new ways.

For example, tea bags had *always* been square since they had been introduced in 1951 to British consumers; no one ever thought of changing the shape. Then, in 1985, Lyons Tetley, one of the leading makers of tea bags in the United Kingdom, began doing research on consumer reaction to round tea bags. Research by Tetley's marketing research firm, Mass Observation, showed that group after group of consumers had a strong preference for the round bags. After an initial marketing blitz in the south of England, Tetley went national with its round bags in January of 1990. Tetley's share of the English tea market rose from 15 percent to 20 percent, slightly behind PG Tips.[27] Not to be outdone, PG Tips launched its own, highly secretive efforts to develop tea bags in a new shape. The result was the PG Tips Pyramid tea bag, which has a 3-D shape that is said to mirror the brewing process in a teapot and to make the brewing process faster than the traditional square (or less traditional round) tea bag. PG Tips introduced their new bag in 1996 and soon reported that sales of Pyramid tea bags had eclipsed Tetley's round bag in many regions.[28] The shape of tea bags didn't change for 34 years until these researchers saw the same old thing in a new way—*vu ja de!*

Young industries and companies can cling to the past just as tightly as old ones. People form vehement beliefs quickly, often on the basis of flimsy or flawed evidence. Worse yet, once most people start acting in a certain way—often without even realizing it—they persist even when presented with evidence that what they are doing is ineffective. This pattern, which psychologists call mindless behavior, happens to companies as a whole.[29] Before the Palm Pilot was invented, for example, product after product developed in the hand-held computer industry failed. Palm Computing, along with half a dozen other companies including Apple, Slate, Go, and Sharp, introduced failed hand-held computers in the 1990s. Palm's first product was called the Zoomer. It was crammed with features just like its competitors'. Palm's competitors responded to slow sales by developing hand-held devices that had even more features, that were more like customers' personal computers. They clung tightly to their ingrained belief that customers wanted an imitation of their personal computers, with as many of the same features as possible. In contrast, after talking to customers, Palm's Jeff Hawkins decided that his industry was operating under a flawed assumption. He realized that "my competition was paper, not computers."[30] The rest is history. By seeing the same problem in a new way, Palm was able to discard flawed beliefs and invent one of the best-selling consumer electronics products of all time.

To break from the past, a company needs varied ideas and *vu ja de,* which provide the raw material and right attitude. But that is just part of the story. As you will see, my weird ideas help companies break from the past through other means as well.

## The Weird Ideas

Table 2 shows 12 (really, 11½) pairs of contrasting practices: The left side lists familiar and conventional management practices for hiring and managing people, making decisions, dealing with the past, and interacting with outsiders. These practices help companies do routine work by driving out variance, seeing old things in old ways, and replicating the past. You probably aren't surprised, and may be bored, by recommendations that companies should hire people they need, use old-timers to indoctrinate newcomers, reward success and punish failure, think of some practical things and plan to do them, replicate past successes, and so on.

Things get more interesting, however, when you realize that these practices—most of which are widely accepted as right for managing any

TABLE 2 **Management Practices That Work:**
*Organizing for Exploitation vs. Exploration*

| **Exploiting Old Ways:** Conventional Ideas That Work | **Exploring New Ways:** Weird Ideas That Work |
|---|---|
| 1. Hire "fast learners" (of the organizational code) | 1. Hire "slow learners" (of the organizational code) |
| 1½. Hire people who make you feel comfortable, whom you like | 1½. Hire people who make you uncomfortable, even those you dislike |
| 2. Hire people you (probably) do need | 2. Hire people you (probably) *don't* need. |
| 3. Use job interviews to screen and, especially, to recruit new employees | 3. Use job interviews to get ideas, not to screen candidates |
| 4. Encourage people to pay attention to and obey their bosses and peers | 4. Encourage people to ignore and defy superiors and peers |
| 5. Find some happy people, and make sure they don't fight | 5. Find some happy people, and get them to fight |
| 6. Reward success, punish failure and inaction | 6. Reward success and failure, punish inaction |
| 7. Decide to do something that will probably succeed, then convince yourself and everyone else that success is certain | 7. Decide to do something that will probably fail, then convince yourself and everyone else that success is certain |
| 8. Think of some sound or practical things to do, and plan to do them | 8. Think of some ridiculous or impractical things to do, then plan to do them |
| 9. Seek out and be attentive to people who will evaluate and endorse the work | 9. Avoid, distract, and bore customers, critics, and anyone who just wants to talk about money |
| 10. Learn everything you can from people who seem to have solved the problems you face | 10. Don't try to learn *anything* from people who say they have solved the problems you face |
| 11. Remember and replicate your company's past successes | 11. Forget the past, especially your company's successes |
| Summary: Efficiency indicates effectiveness in the implementation and use of proven ideas | Summary: Creative companies and teams are inefficient (and often annoying) places to work |

kind of work—are drastically different from my 11½ weird ideas for sparking innovation (on the right-hand side of the table). Indeed, most are the exact opposite of practices that are well suited for routine work. These weird ideas work because they help increase variance in knowledge, help people see old things in new ways, and help companies break from the past. These weird ideas also work because each is grounded in sound academic theory and research. I combed through existing academic writings to support (and refute) my emerging ideas, to get inspiration for more ideas, and to make them more powerful to use and more fun to talk about. I also did original research on these weird ideas, and talked about them constantly with students and colleagues at Stanford University and elsewhere.

But that wasn't enough. I wanted to develop ideas that people could actually use. So I picked weird ideas for this book that had actually been used, in some form, by real companies. I also gave ever-changing versions of my "Weird Ideas Talk" to over a hundred groups of senior executives, managers, engineers, scientists, lawyers, and other professionals during the last decade. I goaded each group to argue with me about the ideas and point out flaws. They offered constructive criticism, told me how the weird ideas were already used in their companies, and suggested their own strange practices. The result is that the weird ideas in this book have both sound academic and practical underpinnings.

## Why These Ideas Seem So Weird

The 11½ weird ideas developed in this book are based on sound theory and evidence. Many are used in companies where innovation is a way of life. But the question that I raised at the outset of this chapter hasn't been answered yet and may seem even more puzzling if you believe that these ideas work: Why do these ideas strike so many people as weird? One reason, as I confessed, is that I made them sound weird to engage and amuse you. But that doesn't explain why I could generate so many well-supported ideas that strike so many people as strange, even downright wrong, at least at first. It also doesn't explain why people in so many companies reject these and other sound ways to spark innovation, regardless of how blandly the ideas are described.

There are several reasons that the 11½ conventional ideas are treated as good generic management practices, as the right thing to do under all circumstances. For starters, people almost everywhere believe that making money is good and losing it is bad. Yet, in most companies, most of the time, generating and testing ideas is something that loses money *right now*. The only way to make money *right now* is by repeating a proven service or making a proven product over and over again. There are exceptions, including firms that commodify creativity, such as advertising agencies and design firms. For the most part, however, people who do and manage routine work—who use the practices on the left side of the table—have more influence and prestige in their companies than people who do innovative work. After all, they make money while those mavericks keep losing it! There are companies like 3M and Novartis (a Swiss pharmaceutical company) where people who generate ideas have substantial power, but these are exceptions.

To make matters worse, most companies use the same standards for evaluating both routine and innovative work. They use conventional idea #6: Reward success, punish failure and inaction. This is fine for routine tasks. When known procedures are used by well-trained people, failure does signal improper training, weak motivation, or poor leadership. But applying this standard to innovative work stifles intelligent risks. The usual reward scheme means that, because people who do routine work succeed most of the time, they are glorified as winners. In contrast, people who do innovative work fail a lot. So they not only get few rewards, they may be denigrated as losers. In many companies, people who do routine work complain that "if those creative types just acted more like us, they would be more efficient and wouldn't make all those mistakes!"

Finally, my ideas seem weird because companies don't use them very much compared to the conventional practices. Most companies devote the lion's share of their people and money to supporting routine rather than innovative work. The right balance between exploration and exploitation varies across industries. But even in companies that are much ballyhooed for innovation, only a small percentage is usually devoted to generating and testing new products and services. The percentage of corporate budgets devoted to research and development (R&D) versus more routine tasks like manufacturing, marketing, and finance is one indicator of this imbalance. This is a crude measure, as there is routine work in R&D, and innovation elsewhere. But it is instructive. Most public companies spend less than 2 percent of their annual budgets on R&D. Even companies renowned for innovation, like IBM, Lucent, Hewlett-Packard, Siemens, Xerox, and General Electric, rarely spend much more than 5 percent or 6 percent.[31] William Coyne, 3M's former vice president for R&D, points out that 3M's financial success depends largely on new products, but most of what 3M's people do (and most of what 3M spends money on) are activities like manufacturing and marketing, which enable them to cash in on these new ideas. In 1999, over 30 percent of 3M's sales revenue was from products less than four years old, but the R&D budget was 6.6 percent of sales, a ratio that has held fairly constant over the past five years.[32] If you consider parts of these companies that do path-breaking work, such as research labs, the percentage is far lower. Xerox PARC in Palo Alto is famous for inventing many of the technologies that made the computer revolution possible, everything from bit-map displays to pull-down menus to laser printers. Yet Xerox has never spent more than one-third of 1 percent of its budget to support PARC's activities in any year.[33]

This comparative rarity helps explain why practices that support innovation may seem odd and provoke discomfort, and why managers hesitate to use them even when they should. Study after study shows that, independent of other factors, the more people are exposed to something the more positive they feel about it, and the less they are exposed to something the less positive they feel about it.[34] This "mere exposure effect" has been found for "geometric figures, random polygons, Chinese and Japanese ideographs, photographs of faces, numbers, letters of the alphabet, letters of one's own name, random sequences of tone, food, odors, flavors, colors, actual persons, stimuli that were initially liked and initially disliked stimuli."[35] This effect is found when people have no idea it is happening and deny that it is happening. It is found in all populations and all cultures, even in prenatal research on fetuses. One of the most interesting studies

> asked subjects which of two photographic prints of their [own] faces they liked better—a normal or inverted print. The inverted prints portray people as they see themselves in the mirror, whereas the normal prints portray people as other people see them. Predictably, the subjects preferred the inverted prints of themselves, but the normal print of their friends.[36]

### The Best Way to Learn from the Weird Ideas

So how can you avoid getting trapped in routines that smother innovation? The best way to learn from this book—and from other counterintuitive ideas—is to keep asking yourself: *What if these ideas are true?* How might I help organize or manage my company differently to make it more innovative? How should I act differently to make myself more creative? My ideas are designed not only to provoke readers to try them; I want to provoke you to imagine and try your own ideas about sparking innovation, especially ideas that clash with the accepted dogma in your company or industry.

Play with these ideas in your mind and experiment with a few in your company. Treat them like toys that you might buy to mess around with: Try to break them, try to take apart the pieces to see how they work, try to improve them, and mix them (or parts of them) with your other toys. I offer these ideas not as immutable truths, but as methods that have helped other companies produce beautiful and profitable mutations, and that just might help your company as well. These are ideas about building innovative groups or businesses in any company, or about injecting innovation in companies that focus on exploiting tried-and-true ways. Even if your group or business thrives by doing mostly routine things, many of the practices here can still help you and your colleagues switch cognitive gears for a while, so you can learn some new things, see old problems in new ways, and break from the past.

One big question remains before the journey through the 11½ weird ideas can start, before I show why each one works, how it is already used in companies to spark innovation, and how it might be used in your workplace. I've talked about the importance of creativity, but I haven't said what it means. As the next chapter shows, much of the mystery about what it takes to build an innovative company disappears when you realize what creativity entails.

### CHAPTER 2

# What Is Creativity, Anyway?

All geniuses are leaches, so to speak. They feed from the same source—the blood of life. . . . There is no mystery about the origin of things. We are all part of creation, all kings, all poets, all musicians; we only have to open up, only have to discover what is already there.[1]

*—Henry Miller, novelist*

In a sense, I put together elements that were already there, but that is what inventors always do. You can't make up new elements, usually. The new element, if any, it was the combination, the way they were used.[2]

*—Kary Mullis, on the process used in
his Nobel Prize–winning work on
polymerase chain reaction (PCR)*

You can have the best new technology in the world, but if you can't convince someone to buy it, that enough people will want it, it is worthless.

*—Audrey MacLean, former CEO of
Adaptive and an "angel" investor
in many new companies*

CREATIVITY IS OFTEN PORTRAYED as something that cannot be defined, described, or copied. Yet it is actually far less mysterious. Novel products, services, and theories are not conjured out of thin air. Creativity results from using old ideas in new ways, places, or combinations.

The three keys to exploration introduced in Chapter 1 all involve using old knowledge in new ways. *Variance* is enhanced by bringing ideas that are old in other places but new to the company or some part of the company. *Vu ja de* means seeing old things that are inside and outside the company in new ways. And *breaking from the past* usually means borrowing new ways of thinking and acting from other people and places. New ideas come from old ideas. This is why Thomas Edison needed a "pile of junk" at his labs—some existing things—to invent new things. If you ever visit Edison's reconstructed laboratory in Dearborn, Michigan, notice that many of the inventions in the display cases have missing parts. This isn't because visitors have stolen them; it is because Edison's engineers and model makers took pieces from their old creations to build new ones.

Like beauty and other good things, creativity is in the eye of the beholder. An idea that has been around a long time will seem creative to people who encounter it for the first time, as long as they believe it might be valuable.[3] And a new idea can seem creative to some people, but not to others. I find little value in a toy that my kids own called the Water Talkie, which is supposed to allow them to talk underwater. I don't think it works very well. I don't understand why they can't just stick their heads above water to talk. The Water Talkie was the first product developed by a toy company called Short Stack in Moraga, California. It was invented in 1996 by then-11-year-old Richie Stachowski and Richard Stachowski Sr., his father. When his mother (and experienced entrepreneur) Barbara Stachowski saw the invention, she believed it would sell. She was right. In October of 1996, after Richie and Barbara made a pitch to Toys-R-Us corporate headquarters in New Jersey, the company placed an immediate order for nearly 50,000 Water Talkies. It went on to become a very successful product. Short Stack (which has since hired adult product designers to work with Richie) has developed a line of other water toys, and the firm was sold to Wild Planet, a larger toy company.[4] I may not like it, but I would call the Water Talkie a creative idea. Kids find the marriage of a telephone and swimming to be fun and new.

The Water Talkie story and Audrey MacLean's observation that a great new technology is worthless unless someone buys it show that ideas rarely sell themselves. People need to be convinced that a new idea is worthwhile. In fact, selling—rather than creating—inventions may have been Thomas Edison's greatest talent. Many of the famous inventions from his laboratory were imagined and developed by his staff, not Edison. His assistant, Francis Jehl, lamented that Edison was a more skilled pitchman than inventor, that his "genius" was most reminiscent of master huckster and showman P. T. Barnum. But inventions like electric lighting systems for cities would never have succeeded without Edison's knack for generating publicity as "The Wizard of Menlo Park" and for securing financial backing from wealthy people.

So, if you want to build a team or company that is constantly creative, you need to keep finding new places and ways to use existing ideas and keep persuading others that your ideas are new and valuable.[5] There are three intertwined ways that people, groups, and organizations accomplish these ends.

### Bringing Old Ideas to People Who Have Never Seen Them Before

The first way to convince people you have done something creative is to show them an old idea they don't know about. People, groups, and companies that do this over and over again, and do it well, act like curious pack rats who collect diverse and strange things that seem to be of no immediate use. They keep unearthing old ideas and storing them where they can be easily found. That way, they are always ready to show ideas that have been shelved to people who might find them new and useful.

When people or companies have ties to scattered industries, companies, or locations that otherwise have little contact with each other, they are in an especially good position to keep surprising others in this way. The same thing happens when business units in large decentralized firms like Hewlett-Packard, IBM, and 3M operate as isolated kingdoms. Insiders who are linked to these otherwise disconnected kingdoms are in a good position to demonstrate old ideas—often from other parts of their own company—that they have never seen before. Such people and groups are sometimes called "knowledge brokers." They survive and thrive by transferring ideas from where they are proven and plentiful to where they are untested and unknown.[6]

Walt Conti, the CEO of Edge Innovations, is a good example of a broker. Edge makes realistic mechanical beasts that appear in movies, like full-size killer whales for *Free Willy*. Conti started out working at IDEO, where his consulting with diverse high-technology firms taught him about sophisticated control systems and electromechanical technologies. When he later went to work for filmmaker George Lucas at Industrial Light and Magic, he discovered that the movie industry was using less sophisticated technologies to make mechanical beasts than he had seen at IDEO. Conti formed Edge to fill this gap and hired IDEO to help his engineers develop better beasts. Edge has made superior "animatronic" creatures by transferring knowledge from high-technology firms to the movie business. The life-size 8,000-pound mechanical killer whale in *Free Willy,* for example, looked so realistic that audiences couldn't tell when Keiko (the real whale) or Edge's creation was on the screen. This fake whale looked so real, in fact, that Keiko tried to mate with it. Edge produced other mechanical beasts, including the killer whales for the next two *Free Willy* films, the bottle-nose dolphin in *Flipper,* and a 40-foot, 5,500-pound snake that contained more than 40 miles of wire and over 70 microprocessors for the horror film *Anaconda.*[7]

IDEO itself innovates in much the same way, capitalizing on its position as a broker between different industries. By designing more than 4,000 products, IDEO has worked with hundreds of different firms in dozens of industries. IDEO's designers have seen so many different technologies, products, and design tricks that they constantly bring solutions to clients that are new to their companies or industries, but have been proven to solve similar problems in other places. For example, they developed a "slit valve" for an innovative water bottle for Specialized, the bicycle company. This is a one-way plastic valve that fluids can only flow through when pressure is applied—in this case, only when the bottle is squeezed. IDEO engineers got the idea from a heart valve that was used in the medical products industry. When they showed a prototype of the slit valve to Specialized executives, it came across as a new idea because it had never been sold before in the bicycle industry. The Specialized executives believed that customers would buy water bottles with such valves. They were right. It became a successful product.

You don't have to be a world-renowned expert to accomplish this kind of creativity. You don't even need to work in an area for years or come to it with formal training. You just need to be skilled and motivated at gathering knowledge from diverse sources, and then at figuring out how it might be put to new uses. If you keep doing this, you will develop a reputation for creativity within your company or industry. And if you (or your group or company) is lucky enough, smart enough, or well-enough situated to keep unearthing old ideas that others find new and valuable, then you *deserve* to be called creative as well.

### Finding New Uses for Old Ideas

The second way to spur creativity is to find new uses for old materials, objects, products, services, or concepts. When the light bulb was developed in Thomas Edison's laboratory, finding a long-lasting and inexpensive filament was only one of the design challenges his inventors faced. Another problem was that now and then the bulbs fell out of their fixtures. One day, an inventor at the lab wondered whether a light bulb could be attached to a socket the same way that a screw-top cap stayed on a kerosene bottle. This simple and effective design solution persists to this day.

IDEO did something similar when they took a reliable and inexpensive motor they had seen in a Chatty Cathy doll and fitted it to a docking station for an Apple laptop computer. Another product design firm, Design Continuum, used an old idea in a new way to develop an innovative medical product for cleansing wounds. It would be used in emergency rooms to clean wounds with a pulsating flow of saline solution. The new product, called a pulsed lavage, had to meet strict guidelines for cleanliness and safety. And it had to be low-cost and disposable. The Design Continuum engineers recognized similarities between the pulsed lavage and a battery-powered squirt gun. On the surface, an emergency-room tool and a children's toy seem unrelated. But once these engineers recognized the similarities between the two products, they were inspired to modify the inexpensive electric pump and battery of the squirt gun to meet the guidelines for the new medical product.

Another example comes from Gary Hamel's research on Marks & Spencer, one of Europe's leading retailers. There is a Marks & Spencer food store in most English towns of any size. When the company got into the sandwich business a few years ago, they realized it was a massively inefficient process. In particular, the English like sandwiches with butter, which means that, every day, people in sandwich shops throughout the country spread soft butter on bread slices by hand. Martin van Zwanenberg, then Marks & Spencer's head of home services and food technology, realized that "if we wanted to expand, this was unacceptable—we'd have to have everyone in the company buttering bread." A few days later, van Zwanenberg visited a supplier who made bed sheets for Marks & Spencer and noticed they were using a silk-screen process to print patterns. He tried an experiment: "We filled up one of the ink vats with butter and screen-printed butter onto cotton." Marks & Spencer now silk-screens butter onto bread, which is one reason it is now a major player in the sandwich business in England.[8]

The way that Play-Doh was invented is one of my favorite examples of finding a new use for an old idea. In 1954, Kay Zufall was a nursery school teacher and mother living in upstate New York. She was always looking for fun new things for kids to do. In particular, she didn't like the modeling clay sold for children because it was too hard for little hands to squeeze. It happened that her brother-in-law, Joe McVicker, owned a small factory in Cincinnati that made a doughy mixture people used to clean the soot off wallpaper. Zufall got a can of McVicker's wallpaper cleaner, and after finding out it wasn't toxic, discovered that it could easily be rolled out and cut into shapes. When McVicker saw the little stars and birds hanging on Kay Zufall's Christmas tree that were made out of the dried wallpaper cleaner, he was impressed by how easy the stuff was to work with. At Zufall's suggestion, he went back to Cincinnati where he had the product reformulated as a safe and colorful product for children. Kay Zufall and her husband, Bob, then came up with the name "Play-Doh," and Joe McVicker went on to make and market one of the most successful and enduring children's products of all time. More than 2 billion cans have been sold since 1956.[9]

This technique of borrowing an existing idea and modifying it for another purpose was used to design Whirlpool's imaginative training program for new employees who will eventually train salespeople at places like Sears to sell the company's appliances.[10] This program is called "The Real Whirled," and is inspired by *The Real World,* a popular "reality-based" MTV series where viewers become voyeurs, and get to see what happens when seven young people share a fancy house in an exotic location for five months. At Whirlpool, seven young recruits are "sentenced" to live together for two months in a large house in Benton Harbor, Michigan. These young men and women use Whirlpool appliances day and night because "we want them to have a better appreciation of what a consumer goes through," says national training manager Jackie Seib. The group that stayed in the summer of 2000 "prepared more than 900 plates of food, washed no fewer than 120 bags of laundry, and performed countless hours of loading and reloading of the company's refrigerators, washers, and dryers." They also visited local stores, went on house calls with appliance repair crews, and visited Whirlpool manufacturing plants and research centers. By September of 2000, four groups had experienced "The Real Whirled." The value of this program will take years to fully evaluate. But it appears so far that this blend of live theater, training, and indoctrination is helping Whirlpool recruit top employees, get them excited about the company, and provide them with a deep understanding of its products and customers. "The Real Whirled" has also helped Whirlpool get some good publicity for being more trendy and innovative than customers and employees might expect from an 89-year-old appliance company.

The process of finding new uses for old things is not always intentional. Accidental discoveries sometimes enable firms to serve unexpected customers. Viagra and Minoxidil are examples of such happy accidents. The discovery that Viagra usage was associated with penile erections in some men was initially given little attention by researchers from Pfizer Pharmaceuticals when this "side effect" was first noted in clinical trails. The drug was originally developed to be a treatment for hypertension, and after that failed, it was tested as a treatment for angina. Once again the drug failed. But this time Pfizer researchers followed up on the side effect from their earlier study. They ran clinical trials of Viagra as a treatment for erectile dysfunction, which led them to discover a new application for this existing drug.[11] Similarly, Minoxidil was originally sold in tablet form as a treatment for high blood pressure. A side effect of this medicine was unwanted hair growth. So researchers from Upjohn started examining if it could be applied to the scalp to increase hair growth in balding men. Significant hair growth was observed in more than half the subjects who used it, and Minoxidil is now marketed in the United States by Upjohn as Rogaine.[12] Researchers at both Pfizer and Upjohn didn't anticipate these side effects, but both groups were creative because they were observant and persistent enough to find a new use for an existing medication. In the right hands, nothing succeeds like failure.

### Inventing New Combinations of Existing Ideas

Creativity also means inventing entirely new ideas, products, and services. Most things that appear to be entirely new are not conjured up out of thin air. Rather, they are new blends of old objects, ideas, or actions. The steam engine was used in mines for roughly 75 years before Robert Fulton put it on a ship and invented the first commercially successful steamboat. Fulton accomplished this because he understood how steam engines were used in mining and figured out how to adapt these engines to propel ships. Fulton was also skilled at persuading others that his ideas were valuable, which is one of the reasons that his steamboat was a commercial success, while others working on similar ideas at the time failed to get enough financial backing.

The computer hardware and software that makes the Internet work have been developed largely by people who imagine new blends of existing technologies, build them, use trial and error, and constantly refine them, until it is clear if they will succeed or fail. Sun Microsystems' Java software language is a splendid example. Robert Reid observed, "No one of these features was by itself revolutionary, even new.... But the new language's many features cohered immaculately. And together, they added up to something that was truly unique."[13] One Java creator, "gentle genius" James Gosling, added, "In some sense, I would like to think there was nothing invented in Java." Yet Java was a huge breakthrough, making it much easier for people to write, create, post, and modify Internet content. Gosling borrowed heavily from languages including Smalltalk, C++, Cedar/Mesa, and Lisp.[14] David Roberts, cofounder of Zaplet, is even more explicit about this view. The company has developed a promising technology called Zaplets, a way to "put e-mail on steroids," to make it instant and easy to use for large groups. Roberts says that "all great technologies are blends of other technologies." Zaplets was developed by bringing together e-mail, instant messaging, and the World Wide Web.

Corey Billington, vice president of procurement at Hewlett-Packard, shows how creativity results from combining existing actions in new ways.[15] Billington was inspired by academic research on the "grammar" of organizing activities in restaurants, which examined all feasible permutations of the five basic verbs or "moves" required ("order," "cook," "serve," "eat," and "pay") and the rules for combining them in different sequences. In analogous fashion, Billington created a "supply chain grammar," which he defined as "syntactical units for tasks, activities, and processes, along with the rules for combining them" to analyze the moves required to complete key design, production, and sales tasks at Hewlett-Packard. Billington's Strategic Planning and Modeling Group has used this grammar to identify all feasible permutations of moves that might be used in the company's supply chains to find more cost-effective sequences. For example, there are four moves required to build an HP printer after its engine and basic ink system are assembled: (1) Add paper tray; (2) Add Ethernet and/or Postscript bundle; (3) Add Token Ring (a cable that allows it to attach to a certain kind of computer network); and (4) Add localization (e.g., software for different languages like French, German, or Spanish). Billington and his colleagues did extensive quantitative modeling to discover the optimal sequence for combining these moves. After analyzing every permutation and the associated costs (including obsolescence and demand uncertainty), they found that— contrary to what HP was doing—it was more efficient to add the bundle first and then the Token Ring, and to postpone adding the paper tray and localization until after a customer had ordered the product.

Billington says that the logic of "supply chain grammar" has changed how Hewlett-Packard thinks about supply chains even when they don't do quantitative modeling. They automatically think of every possible permutation instead of assuming that existing ways are best. He says, "We used to believe that, for big customers like Wal-Mart, it was best to make a computer and then sell it to them. Or at least it was best to take orders for computers with rigidly specified parts. Now we sell it to them first and negotiate it so—depending on what parts are available when we make it—there is flexibility in when we build it and exactly what parts are in the machine. This ability to postpone the exact components helps HP: We still can build something different, but equally good, if a supplier lets us down. So we might put in a bigger hard drive if, for example, a supplier can't deliver the chips they promised. Or if we can get an even better component at the same price, and make our customer extra happy, we add that instead. This flexibility also helps a customer like Wal-Mart because they get the best machine we can make for the price, and get it on time."16

An inventive combination may be a new blend of old formulas rather than existing things, concepts, or actions. One example is mathematician Andrew Wiles's eight-year quest to solve Fermat's last theorem. This was one of the great puzzles of mathematics, remaining unsolved for over 350 years. Wiles created a unique blend of mathematical techniques, but the elements he wove together and modified had been developed by generations of mathematicians who came before him.17 Wiles spent most of those eight years working by himself, scribbling on pads and a blackboard, and thinking, thinking, thinking. What he was mostly thinking about, however, was how to modify and weave together the existing ideas. The crucial role of old ideas in this creative process is emphasized in the final scene of the documentary film *The Proof:* A collage of interviews with five fellow mathematicians is presented, who cite over 20 other mathematicians whose prior work Wiles had woven together to solve Fermat's last theorem.

This ability to blend existing ideas in new ways is a hallmark of many scientific breakthroughs. In *Bold Science,* Ted Anton portrays the leaders of seven teams that are doing some of the most innovative scientific work in the world.18 In each case, they have made breakthroughs by borrowing ideas from outside their fields, or creating new fields that blend together key ideas from disparate fields. Craig Venter, cofounder of Celera

Genomics, is often described as the single most important scientist in the human genomics revolution. In an announcement made at the U.S. White House on June 26, 2000, Venter proclaimed that his team at Celera, along with many other scientists throughout the world, had completed the first human genetic blueprint, an index of the 3 million bits of information in the human genetic code. Venter announced in his statement to President Clinton, the cabinet, and members of the U.S. Congress, "Starting only nine months ago on September 8, 1999, eighteen miles from the White House, a small team of scientists headed by myself, Hamilton O. Smith, Mark Adams, Gene Myers and Granger Sutton began sequencing the DNA of the human genome using a novel method pioneered by essentially the same team five years earlier at the Institute for Genomic Research in Rockville, Maryland."[19] The rapid progress that Venter's teams made at Celera, and in the organizations he worked at before, was due in large part to his ability to see links between otherwise disconnected fields. Anton noted that "he envisioned the relations among computers, sequencers, established libraries, and unknown organisms to glimpse each next wave before it happened."[20]

In short, *an idea is creative when it is new to people who use or evaluate it, and (at least some of them) believe it could be valuable to themselves or others.* The ideas that follow are strange but powerful practices that companies can use to spark and cash in on such creativity. My weird ideas focus on building companies that find new uses for existing knowledge, but address the salesmanship problem as well. In particular, the final chapter includes tips for persuading others that you and your company are innovative.

# PART II

# THE WEIRD IDEAS

### CHAPTER 3

# Hire "Slow Learners" (of the Organizational Code)

## (Weird Idea #1)

Darwin disliked school and was quite content to be a mediocre student at the university; yet he was also deeply committed to self-education through extensive reading, scientific explorations of the English countryside, and conversations with established scientists.[1]

—*Dean Keith Simonton,*
*creativity researcher*

The best engineers sometimes come in bodies that can't talk.

—*Nolan Bushnell, founder of Atari*

I AM NOT ADVISING YOU to hire stupid people, or at least, I am advising you to hire people with a special kind of stupidity or, if you prefer, stubbornness. If you want a wide range of perspectives, ideas, and talents in your company, you should find and hire "slow learners" of the organization's code. A code is a company's "knowledge and faiths,"[2] its history, memories, procedures, precedents, rules, and all those taken-for-granted, and often unspoken, assumptions about why things are supposed to be done in certain ways. The heart of an organization's code are shared norms, "those overarching 'shalts' and 'shalt nots' which govern the actions, imply the sanctions, and in time permeate the souls of organization members."[3]

Most companies screen job candidates to bring in people much like company insiders, who learn how to do things "the right way" quickly, and who see things much like everyone else in the company. These criteria make sense if a company wants people who will repeat its tried-and-true ways of thinking and acting. Companies and teams that do innovative work need a different sort of person. They need newcomers who have new ideas and see things differently than insiders, and especially, who won't get brainwashed into thinking just like everyone else. They need people who avoid, ignore, or reject "the heat of the herd," as futurist George Gilder puts it.[4] This is what I mean by a slow learner of the organizational code.

James March has been studying slow learners for over a decade.[5] He shows that companies will focus more on exploring new possibilities, and less on exploiting old knowledge, when a significant percentage of members don't follow the code. When people don't know or don't believe the code, they draw on their own knowledge and skill, or invent new ideas or methods to get their work done. When they do what they think is right, rather than what everyone else does, they produce more variation in what is thought and done. This means it is *smart* to hire slow learners, to tolerate deviants, heretics, eccentrics, crackpots, weirdoes, and just plain original thinkers, even though they will come up with many ideas that are strange mutations, dead ends, and utter failures. The cost is worthwhile because they also generate a larger pool of ideas—especially novel ideas— than you can get from just hiring and breeding fast learners.

March presents impressive formulas and graphs showing that when an organization has a greater percentage of people who are incapable, unwilling, or have not yet learned the way things are "supposed to be done around here," the company is more likely to be innovative. Yet March offers few hints about what kinds of people are likely to be slow learners. Research in personality psychology suggests that three kinds of traits are key: those who are "low self-monitors," those who avoid contact with coworkers, and those who have very high self-esteem.

First, many slow learners are what psychologist Mark Snyder calls "low self-monitors," people who are especially insensitive to subtle, and even not so subtle, hints from others about how to act. Snyder's studies reveal consistent differences between high and low self-monitors.[6] High self-monitors are skilled at observing subtle aspects of what people around them are doing, interpreting what it means for how they should act, and, finally, acting in the expected way. High self-monitors often hold jobs (e.g., in sales, acting, or politics) that require being aware of their own actions and expressed feelings, how others respond to them, and what adjustments are needed to best please, persuade, or comply with others.

Low self-monitors are pretty much the opposite. Their feelings and actions are "controlled by inner attitudes, dispositions, and values, rather than to be molded and shaped to fit the situation."[7] Even when low self-monitors do figure out what others expect, even when they do "get it," they will have trouble producing the "right" response in sincere and convincing ways. For better and for worse, low self-monitors are relatively unfettered by social norms. These mavericks and social misfits can drive bosses and coworkers crazy, but they increase the range of what is thought, noticed, talked about, and done in a company. High self-monitors tend to be yes-men (and -women), who can't stop themselves from telling others what they want to hear. Low self-monitors can't stop themselves from saying and doing what they think is right, because they don't notice—or don't care about—pressures to follow the herd.

Richard Feynman, a Nobel Prize winner in physics, was a creative person who had little interest in what others did, expected him to do, or in pleasing others.[8] He refused nearly all honorary degrees, spent years trying to resign from the prestigious National Academy of Science, and refused to participate in the business of his academic department in any way, including hiring and promotion decisions and writing grants. He was driven largely by his inner thoughts and needs. Some colleagues found him selfish and boorish, but Feynman was proud of his indifference, titling a collection of autobiographical essays *"What Do You Care What Other People Think?"*[9]

Feynman cared so little, in fact, that he routinely violated perhaps the strongest norm in academic circles: When you come up with a good idea, you publish it in an academic journal so that other researchers can learn and build on your ideas, and so you can enhance your reputation. Feynman published enough work to win a Nobel Prize. But many colleagues claimed he would have had a bigger impact on physics, and might have won another Nobel Prize or two, if he had bothered to publish several hundred of his other novel ideas. Feynman once did a hundred or so pages of work predicting that supermassive stars with blazing radiation would be gravitationally unstable. About 20 years later an astrophysicist won a Nobel Prize for independently producing this same conclusion, in part because Feynman never bothered to publish it.[10]

When Feynman was asked to become a member of the Rogers Commission, a prestigious group convened to determine why the Challenger Space Shuttle exploded, his wife, Gweneth, urged him to join because (as a low self-monitor!) he would think and act independently. She told him:

> If you don't do it, there will be twelve people, all in a group, going around from place to place together. But if you join the commission there will be eleven people—all in a group, going around from place to place together—while the twelfth one runs all over the place, checking all kinds of unusual things. There probably won't be anything, but if there is, you'll find it.[11]

As Gweneth predicted, Feynman collected a lot of information on his own, especially by doing interviews and site visits. He ignored what he was told to do by administrators who ran the commission, and questioned guidelines that members were told to follow. At one meeting, he interrupted the proceedings (despite efforts by administrators to stop him) to demonstrate that the shuttle's O-rings lost flexibility when he plunged them into a beaker of cold water, which at 32 degrees Fahrenheit was about the same temperature the day of the Challenger launch. This was crucial evidence because the seal created by the O-rings prevented the escape of hot gasses from the shuttle's solid rocket boosters, and if they didn't remain flexible, the seal could be broken. O-ring failure was eventually identified as the primary technical cause of the Challenger explosion—largely through a series of tests that replicated Feynman's demonstration under more controlled conditions.

Neil Armstrong, the first astronaut on the moon, overheard Commission Chairman William Rogers complain that "Feynman is becoming a real pain in the ass."[12] Feynman, like other low self-monitors, couldn't help himself. He felt compelled to listen to his inner voice rather than to peers or administrators. But the payoff was big.

"Slow learners" are not only low self-monitors; many also prefer to avoid social interaction. They may feel, as Jean-Paul Sartre put it, that "Hell is other people." They don't spend a lot of time talking to coworkers and bosses. They have fewer chances to learn how things are "supposed to be done" in a company. In research conducted at the University of California at

Berkeley, Jennifer Chatman followed 171 newly hired auditors in the eight largest accounting firms in the United States for a year. She examined factors that cause the new employees to have beliefs similar to veteran members of the firms. These "values" included respect for people, flexibility, innovation, team work, risk taking, aggressiveness, and attention to detail. After a year, those new auditors who interacted less with others in the company (by going to fewer social activities and spending less time with their mentors) were less likely to believe and support the firm's dominant values.[13]

My experience (and, I suspect yours) is that these people are often shy. They aren't especially comfortable around others, or at least are happiest when alone, working on their own ideas and lost in their own thoughts. When Nolan Bushnell, the founder and former CEO of the Atari Corporation, remarks that "sometimes the best engineers come in bodies that can't talk," he is talking about people who are low self-monitors and who shy away from social interaction. They may lack social graces. And even when they have such graces, some of the most creative people prefer to spend time away from coworkers, alone with their own thoughts and ideas. They may be difficult to talk to, even to find, and may not like working on teams. But they do increase the range of ideas in a company, and are recognized and appreciated in every innovative company.

Some innovative work—like improvisational theater—requires constant communication and tight coordination between people. Creative people who dislike and avoid others are poorly suited for such work. But many innovative tasks can be divided up so that people can work with limited contact, with the necessary coordination done by management. The design of computer hardware and software is organized this way in many companies, including some work groups at Cisco, Intel, and Zilog. Slow learners can flourish in such settings. Last year, I was teaching a group of executives who were arguing about whether it was possible to do creative work with people who had poor social skills and who preferred to work alone. One executive from a computer hardware firm squirmed and turned red, finally blurting out, "These are exactly the kind of people I manage." He went on to say:

> They hide in their offices, and don't come out. We divide the
> work so they each have a separate part. We slide their assignment
> under the door and run away. They ignore us when we tell them
> it is good enough—they won't let us build it until it meets their
> standards for elegant designs—they don't care what we think.

Finally, slow learners are likely to have high self-esteem. Much research shows that people with high self-esteem (e.g., who have enduring positive evaluations of themselves) lack "plasticity" in their behavior, which means "the extent to which an individual's actions are susceptible to influence by external and, particularly, social cues."[14] Such people have the confidence to do what they think is right, no matter what others ask them, tell them, or expect them to do. This means, among other things, that people with a touch of hubris or arrogance will reject what others think and do, and hold steadfast against it, when they think it is wrong. James Watson's book *The Double Helix* describes how he and Francis Crick discovered the structure of DNA. Watson emphasizes that Crick's hubris was often difficult for him and others in their laboratory to take.[15] The first sentence of this account of their Nobel Prize–winning work is, "I have never seen Francis Crick in a modest mood."[16] Watson shows that Crick's supreme self-confidence, as well as his own (Watson had more than a touch of hubris himself), enabled them to ignore critics, which was crucial to their ultimate success.

The Beatles' John Lennon was an even more famous slow learner. Like Feynman, Crick, and Watson, he didn't care what other people thought of him, and he could be remarkably arrogant. Lennon blamed his teachers, and especially the aunt who raised him, for never recognizing his talents: "I never forgave her for not treating me like a genius when I was a child. Why didn't they train me? Why did they keep forcing me to be a cowboy like the rest of them? I was different, I was always different." A reporter asked Lennon if he missed the music scene because he was staying home and raising his son, Sean. Lennon raged: "It's like asking Picasso, has he been to the museum lately? Picasso didn't go to museums. He was either painting or eating or fucking. Picasso lived where he lived and people came to see him. That's what I did. Did Picasso go down to some studio and watch somebody paint? I don't want to see other people paint. I'm just not interested in other people's work."[17]

The problem with hiring such people—aside from all the headaches they cause—is that their self-confidence and persistence does not insure that a person or company will succeed. It leads most people (and sometimes their companies) to *fail,* because most new ideas are wrong, or at least not as good as the old ideas they are meant to replace. At the same time, the persistent fantasies held by supremely confident people need to be protected long enough to find out if their challenge to orthodoxy is, in fact, one of those rare, superior ideas.[18]

The Xerox researcher who invented laser printing, Gary Stark-weather, is a great example of a person with enough self-confidence to reject the organizational code, and who succeeded because he was protected just enough to bring his idea to fruition.[19] In 1968, Starkweather was hired as a new Ph.D. in optics by Xerox's main technical laboratory in Webster, New York. He kept insisting that the (then new) "technology of lasers could be used to 'paint' an image onto a xerographic drum with greater speed and precision than ordinary white light."[20] This idea was constantly dismissed by other scientists at the Webster lab as impractical and too expensive. Starkweather responded by doing one experiment after another that answered nearly every objection raised by his superiors and peers. When his manager still tried to stop his research, he was confident enough to complain to a senior manager at Xerox about how "laboratory dogma" was ruining both a good idea and his career. He was then transferred to the new (and now famous) research facility in Palo Alto, California, called Xerox PARC; by 1972 he had developed his ideas into a commercially feasible copier.

The commercialization of laser copiers and printers was halted at least three more times by Xerox senior management, who were skeptical of their value. Ultimately, however, when it was "launched in 1977 as the 9700 printer, Gary Starkweather's laser device fulfilled its inventor's faith by becoming one of Xerox's bestselling products of all time."[21] The success of Xerox laser printers and copiers also belies the books, articles, and even a documentary on PBS called *Triumph of the Nerds,*"[22] which claim that Xerox "fumbled the future" by not profiting significantly from any inventions at PARC. These reports are accurate in that Xerox failed to commercialize dozens of inventions that made the computer revolution possible, but they overlook Starkweather's work, which generated huge sales and profits in Xerox's core businesses of copiers and printers.

Most companies automatically search for fast learners, gregarious people with social graces, who are willing and able to bend to the wishes of others. Indeed, for most of what they do, companies need fast learners who will do things as they have always been done. That is how to make money *right now.* But your company can benefit from slow learners if you want to explore new ways of doing things, if you want to break from the past so you can keep making money *later.* Even in parts of your company that do mostly routine work, hiring a few slow learners can be a worthwhile investment in the future.

To make this weird idea work, you need to recruit and hire a different kind of person, and to treat them in ways that might surprise you. You might want to look for smart people with bad grades. Research on creative geniuses suggests that many of them—including Edison and Darwin—were mediocre students or worse. Another weak student was Craig Venter, whose shotgun genomics made him and his research team the most renowned, and perhaps most important, scientists in the Human Genome Project, which is mapping the human genetic code. He was "a poor student who preferred surfing to his California high school."[23] Creativity researcher Dean Keith Simonton points out: "To obtain high marks in school often requires a high degree of conformity to conventional ways of looking at the world and people."[24] People who get good grades are often fast learners of social cues. By contrast, smart people who get bad grades are listening to their inner voice, doing what they believe is interesting and right. Simonton observes that "one of the reasons creative talents often dislike school is that it can interfere with what they really want to know. When faced with the choice of reading a good book or studying for an exam, the extracurricular but still instructive diversion may win out."[25]

A final and essential point about slow learners is that they can have symbiotic relationships with fast learners. Harvard Business School career counselors James Waldroop and Timothy Butler suggest that people who ignore what others think and who have bad social skills should be trained to dampen their offensive behavior.[26] I agree that slow learners should learn to work more smoothly with others. But there are hazards to trying to reform slow learners. The first hazard is that such behavior can have a large neurological and genetic component, so it may be impossible to change. The socially awkward and sometimes defiant Albert Einstein probably never could have learned the social skills that Waldroop and Butler teach Harvard M.B.A.'s and describe as crucial to career success. Some psychologists and other experts have even suggested that Einstein had Asperger's syndrome, a neurological condition related to autism, that makes it difficult to follow social cues and learn social skills.[27] The second hazard is that if it were possible to build a world filled only with gregarious and modest fast learners, it not only would be a dull place, there would also be less creativity. To return to Albert Einstein, if he had been more concerned about pleasing his mentors in graduate school, they might have helped him get a university position, but he might never have developed the theory of relativity.

A better solution is to surround slow learners with the right kind of

*Putting Weird Idea #1 to Work*

*Use Slow Learners to Boost Innovation*

- Recruit smart people who seem slow to learn how things are "supposed to be done" in their current company.

- If a job candidate is smart, but socially awkward, try hiring the person anyway.

- Hire—or breed—a few loners and individualists.

- Take a risk and hire a few people who seem imaginative, but had bad grades.

- Make sure that slow learners are rewarded—or at least not punished—for expressing their deviant views and acting in odd ways.

- Protect slow learners from pressures to learn and blindly follow the local culture; leave them alone for long periods of time.

- Surround slow learners with fast learners who understand how to translate and promote their creative ideas.

- People who manage slow learners need an especially deep understanding of the work. Slow learners often have a hard time communicating their ideas and putting their ideas in context, so their managers often need to do it for them.

- Protect (even isolate) slow learners from each other. Their poor communication skills and arrogance can fuel destructive conflict with each other.

fast learners. After all, most good ideas are developed via interactions between people, not by a lone genius. In Richard Feynman's case, he refused to participate in the business of his academic department, but the fact that other faculty and administrators did so made it possible for him to have the resources to do his work.[28] Successful slow learners are often paired with one or more fast learners who protect and insulate them, and who can translate and promote their ideas. The quirky and independent-minded Bill Joy has developed ideas that led to many successful products for Sun Microsystems. Fast learners like Sun CEO Scott McNealy don't try to change Joy. They leave him alone to develop his ideas until he needs help translating them into products and selling them to others inside and outside the firm.

John Lennon's boasting and insults infuriated the fast learners around him, especially fellow Beatle Paul McCartney and band manager

Brian Epstein.[29] Lennon would "disagree out of sheer whim and perversity."[30] But Lennon realized that he desperately needed them, admitting, "Paul and Epstein did have to cover up a lot for me. I'm not putting Paul down, and I'm not putting Brian down. They did a good job in containing my personality from causing too much trouble."[31] McCartney's hurt feelings and his admiration were both evident in his comment after Lennon's murder. "He was pretty rude about me sometimes, but I secretly admired him for it. There was no question that we were friends; I really loved the guy. In years to come I think people will realize that John was an international statesman. He often looked a loony and even made a few enemies, but he was really fantastic. His record 'Give Peace a Chance' helped stop the Vietnam War. He made a lot of sense."[32] Lennon was gifted, but his talents would never have been developed and known without McCartney's charm and diplomacy.

### CHAPTER 4

# *Hire People Who Make You Uncomfortable, Even Those You Dislike*

## *(Weird Idea #1 ½)*

Hire people who make you squirm; that's how you get new ideas.

—*Peter Skillman, director of product design engineering, Handspring*

I have this guy who is a left-wing radical who works for me. He makes me uncomfortable. He tells me I am wrong. He compensates for my blind spots. I need him desperately.

—*Rey More, senior vice president, Motorola*

I CALL THIS WEIRD IDEA #1½ because it is really an extension of idea #1. Hiring people who make you uncomfortable, even those you don't like, is another way to find a few useful misfits who will ignore and reject the organizational code. And if you start hiring newcomers who make insiders squirm, chances are that some will be slow learners. If a company hires only new people whom insiders like and feel comfortable being around, it is probably hiring imitations of those insiders. One of the most persistent findings in the behavioral sciences is that people prefer to spend time with, and have positive feelings about, people who are similar to themselves. In the battle of clashing clichés, study after study of "similarity" and "attraction" confirms that "birds of a feather flock together," while there is little evidence that "opposites attract."

Even when people try not to be influenced by this "similarity-attraction" effect, or aren't aware it is happening to them, they still have warmer feelings (and offer more positive evaluations) when another person looks like them, acts like them, went to the same school they did, has the same birthday, or is similar on virtually any dimension that they notice. Conversely, no matter how confident, intelligent, or skilled the person is, differences can provoke negative feelings, which can lead to subtle rejection like avoiding conversation, or less subtle rejection like deciding not to hire the person. Many people don't even realize that such differences are driving what they feel and do. And even if they are aware of their biases, they usually vehemently deny that such biases are shaping their actions.[1]

This preference for similarity shapes hiring and promotion, resulting in what Harvard Business School professor Rosabeth Moss Kanter calls "homosocial reproduction."[2] Kanter focused on how executives in big companies rely on "outward manifestations to determine who is the 'right sort of person' . . . to carefully guard power and privilege for those who fit in, for those who they see as 'their kind.'"[3] Kanter especially focused on executives, mostly white males with similar educational backgrounds, who "reproduce[d] themselves in their own image."[4] But homosocial reproduction occurs in thousands of other ways; all human beings suffer from this tendency, not just white males.

Our emotional responses to a job candidate are like a divining rod. When we have negative emotional reactions to people, it may not have anything to do with whether or not they can do the job. Rather, it can be because they have different beliefs, ideas, and knowledge from us. I am not suggesting that you actively seek out rude, insulting, or incompetent people for your company. But I am saying that, if you find a candidate who seems competent and has skills your firm needs but has different beliefs, knowledge, and skills than most insiders, negative emotional reactions or evaluations are reasons *in favor* of hiring the person. It will help bring in some new ideas.

When I present this weird idea to executives, managers, and engineers, as I have many times, it provokes three waves of reactions. The first is nonverbal rejection: They look at me as if I am out of my mind. The second is verbal rejection: They tell me that if their firm hired people who didn't like one another, it would undermine teamwork and make it a horrible place to work. (A recent response by a television network executive is typical: "Well, Professor Sutton, this is a cute idea, but those of us in the real world actually have to get something done now and then.") The third wave is the most intriguing: Just as the group is about to dismiss the idea as absurd, a few people respond with stories about how their company has benefited from people who make everyone uncomfortable, even who are widely disliked, because they think differently, act differently, have different backgrounds, or advocate unpopular ideas.

The virtue of this weird idea is seen in the success of Will Vinton Studios in Portland, Oregon. This company specializes in the Claymation technique, where clay, instead of illustrations, is used to make animated films. It also uses Foamation, where the clay is replaced with foam. Artists at Vinton Studios have won two Academy Awards for work in films, six Emmy Awards for television, and numerous Clio awards for television commercials. Their most famous commercials are the singing California raisins, and they produced a prime-time television show called *The PJs*, which starred Eddie Murphy as the voice of a housing-project superintendent. Vinton Studios had been able to attract the finest artists in the world since it was founded in 1975, and kept winning awards, but it wasn't making much money. Founder Will Vinton said, "I was an artist, and I only hired people who were fellow artists." This meant that "whenever we took on a project, we failed to ask whether that project would make us enough money to build the infrastructure necessary to do longer projects in the future."

Vinton eventually realized that he was engaging in homosocial reproduction, and to make money, the company needed people with business skills. In 1997, Vinton overcame his natural aversion to business types and hired former Goldman Sachs banker Tom Turpin to bring business sense to the company. Turpin's business discipline (especially planning how people spend time on projects) in combination with the creative people at Vinton resulted in a 50 percent increase in revenues between 1997 and 2000. Even more impressive, the company was earning profits by mid-2000, unlike past years, when it barely broke even. At the same time, Turpin was careful to leave in place policies that spark artists' creativity, like allowing them to take 13-week paid breaks (called "Walkabouts") to pursue their own ideas, and encouraging them to use company equipment to work on their own projects.[5]

I've found other managers who seek out job candidates and colleagues who make them uncomfortable because it sparks needed innovations. Peter Skillman, director of product design engineering at Handspring, says, "Hire people who make you squirm; that's how you get new ideas." Rey More, an executive vice president at Motorola, has a similar view. He looks for people who will annoy him, who will tell him he is wrong over and over again. More commonly, however, an unpopular newcomer is forced on a group or organization by superiors. Quite a few managers have told me that, when they are trying to bring in some new ideas, they hire people that they expect other insiders will dislike, or at least will feel uncomfortable around. So, perhaps this weird idea should be expanded to "Hire newcomers that *other* people in your company will dislike."

David Kelley, founder and chairman of IDEO, enjoys telling me (and others, including business reporters) that when the designers in his firm dislike or at least feel uncomfortable around a new employee, it is a sign that IDEO has done something right. To illustrate, IDEO is populated largely by engineers, industrial designers, human factors experts, and other designers who develop great products, but who are less skilled at marketing. IDEO has been compensating in recent years, in part, by hiring people with marketing and consulting backgrounds. A couple of years ago I reported to Kelley that engineers were complaining that a new marketing person talked way too much, asked way too many questions about the marketing aspects of design, and gave people advice about marketing they had not asked for. I wasn't thinking about this weird idea when I told Kelley about this "problem." He laughed at me. "Sutton, I am just doing what you told me to do. I hired the guy because he has different ideas and acts different. The things designers don't like about him are the things that we need more of in our culture."

Another variation of hiring people who make you uncomfortable happens in start-ups that are founded and populated largely by young people. In order to get funding from venture capitalists and others, young founders are coaxed—or even forced—to hire older, more experienced executives even though they are less knowledgeable about the technology than the people they manage. This practice has been used in high-technology start-ups for decades. In 1976, venture capitalist Don Valentine told Apple founders Steve Jobs and Steve Wozniak that he wouldn't invest in the company unless they found someone with marketing expertise to help them run it.[6] So, with Valentine's help, these two grubby young hippies found straight-laced former Intel executive Mike Markkula and convinced him to join because their technology was so promising. The relationship between Mike Markkula and Steve Jobs was tense; one of Jobs's biographers reported that "Markkula absolutely could not stand to work with Steve."7 The conflict got worse when Markkula brought in Mike Scott, another older and experienced manager, to serve as president. Jobs and Scott disliked liked each other immediately. They battled over everything from the Apple logo, to awarding employee numbers, to whether bean bags were acceptable office furniture. At best, there was tense discomfort between Jobs and these two older managers; at worst, there was open anger, disdain, and yelling that drove Jobs to tears. But without Markkula's and Scott's financial savvy, marketing expertise, and operational skills, Apple's inventive technology might have remained an obscure footnote in the history of the computer industry.

Similar tensions and benefits have been seen in more recent high-tech start-ups like Netscape, Yahoo!, and Zaplet, as investors routinely mix young technologists and older managers with business experience. The friction between the different generations is sometimes destructive, and even in the best of situations, there is discomfort between Gen Y (20ish), GenX (30ish), and baby boomers (40ish and 50ish). Yet, as with Apple, even though employees are more comfortable with people their own age and sometimes engage in generational warfare, people from these different generations need each other because they have complementary skills and experience.

I've yet to hear managers admit that they try to recruit coworkers because they are disliked (although I believe they should), but the imperfections of job interviews can cause organizations to unwittingly hire people who are different from insiders. Successful job candidates may listen carefully to the opinions expressed by people who interview them, and they use what they learn to create false impressions that they are similar to company insiders. They may also say things they don't believe during interviews just to get the job. Candidates use tricks much like those used at automobile dealerships. Robert Cialdini describes how this is done in his book on the psychology of persuasion:

> Car salesmen, for example, are trained to look for evidence of such things while examining the customers' trade-in. If there is camping gear in the trunk, the salesman might mention, later on, how he loves to get away from the city whenever he can; if there are golf balls on the back seat, he might remark that he hopes the rain will hold off until he can play 18 holes he has scheduled for later in the day. . . . Because even small similarities can be effective in producing a positive response to another and

## Putting Weird Idea #1½ to Work

*Innovate by Hiring People Who Make You Uncomfortable,*
*Even Those You Dislike*

- If you have a negative reaction to a job candidate, ask yourself:

  Is it just because the candidate is different?

  If hired, can this person bring in valuable new ideas, see things in new ways, and help the company break from the past?

- Teach people the hazards of sameness and homosocial reproduction.

- If people want to hire a candidate because "I like her" and "She is just like us," these might be reasons *not to hire* the person if the job requires creativity.

- If you are young, hire people who are old. If you are old, hire people who are young. Be aware that the age difference alone can cause discomfort and conflict.

- If a group isn't creative enough, hire someone with different skills and new beliefs about how to do their work, assign the newcomer to the group, and tell them that even if they dislike the newcomer, they need him or her.

- Develop and monitor signs that people are hiring too many others like themselves (e.g., percentage of graduates from the same schools, parts of the country, discipline, functional backgrounds, and former employers, who have the same hobbies and belong to the same clubs, as well as traditional demographics like age, race, and gender).

- If someone comes across as likable in an interview, but starts making enemies, try to determine if it is because the person lacks competence, or is challenging existing dogma.

- If you hire people who prompt discomfort in yourself and others, take extra care to listen to their ideas and insist that others do so as well.

- Warn people that they will find it frustrating and annoying to work with people who are "different" and teach them to cope with these negative feelings.

- Provide extra protection and support for newcomers who are disliked because they think differently. Their value is lost if they are silenced, start thinking and acting like everyone else, or quit.

because a veneer of similarity can be so easily manufactured, I would advise you special caution in the presence of requesters who claim to be "just like you."[8]

Cialdini rightly focuses on the downside of creating a veneer of similarity when none exists. But candidates who create a false veneer of similarity may not be such a bad thing for the organization, at least for sparking innovation. This may be a "bait and switch" tactic, but it can also mean that more varied ideas and perspectives will be imported into the company.

A senior executive in a toy company once told me that her firm kept hiring people who pretended to "think like us" during job interviews. Once hired, however, they would start pointing out how bad the company's products were, which in her words, "makes us hate them." This executive said she fired those toy designers who criticized old products and ideas for new products, but never came up with better ideas. She went on to say, however, that the complainers who kept coming up with great ideas for new toys ("probably just to spite us") were crucial to her firm's success. She admitted that, while the success of her company was due, in part, to people who "fooled us during interviews," she still couldn't quite bring herself to like such people. Of course, the next step, which I recommended to her, is to intentionally hire people that she and others in her firm dislike!

Even if I have convinced you that hiring slow learners and people who make you uncomfortable is a good idea, it may be a lot harder to convince others in your company. These two practices not only clash with those practices used and taught by most human resource management departments, they clash with an ingrained human tendency for like to attract like, and the natural avoidance of people who provoke negative feelings. The only argument for experimenting with this weird idea is that it works.

### CHAPTER 5

# Hire People You (Probably) Don't Need

## (Weird Idea #2)

We look for people who are smart and who have the right attitude. Even if we don't know how we are going to use their skills, we figure they can teach us something new we just might need, even if we don't quite know why yet. And we always assume that they can learn new skills. That is why we hired a lawyer last year, even though we didn't need one. She eventually became head of human resources, although she had no prior experience in that kind of work.[1]

—Justin Kitch, CEO and founder of
Homestead

THIS IDEA STARTED AS A JOKE. In talking to executives, I'd say something silly like, "If creativity means hiring people who do things that usually fail or prove unnecessary, you might hire some people you don't need on purpose so you won't be disappointed in the end." Some would laugh, others would look at me as if I was crazy. But I began wondering if this was more than a joke after several executives who managed creative work—including those from a toy company, a TV show, and a research and development lab—told me that this practice was actually used in their companies. They reported that, every now and then, they hired a smart, interesting, or strange person with skills their firm probably did not need at the moment and might never need, sometimes over the objections of their superiors. They told me that such "experiments" were often hired on a trial basis (as temporary or contract employees), and while many failed, they sometimes produced useful new products or ways of working that people who had the "right" skills never would have dreamed up.

The main reason for hiring such "unnecessary" people now and then is that they bring in ideas that a company lacks, broader knowledge that makes possible more varied experiments. They can bring in fresh perspectives, a constructive ignorance or disdain for accepted dogma. If you hire such people, it is especially important to heed Weird Idea #4: Teach them to ignore advice from coworkers or bosses, instead of learning how company and industry insiders are "supposed to" think and act. The idea is to hire them (at least on a temporary basis) and see if they can come up with something different.

IDEO's David Kelley describes another way to use this tactic: "Hire people you know you don't need now, but you think you *might* need later." These are people who bring in skills from other places, which aren't needed to do current work, but could be valuable in the future. Kelley calls them "Indian scouts, people who are ahead of everyone, trying things that might be important in the future." In IDEO's early days, he hired a person who was skilled at using a CAD (computer-aided design) machine long before any of his competitors or customers were using this technology; they still drew designs by hand. Kelley says, "It would have cost us quite a bit of money if CAD machines had not taken off, we could have found some use for the guy, but we bought him some expensive machines as well." As it turned out, CAD machines did become the standard for doing design, so this was a worthwhile risk.

This same attitude led IDEO to hire people who started new and profitable services. Kelley described how it led them to hire Craig Syverson. They hired Syverson because they liked him, and he seemed to have a lot of skills, but they weren't quite sure what he was going to do when they offered him a job. He soon started taking videos of company meetings and other events, which they thought was "cool," but no one imagined that this was a service that IDEO could sell to clients. Within a few years, however, Syverson had developed a profitable service (and now has an assistant to help him) videotaping, editing, and selling videotapes of how people use different products and places. Kelley explains, "When we started getting beyond prototyping products, and started prototyping user experiences, we needed videos of how people used things like heart defibrillators and furniture. Syverson turned out to be one of our most successful scouts, even though we were not quite sure what he would do when we hired him."[2]

Kelley went on to say that IDEO "got lucky" with CAD machines and Craig Syverson for the same reason they have been "unlucky" with other experiments.[3] They hired a management consultant to help IDEO develop its innovation consulting services. He proposed a way of doing business that was new to IDEO (management consulting while living at the client's site), and he used business terms that were foreign to them, like "core competence" and "business processes." He decided to leave IDEO because his approach was not attracting many clients and few IDEO designers were interested in becoming management consultants; they preferred to design products. Tom Kelley (David's brother) is a senior manager at IDEO. When I asked him about this experiment, he said, "I didn't think there was a big chance it would work, but I agreed it was worth a try."[4]

Some creative firms prefer to hire people with interesting back-grounds but who actually don't know how to do the job they will be given. The theory is that smart people can always learn new skills, and having a broad mix of skills—for reasons not necessarily foreseen—may help the firm come up with new ideas or move into new markets in the future. Given how fast technical skills become obsolete these days, finding people who can learn new skills fast might be essential for all companies, creative or not. Homestead CEO Justin Kitch says, "We look for people who are smart and who have the right attitude. Even if we don't know how we are going to use their skills, we figure they can teach us something new we just might need, even if we don't quite know why yet." This logic led them to hire a physician to work as a programmer and a lawyer to work in human resources, even though each had little formal training or work experience for their new jobs. Kitch's theory is that if interesting people like these are smart enough to learn the job they applied for, it is worth devoting the time to train them because their other skills might prove useful someday.

Here is a useful rule of thumb: When choosing among experienced and qualified candidates, select those with additional skills that might help the firm in as-yet-unknown ways. Design Continuum is a product design firm that, like IDEO, brings in new ideas by hiring people with varied, even offbeat, backgrounds. They have hired engineers who moonlight or have worked as sculptors, carpenters, and rock musicians. They like to hire people such as Joseph Graney, who grew up as a machinist in his family's shop, and David Cohen, who worked as an aircraft mechanic. These diverse experiences give the firm a broader palette of ideas to try in new ways and places. Design Continuum also takes a flyer now and then on someone with skills that they aren't sure they need. They have hired anthropologists, literature majors, even a theater designer.

There are other times when managers believe that a candidate's skills aren't needed, but the person is hired anyway. There is a myth, especially in the United States, that senior managers have almost total control over what happens in organizations.[5] Yet many things happen in organizations that managers don't know about or cannot stop. So they may never learn that people with skills they would consider irrelevant have nonetheless been hired. The managerial chain of command may be subverted to bring such "unnecessary" people aboard. Or managers may simply step aside despite their reservations, and wait to see if the new hires can prove them wrong.

All of these things happened at Xerox PARC in 1974 when they brought in Alvy Ray Smith, an abstract artist who had abandoned a promising career as a computer science professor at New York University. PARC engineer Dick Shoup wanted to hire Smith to help him develop his invention "Superpaint," the first color computer that could "grab a frame from a videotape, disc, or directly off a television screen and manhandle it by changing its colors, flipping or reversing the image, bleeding it across the screen, even animating it."[6] Shoup believed that Smith's talents as both a computer scientist and an artist "uniquely qualified him to develop Superpaint's full potential, like a test pilot pushing a new fighter plane to the edge of the envelope."[7] Unfortunately, Xerox wouldn't even allow Smith to be hired as a temporary employee or contract worker. This was apparently because PARC's management, especially Bob Taylor, the influential associate manager of the computer science lab, viewed Shoup's color computer as being at odds with PARC's emphasis on the "office of the future." Besides, PARC had no budget for an artist, let alone a "rootless hippie" like Smith.

With help from PARC computer scientist Alan Kay, Shoup subverted such resistance, by treating Smith "virtually as a piece of furniture—executing a purchase for his services for a couple thousand dollars."[8] Bob

Taylor believed that Superpaint, and especially Alvy Ray Smith, were a wasteful distraction from PARC's primary mission, but he tolerated Smith's presence for a couple of years before he was fired, or more precisely they cancelled his purchase order. Xerox management did not support color printing; they believed that the "office of the future" would only need black-and-white text and documents. Smith went on to develop Superpaint with the group that eventually founded Pixar (now led by Steve Jobs), which produced award-winning computer-generated films like *Toy Story, Toy Story 2,* and *A Bug's Life.* An ironic twist is that Shoup and Xerox were awarded a technical Emmy by the National Academy of Television Arts and Sciences in 1983 to recognize Superpaint as a pioneer in video animation technology.

PARC's management can be criticized for lacking foresight, but I see this example in another light. Even at its most rigid and short-sighted, PARC was flexible enough to bring in a person who had "unnecessary" skills. Bob Taylor and other managers put up with Smith for a long time given that they had unpleasant interactions with him and found his work unnecessary. During one of their first conversations, for example, Taylor was rebuffed by Smith for not understanding that Superpaint was "revolutionary," a lecture that annoyed Taylor because he considered himself—and is considered by most experts—a key visionary in the computer revolution (he was a leader in the development of the personal computer and the ARPANET, the forerunner of the Internet). And Taylor let Shoup stay on even though he had no interest in color computing and believed that Shoup was wasting PARC's resources on Superpaint. I would argue that Taylor's willingness to let people prove him—and one another—wrong was a primary reason that so many technologies that sparked the computer revolution were developed under his leadership.

The notion that creativity can be sparked by hiring people with skills that probably aren't needed may have started out as a joke, yet the more I learn about how creative organizations operate, the more reasonable it sounds to me. Clearly it is a tactic that is best used only on occasion. Creative companies do sometimes hire smart but naive outsiders who don't know the accepted dogma about what can and can't be done in a given company or industry, or with a given technology. They hire "scouts" to learn about possible futures and to be better prepared if such futures become the present. I also suspect that effective leaders of creative organizations act a lot like Bob Taylor did toward Alvy Ray Smith. They may disagree with people who work for them, but they get out of the way for a

*Putting Weird Idea #2 to Work*

*Innovate by Hiring People You (Probably) Don't Need*

- Interview candidates who look interesting, but who have skills that seem unrelated to what your company does. Ask them how they can help; you might be pleasantly surprised.

- Every now and then, even if you don't know how an interesting candidate can help you, hire him or her as a contractor, consultant, or temporary employee to see what happens.

- When trying to decide whom to hire from among people with skills your company *does need,* hire those who have broader training, skills, and experience in areas that *appear to be* unrelated to the job.

- If you believe that a candidate's skills are useless, but others in your company argue otherwise, hire the person, get out of the way, and see if he or she can prove you wrong.

- Take a look at your company's current job titles and descriptions. Think about what is missing and then brainstorm about some off-the-wall skills that just might help your company be more innovative. Then interview some people with those skills.

- Don't view it as a mistake when one of these "oddball" hires doesn't come up with anything useful. Think of it, and talk about it, as a cost of having an innovative company, where success comes from trying a lot of different things.

little while to see if they can be proved wrong.

Even if a company never derives any new and valuable ideas from using this tactic, making such hires can help support a culture of innovation. Senior executives who take an occasional risk on a smart, interesting, or offbeat person with skills the company probably does not need at the moment convey that they are not just talking about experimenting, taking risks, and accepting a high failure rate. They are setting an example for others to follow. It also conveys to people at all levels of the company: Be wise enough to realize that, because creative work is so inherently unpredictable, you will often misjudge what knowledge will be useful and what will be useless.

More generally, innovative people and companies are pack rats, collecting ideas, people, and things they don't seem to have any immediate use for, but they can't bring themselves to forget or discard. No matter how inefficient it might seem, it may ultimately pay off because it enhances variance, brings in people who see the same old things in different ways, and provides material for replacing old ways of thinking and acting with new ways. This is why the BrainStore in Biel, Switzerland, uses a network of young people from 13 to 20 years old from all over the world to work on products and advertising campaigns for clients like Coca-Cola, Nestlé, Novartis, Sony, and the Swiss Railway. This is why Xerox PARC hires children, along with artists, science fiction writers, sculptors, and other people with backgrounds that, at least on the surface, don't have much to do with copiers. This is why research organizations like 3M hold seminars and buy books on interesting topics that seem only tangentially related to what they are doing. This is also why places like Edison's lab, IDEO, and Design Continuum that develop products have large collections of strange tools, toys, and materials that don't seem to have any immediate use, but might prove valuable someday. This is also why Design Continuum vice president Eric Cohen thinks it is cool to "spend time in the dump looking for treasures." These are all signs that a company has a broad palette of ideas that might be applied to unknown problems in the future, and that it can create new combinations of old things.

### CHAPTER 6

# Use Job Interviews to Get Ideas, Not to Screen Candidates

## (Weird Idea #3)

The job market is so tight right now that, by the time someone interviews with me, they are going to get a job offer unless they do something really stupid. So I use job interviews for two things. First, to recruit people. Second, to get some help with my work. I give job candidates problems I can't solve. They often have great ideas, so even if they turn down the offer, I still get to use their brains for a little while.

> —*Anonymous executive, commenting on weird idea #3 at a Stanford executive education program*

It was a bizarre interview. He didn't ask me about myself and he didn't tell me a thing about the company. He just kept asking for advice about how to design his Web site.

> —*A Stanford engineering student*

PEOPLE SOMETIMES GET ANNOYED when I say job interviews are a weak, often useless, way to select new employees. I've had executives, middle managers, engineers, scientists, lawyers, a fire chief, and a minister respond with anecdotes that "prove" how skilled *they* are at using interviews to pick which job candidates will succeed and which will fail, even if *others* are lousy interviewers. Their confidence clashes with literally hundreds of studies, going back to before World War I, showing that there is rarely much agreement about who should be hired or who will perform best (and worst) when several interviewers talk to the same job candidate. These studies conclude that the typical "selection interview" is a bad method for deciding which employees to hire.[1] A much better way to pick good employees is to just see if they can do the job, or at least crucial parts of the job—to give them "job sample tests."

Most companies interview candidates something like this: An untrained interviewer leads a job candidate through an unstructured, unplanned conversation. No record is kept of what questions were asked or answered, and the person who ultimately makes the decision to hire the person—or not—sometimes has only a dim understanding of the job skills needed. Despite these flaws, the interviewer has great confidence that he or she can distinguish between good and bad candidates. Unfortunately, research shows that job interviewing is a lot like driving, where 90 percent of adult drivers report that they have "above average" skills.[2] The truth is that the typical interviewer learns little useful information for predicting job performance beyond what is available on the applicant's job application and résumé.

Nonetheless, the typical interview does have a big impact on which candidates get job offers. Candidates who are similar to the interviewer—who went to the same schools and are of the same race and gender—are more likely to get offers, as are those who are more physically attractive and taller. These and a host of other biases shape the selection process. One interpretation of these findings is that firms should not bother to interview at all; they should just hire people based on résumés and objective information like college transcripts. Most managers don't like this idea, usually because they have so much faith in their ability to pick good hires. I agree that getting rid of interviews is a bad idea, but for different reasons: Interviews are useful for other things besides screening candidates.

For one thing, interviews are an important recruiting tool. Few employees will take a job at a company if they are not given courtesy and attention during an interview. Interviews are also useful for giving prospective employees a realistic preview of the job and the company, so that candidates can decide for themselves if they fit the job. Interviews can also foster success because, when an interviewer believes a newcomer will perform well, the interviewer may help that person succeed, creating a self-fulfilling prophecy even if other candidates were initially better suited for the job.

A little-known benefit of job interviews is that they can spark creativity and innovation. When done properly, interviews increase the number of ideas floating around the company. This kind of learning happens accidentally in many companies where job candidates (in their efforts to impress interviewers) talk about the technical knowledge they acquired in college or from current and past jobs. When candidates interview at multiple firms, or have friends who are working for an even broader array of companies, they may reveal "intelligence" about what's going on at competing firms.

This intelligence is not necessarily about proprietary information. It can be about changes in personnel, product lines, and strategy that are not meant to be secret. You should know, however, that the executives I teach sometimes tell stories about candidates who violate their nondisclosure agreements with current and past employers by discussing sensi-

---

## Putting Weird Idea #3 to Work

### Sample Interview Questions for Job Candidates

- What promising technologies, business practices, and business models did you learn about in school?

- What interesting technologies, business practices, and business models are being used in your current company?

- Who are the most interesting people you have interviewed with at other companies? Why?

- What are the most interesting gossip, rumors, and stories that you—or your friends—have heard during interviews with other companies?

- What are some of the most interesting things happening at the companies where your friends or clients work?

- What have you learned about our company that might surprise me?

- Who are our toughest competitors now? Who are going to be our toughest competitors in the future?

- Do you know what our competitors are doing or planning to do?

- What do you think are some of the most important trends in our industry? What is hot, what do you see happening in the future, and why?

tive intellectual property during job interviews. Silicon Valley engineers are infamous for violating NDAs. These indiscretions provided material for Robert X. Cringely's weekly *Info World* column for years because, as he put it, so many engineers are "fragile geniuses who want their greatness to be understood and acknowledged."[3] The same thing happens in job interviews: People want to talk about the great things they know and have done, and they don't know, can't remember, or don't care about what they are *not* supposed to say. I am not suggesting that companies use interviews for espionage, and I suspect that most of the valuable information learned from candidates are not trade secrets. But I am suggesting that companies collect and use the valuable information that can be gleaned when interviewers know how to press the right buttons.

At least a few companies intentionally use this technique to bring in new ideas. I got this idea in the early 1980s when I interviewed Nolan Bushnell (the founder of Atari, an early computer game company). When he heard that I was a professor at the Stanford Engineering School, he told me that he routinely interviewed our young graduates because "I learn a lot from those kids. They tell me what they are learning about technology in their engineering classes and they have their own crazy ideas I never would have thought of." He added that many of these engineers were interviewing with his competitors, so he could gain information about the technologies and new products that his competitors were developing, which were often shown to the young engineers to entice them to join those firms. I have since heard similar arguments about the virtues of interviewing young engineers from other senior executives in Silicon Valley, including Andy Bechtolsheim (cofounder and former chief technology officer of Sun Microsystems, founder and CEO of Granite systems, and currently a senior executive at Cisco Systems) and Bill Campbell (former CEO of Intuit and Apple senior executive).

Since you probably can't avoid using selection interviewers for a variety of irrational and rational reasons, you might as well use them to learn something, especially to bring in new ideas to your company. This means asking job candidates about many of the usual things, like the kinds of things they learned in college and the projects they worked on in past and current jobs. But you need to listen to different parts of their answers, to devote special attention—and to ask follow-up questions—about the technologies, business practices, and business models that they talk about. As the sample interview questions on the prior page show, this method entails asking candidates about a broader range of topics than are

*Putting Weird Idea #3 to Work*

*Use Job Interviews to Spark Innovation*

- Have senior people interview entry-level candidates, even if your company is large. It is a quick and cheap way to accomplish technical training, and helps with recruiting too!

- Prepare for interviews differently. Think about the things you and your company might want to learn from this candidate, regardless of the specifics of the job opening.

- Ask job candidates how they would use things they learned elsewhere to solve real problems that your company faces, even problems that don't have anything to do with the job opening the interview is about.

- Make sure that a small, but significant, percentage (say 10 percent) of the candidates that you interview have skills and experience that seem irrelevant to your company. Ask them how their expertise could be used to solve current or future problems or create new opportunities. (See Weird Idea #2.)

- Listen as much you can, and talk as little as you can—and don't hold it against the candidate just because talking is more fun than listening.

- When you discuss job candidates, set aside time to discuss and record what new ideas were learned and how your company can benefit, and spread the word to the rest of your company.

raised in most interviews: about the other companies with which they are interviewing, about the companies with which their friends are interviewing, and about what their friends are doing at other companies. You might decide to hire some of these folks as well, but even if you don't, you might learn something.

This weird idea will work better if (at least every now and then) you ask the human resources management department to stop using the usual "normality filter." American author and poet Paul Goodman commented that "Few great men could pass personnel."[4] I agree, but hasten to add that many incompetent men and women have been screened out by personnel (and human resources) departments as well. HR professionals are often wise to screen out misfits with poor manners, who dress poorly, who don't look and act like everyone else in the company, or who seem interesting, but have the "wrong" background for the job. Such screening typically increases the odds that candidates will fit in and perform well at most companies, but it also eliminates slow learners and others who can teach you new ideas and new ways of looking at old ideas.

Finally, if you decide to use selection interviews to get some new ideas, you should know about the "blabbermouth theory of employee selection." Just listening—rather than talking to—job candidates may make you like them less. For nearly all human beings, talking is a more pleasant experience than listening. This is why many people want to be professors like me; we get to stand in front of classes all day and "profess." Our students might be bored, but we love hearing the sound of our own voices. This happens in job interviews, too. I tell my students who come from interviews where they didn't have a chance to get a word in edgewise, and where the interviewer has not learned a thing about them, that it probably means they will get the job. In fact, one study showed that, once an interviewer decides to hire someone, he or she starts talking a lot more than the candidate (probably in an attempt to recruit the employee).[5] This is a problem, however, if you want to learn something from a candidate. So if you want to use selection interviews to get new ideas, ask questions about the topics you want to learn about, shut up, and listen. But remind yourself that listening may lead you to be biased against qualified candidates.

Writings by philosophers and psychologists on the differences between intelligence and wisdom might also encourage you to become a better listener. Intelligent people say lots of smart things and produce the right answers to questions more often than less intelligent people, but they are not necessarily good listeners. In contrast, wise people are better listeners and are better at formulating questions than people who aren't so wise.[6] So, if you and your firm want to get smarter, the wise thing to do is to shut up, listen, and learn to ask smart questions—not to keep showing off how much you know and how fast you can think.

### CHAPTER 7

# Encourage People to Ignore and Defy Superiors and Peers

## (Weird Idea #4)

Cultures can have powerful consequences, especially when they are strong. They can enable a group to take rapid and coordinated action against a competitor or for a customer. They can also lead intelligent people to walk, in concert, off a cliff.[1]

—*Professors John Kotter
and James Heskett*

[CEO McKnight] ordered Drew to abandon the project, insisting it would never work. Ignoring the order, Drew went on to invent masking tape, one of 3M's breakthrough products. Drew's perseverance also put us on track for our defining product, Scotch tape.[2]

—*William Coyne, former 3M
vice president of research
and development.*

The most successful group I worked with was a "submarine project." After senior management vetoed it, we worked on it in secret, while claiming to work on something else, until we came up with something good. Then, we surfaced and showed the product to the same executives who tried to stop it; they joked about our insubordination, but thought it was wonderful. It went into production right away.

—*A manager from Siemens, the large
German engineering company*

THE BELIEF THAT "a strong culture leads to performance" is a mantra chanted again and again by management gurus, consultants, human resources executives, and experts of many other stripes. They cite cases like Disneyland, General Electric, Southwest Airlines, Mary Kay Cosmetics, Starbucks, Toyota, and the Men's Wearhouse to show that if you want a strong culture, you need to brainwash, nag, praise, delight, and bribe employees so they will embrace the firm's traditions and imitate its tried-and-true ways.[3] Firms with strong cultures like the Men's Wearhouse and Toyota do more formal training than their competitors, in part, because they teach employees more than just job skills. Much of their training is aimed at imparting company history and philosophy, along with ways that employees are expected to treat customers and one another.

The formal training that newcomers get from such successful companies is just the beginning of the socialization process, a first step toward starting a new way of life. Leaders of these companies know that a strong culture depends on having oldtimers who provide newcomers (and each other) with relentless guidance about how to think, talk, and act.[4] Mentoring programs, or even just informal interaction, are used to help newcomers understand how things ought to be done—or not be done—and why. Jennifer Chatman's study of new auditors in eight large accounting firms provides quantitative evidence on this point. After following these new auditors for a year, Chatman found that "those who experience the most vigorous socialization fit the firm's values better than those who do not." She also discovered that auditors who remained cultural misfits got less glowing performance evaluations from their bosses, and were more likely to leave their jobs.[5]

The subtle and relentless ways that companies drive out unwanted variance and teach employees to see things from the same vantage point is demonstrated by what happened a few years ago when a new employee tried to undermine the Toyota Production System at the New United Motors Plant (NUMMI) in Fremont, California.[6] Toyota is famous for having a robust and powerful culture, where members are indoctrinated to uphold the system, which emphasizes, among other things, driving out unwanted variance. NUMMI is a joint venture between Toyota and General Motors (GM). NUMMI uses the Toyota production system (under Toyota management) to produce cars that are far superior in quality and lower in cost compared to most General Motors plants in the United States; only the Saturn plant in Springhill, Tennessee, comes close. The quality and cost of NUMMI nearly match cars produced in Toyota's best plant in Japan.

Jamie Hresko, an executive and 15-year veteran at General Motors, was brought in as a production worker at the NUMMI plant in early 1997. A few of NUMMI's top managers knew about Jamie's background. His fellow workers and supervisor did not know who he was, or why he was there, so he was treated like any other new employee. Hresko *tried* to mess up the system: "For two weeks, Jamie worked on the line and, using his knowledge of the assembly line, tested the NUMMI system to see whether it was as good as the numbers suggested. He did everything he could to subvert the process and test its limits."[7] Jamie violated the NUMMI way by doing things such as building up a buffer of extra parts, stacking parts on the floor (a safety violation), extending his lunch break by two minutes, and slacking off on some quality checks. *Every single violation was noticed and commented on immediately.* This "guidance" always came from fellow workers rather than from his supervisor (whom he rarely saw).

> When I came back two minutes late from lunch, I was told that others would cover me if it was important, but that I hurt the whole team when I did this and I had better not do it again unless there is a good reason. When I missed a couple quality checks an operator down the line picked them up and stopped by to make sure I didn't do it again. But there was also a willingness of operators to help me fix errors and do a better job.[8]

Companies that want employees to exploit existing knowledge, want to drive out variance, and want their people to have shared worldviews ought to use potent and relentless socialization practices like those at NUMMI. They ought to treat most new and untested actions as deviance rather than creativity. The great virtue and horrible drawback of such places, as leadership guru Warren Bennis once told me, is that "the best you can be is a perfect imitation of those who have come before you." Socialization in such places is meant to produce one replicant after another.

If, however, a company wants lots of variance in ideas and actions, teaching people to believe in and imitate old ways is problematic.[9] Even if the goal is to improve a routine process, switching cognitive gears so that people generate and evaluate a broad range of possibilities is the way to go. That is why at NUMMI, like all Toyota plants, employees do group brainstorming and are rewarded for making group and individual suggestions about process improvements. Diverse, even wild, ideas are encouraged to develop better ways for doing routine production tasks, including better ideas for driving out unwanted variation. If your company's or business unit's primary mission is to explore new possibilities, then your goal should be to build a culture that supports *constant* mindfulness and experimentation, not the ability to generate new ideas now and then. If so, you might want employees to have religious zeal, but of a much different kind. Your company—or more likely part of it—needs to be a place that generates many disparate ideas. It should be an arena, a constant and constructive contest, where the best ideas win. If you want exploration, don't teach people the right and wrong ways to do things. Otherwise they might end up like the men wearing those silly hats in the cartoon below, who do it because it is part of the company culture, but don't know when or why the tradition started.

Some companies create mindful cultures accidentally. I know of several successful high-technology firms that (unwittingly) used hiring processes that were so ill-defined and ambiguous that employees had to invent their own tactics and rules to get a job, and after they got it, to do the work. David Bowen and his colleagues described what newcomers

*"I don't know how it started, either. All I know is that it's part of our corporate culture."*

faced at Sun Microsystems during 1985 to 1990 when it was the fastest growing U.S. company.[10] Sun was growing because it was inventing and selling innovative computers and related products. Job candidates were given numerous interviews, but "The process is full of ambiguity, lacks formal rules, and demands that all employees engage in problem solving to get themselves hired."[11] The lack of standardization in the hiring process at Sun was due, in part, to its nearly out-of-control growth. But this messy process also helped ensure that employees who were hired would rely on their distinct individual skills, abilities, and judgment to get their work done. People who figured out how to get themselves hired had the confidence and ability to make up solutions as they traveled through organizational life, rather than waiting for others to tell them how to think and act. They didn't expect or need established and proven systems to get their work done.

Some companies also take deliberate steps to create a culture where people don't look to company traditions, bosses, or even other insiders for guidance about how to do their work. Such companies can have strong cultures, but they are cultures that glorify people who try different things, who see old things in different ways, and who defy and ignore precedent. You want people to draw on their diverse individual experiences, not company history. You want a culture with mantras like: "Be yourself," "Ignore your boss," "Ignore what the firm has done in the past," "Defy organizational history," "Invent your own procedures." To do so, companies use some strange, but effective, practices when they hire newcomers, educate employees, or orchestrate and reward employee action.

### Hire Defiant Outsiders

Companies sometimes hire people who are given a mandate to defy established ways of doing things. Outsiders can get such a mandate when they have skills that the firm lacks but desperately needs. Anointed by top management to implement their knowledge, they can be powerful deviants whom veteran insiders find threatening. Several senior managers have described to me how they hired newcomers and gave them the authority to challenge the "trolls," "traditionalists" or "sacred-cow protectors," to take on those veteran members who sustain ingrained but dysfunctional practices. These anointed newcomers may be given the power to ignore, overwhelm, or fire insiders who get in their way, especially when the firm has failed to accomplish something in the newcomers' areas of expertise. Managers are especially prone to give newcomers such license after a conspicuous and costly failure. Like other people who have failed, such managers will be more open to new ideas than those who have succeeded, because they have good reason to believe that things are broken and need new fixes.[12]

In a Fortune 500 firm that my colleagues and I studied, an information technology (IT) manager was hired to help plan and oversee the implementation of a series of SAP software systems.[13] So-called enterprise-wide software systems like SAP are integrated systems that help companies communicate, store, and retrieve information in more efficient ways than had been possible before, enabling them to automate tasks in areas such as finance, materials management, production planning, sales, and human resources. These complex software systems have helped many companies handle information in more reliable and less costly ways, but they are notoriously difficult to implement.[14] Executives in this large firm decided to bring in this skilled outsider who had more than 10 years experience implementing these kinds of systems in other firms, because they had such a "miserable failure" on a related project a few years earlier.

This outsider and the rest of his project management "office" (which, besides him, included two other employees and a consultant, who all shared power equally) implemented a series of SAP projects on time and under budget. An internal survey also indicated that employees who used the first of these SAP system were overwhelmingly satisfied with the way it was implemented, the system itself, and its ease of use. We interviewed the managers and other employees at this first site, and they confirmed that the system worked well and the implementation had been well managed. Our interviews confirmed that several other SAP projects had subsequently been implemented by this team with equal success. The IT manager who was brought in from the outside argued that these implementations were so successful because his team could ignore and defy ingrained ways of doing things.

> Every single thing we do on a daily basis goes against every standard policy and procedure of this organization. Everything we do just goes against the grain of how [the corporation] does things. . . . I have no idea how we were able to get away with it as

long as we have . . . Now people are trying to reel us back in and they can't. [They are saying] "Come back, go on another path." We are saying, "No." Why? You've got successes behind you. GL [general ledger] went live, on time, under budget. AP [accounts payable] went live, on time, under budget. Project systems went live, on time, under budget. Fixed Assets is on track to go and AR [accounts receivable] is on track. Why change?

Top management's sheer desperation forced them to anoint these deviants, to give them the clout to defy ingrained ways of doing things, at least until the crisis had past.

## Use "Backward" Socialization

You might want to take the idea of using newcomers to increase the range of ideas and perspectives a step further: Have newcomers teach old-timers how to think and act. I call this "backward" socialization. It includes reverse mentoring. Newcomers are assigned to veterans as in any mentoring program, but newcomers do the teaching and veterans do the listening, learning, and imitating. The formal socialization process might also be reversed, with newcomers teaching classes to old-timers. Backward socialization happened at times during the SAP implementation described above. The new IT manager was far more knowledgeable about implementing these systems than other members of the firm, so many insiders did listen to and learn from him.

The notion that experienced insiders should defer to outsiders who are ignorant of their organization's culture and practices sounds less absurd if you think about the powerful outsiders whom firms bring in (and pay handsomely) to change how insiders think and act.[15] The most obvious case is bringing in a new CEO from the outside to destroy the past and create a new future. Much research shows that when a firm is in financial or legal trouble, or is stuck in the past, a CEO from outside rather than inside will probably get the job. Lou Gerstner is an example of an outsider hired by IBM to help change its ways. He had worked at McKinsey & Company, was president of American Express, and had been CEO of RJR Nabisco. Gerstner started challenging the IBM culture on his first day simply by wearing a blue shirt (IBM was famous for its white-shirt uniform). He eventually led other, more substantive, countercultural changes, notably transforming IBM into a firm that currently profits more from selling consulting services than products.[16]

Carly Fiorina was president of Lucent Technologies' Global Service Provider Business when Hewlett-Packard recruited her to be their new CEO. Fiorina had also led the implementation of Lucent's 1996 initial public offering and subsequent spin-off from AT&T. She was hired to change HP's culture and business practices so it could compete better in the fast-moving Internet and computer markets.[17] Fiorina used language that conveyed a new sense of urgency: "This brave new world is not for the faint of heart. It is not for the weak of stomach, but it is a world where technology can make truly amazing things possible."[18] She focused HP's strategy—which had been unclear to both insiders and outsiders—on being an integrated provider of information appliances, information technology infrastructure, and e-services. And Fiorina quickly altered HP to make it more centralized, and emphasized that she would not tolerate the slow decision making, risk aversion, and internal bickering that had plagued the company in recent years. Fiorina also raised employees' aspirations, emphasizing that she wanted HP to become a winning company with a shining soul.

Executives like Gerstner and Fiorina are brought in from the outside because stockholders and board members believe that troubled firms need an infusion of new ideas. In 1997, Steve Jobs was brought back to lead Apple Computer after being absent for a decade. Jobs was one of the firm's founders, yet he was brought in to destroy much of what Apple had become in his absence and to invent a new future. He eliminated every existing line of computers that Apple made during his first year, focused the firm's attention on designing computers that were fun and interesting, and brought out four entirely new lines of computers by the end of his second year.[19] Apple's recent success may not last, and even if it does, it may never seriously challenge the dominance of Microsoft Windows-based computers. But his accomplishments are impressive nonetheless. Most industry experts believed that Apple was in a death spiral when he took over as CEO. Jobs, along with other outside senior executives and board members he brought in, made more strides during the first three years they ran Apple than even the most optimistic observers believed possible in 1997.

External consultants are another kind of outsider hired ("rented" is probably more accurate) to bring in new ideas. U.S. corporations spent over $43 billion on management consultants in 1996, and all signs suggest that the amount has grown considerably since then.[20] Consultants like McKinsey and Accenture are hired to teach and transfer knowledge from other companies, to convince veterans to discard old ways, and to adopt "best practices" from other firms. These are the same benefits that a company gets from backward socialization. In other cases, corporations hire trainers from other corporations that have "best practices" to teach their people new ways of thinking and acting. Motorola University, which is famous for teaching quality management methods, was "rented" by Citigroup (formerly Citibank) a few years ago to import Motorola's philosophies and methods to an entirely different product environment. The Disney Institute, at Disney World in Florida, sells its training services to other companies and government agencies. They hold classes, and take people backstage at Disney World, to show how Disney's methods generate loyalty and satisfaction in customers and employees. It is advertised as a chance to "benchmark with a world-class organization."

> The most unique element of our programs is that you not only learn concepts, philosophies, techniques, and strategies, but you use the Walt Disney World® Resort as a model to see them in action. It's an unparalleled opportunity to learn new ways to apply core business best practices from a world-renowned business leader.[21]

When firms bring in outside consultants, or "rent" training units of other firms, they want an effect that is akin to backward socialization. As one manager who hired an external consultant to improve his firm's customer service put it: "We are doing this to change our DNA a bit." Yet there may be a cheaper way to implement change that achieves more enduring effects: Bring in new employees with new skills, and find ways that they can actually use and spread their knowledge. Consultants and trainers from other firms may have good ideas, but they usually leave before these ideas are customized or tested by the people and firms they advise. Most external consultants and trainers focus on transferring knowledge, not on making sure that it is turned into action by their clients.[22] In contrast, regular employees who bring in new ideas can actually implement their ideas, as long as they are not ignored or banished because they are deviants, or are brainwashed to accept and imitate the organization's code. If these misfits are given some power, or at least left alone, they can change the corporate code so that other members have a broader "menu" of ideas for solving new problems and can see old problems in new ways. And it just might be a lot cheaper—and more effective—than renting some outsiders who won't stick around.

---

### Putting Weird Idea #4 to Work

*Innovation via Weak, or "Backward," Socialization*

- Don't teach newcomers company history or procedures.

- Teach newcomers to ignore what veteran coworkers say and do.

- Teach newcomers that company history and procedures won't help them; tell them to do their jobs *however they choose*.

- Newcomers should talk, veterans should listen.

- Assign newcomers to mentor and teach classes for veterans.

- The first days and weeks after a newcomer arrives are the best time for veterans to learn from them, because they aren't yet brainwashed about the "right way" to think and act.

- Hire corporate trainers from other companies, especially other industries, to teach classes about solving technical and managerial problems.

- Hire senior managers from other companies and industries, and give them the power and resources to destroy old practices and business models, and to teach—and require—people to do things in new ways.

- Bring in consultants to teach you effective practices from other companies and industries, but don't expect them to be nearly as effective at implementing their ideas as new employees.

---

## Encourage People to Ignore and Defy Authority

Weak socialization practices and backward socialization can be used to help bring varied people and ideas into a company. But if a company wants to maintain an innovative culture, it is even more important to routinely encourage people to defy authority figures and established procedures. Organizations—including so-called flat organizations—are hierarchical, with a few bosses and many subordinates. This means that if people only talk about and do what their bosses expect, ask, and order them to do, relatively few ideas will be discussed and tried. In the lingo of evolutionary theory, the variance in the gene pool is reduced. People who do what they think is right, rather than what they are told or anticipate their superiors want, can drive their bosses crazy and can get their bosses and companies in deep trouble. But they also force companies to try promising ideas even though some boss or powerful group has rejected them as a waste of time or money, or finds them threatening. These deviant, insubordinate, and stubborn people not only take enormous delight in proving their superiors wrong, they sometimes come up with wonderful new ideas, and sometimes even help the same people to get rich who squelched their ideas to get rich.

This may sound like incompetent management if you believe that effective leaders are smarter than their subordinates and should have nearly complete control over their underlings. No doubt organizations have been damaged or even destroyed by defiance of authority and established procedures. And some risks are downright idiotic, like the Aeroflot pilot I mentioned in Chapter 1 who let his teenage son fly a passenger plane, resulting in 75 deaths. Rather, I am talking about allowing intelligent risks by skilled people, or even risks that seem dumb—including those by naive or ignorant people—when serious harm cannot be done.

There is quantitative evidence that innovation increases when managers don't devote constant attention to employees and allow them to act without getting permission first. A study by Anne Cummings and Greg Oldham of 171 employees in a manufacturing plant compared those with controlling and noncontrolling supervisors.[23] Cummings and Oldham found that, especially for creative employees in complex jobs, those with noncontrolling supervisors made considerably more novel and useful suggestions. Regardless of what managers do, innovation also increases when employees don't ask for permission before doing things, don't bother to tell managers what they are doing, and even defy their superiors' orders. Michael Kirton has led a series of studies that contrast the problem-solving styles of *adaptive* people (who make small improvements within existing frameworks) with *innovative* people (who ignore existing frameworks and reframe problems). He used the 32-item Kirton Adaptation-Innovation Inventory (KAI) to measure this distinction, which categorized innovators as people who bend or break rules, risk doing things differently, and act without proper authority. Research with the KAI shows that innovators produce more novel ideas than people with adaptive styles.[24]

I have found dozens of cases where creativity happened because of, not despite, underlings who ignored, defied, or even misled their superiors. About 15 years ago, several of us at Stanford did a case study of the rise and decline of the Atari Corporation.[25] Chris Crawford was the most interesting person we interviewed. He was a charismatic software designer who became an evangelist for Atari products.[26] He explained that Atari made hundreds of millions of dollars in the late 1970s and early

1980s, partly because software designers ignored, misled, and even lied to executives about which products they were developing for the VCS 2600 (a programmable home video player that attached to a television). Crawford told us that Warner brought in executives from other industries "who were always trying to get rid of games." When Crawford wanted to spend more time designing games, his boss told him, "There is no market for games. Atari is not interested in doing games for its computer." This advice troubled Crawford and other engineers. Atari had been successful largely because former CEO Nolan Bushnell hired people who loved designing computer hardware and software for playing video games. But many of the new managers that Warner brought in saw games as frivolous and insisted that designers develop "more practical" programs for keeping track of recipes, balancing checkbooks, and other chores.

Many Atari designers, and sometimes their immediate bosses, responded to these demands by pretending to work on the practical programs, while actually working on the games. One designer proposed to develop "Star Raiders," which became a best seller. The idea was rebuked by top management who, according to Crawford, told the designer, "A game in which you fly around in space and shoot up other space ships? That is the stupidest idea that we have ever heard. . . . Kill the project. There is no way we are going to allow that kind of junk." Star Raiders was completed only because the designer's immediate boss misled senior managers, telling them, "Oh yeah, he's working on a checkbook balancing program." Crawford reported this was just one of many incidents where designers didn't tell senior management, or lied to them, about the games they were developing. Crawford also said that when the games turned big profits for Atari and fueled the sales of the VCS 2600, which become the (then) largest-selling home electronics product of all time, the formerly critical executives claimed credit. These executives who were so skeptical about games in the 1970s would never have believed it could happen, but industrywide revenue from computer games was $7.4 billion in 1999, compared to $7.3 billion from motion picture box offices.[27]

Such defiance hasn't helped only companies where executives have little or no technical knowledge about the work they are managing. Masking tape, one of the most successful products in 3M's history, paved the way for the development of Scotch tape, 3M's most successful product line. Masking tape was invented and commercialized because a young employee named Richard G. Drew defied a direct order from CEO

William McKnight to stop his unauthorized work on the product and return to his assigned tasks in quality control.[28] Similarly, in David Packard's autobiographical book *The HP Way: How Bill Hewlett and I Built Our Company,* cofounder Packard admits to—actually seems to brag about—an engineer's defiance:

> I mentioned that sometimes management's turndown of a new idea doesn't effectively kill it. Some years ago, at an HP laboratory in Colorado Springs devoted to oscilloscope technology, one of our bright, energetic engineers, Chuck House, was advised to abandon a display monitor he was developing. Instead he embarked on a vacation to California—stopping along the way to show potential customers a prototype of the monitor. He wanted to find out what they thought, specifically what they wanted the product to do and what its limitations were. Their positive reaction spurred him to continue with the project, even though on his return to Colorado, he found that I, among others, had requested it be discontinued. He persuaded his R&D manager to rush the monitor into production, and as it turned out, HP sold more than 17,000 display monitors representing sales revenue of $35 million for the company.
>
> Some years later, at a gathering of HP engineers, I presented Chuck with a medal for "extraordinary contempt and defiance beyond the normal call of engineering duty." . . . "I wasn't trying to be defiant or obstreperous. I really just wanted a success for HP," Chuck said. "It never occurred to me that it might cost me my job."[29]

Innovation also happens when senior managers don't bother to stop people who are doing unauthorized work, or even to check into what they are doing. Innovators often find a "crack" in a company's procedures or structures where no one has clear authority—or at least a clear incentive—to stop them. This happened a lot at Atari; many video games were written by people who, rather than openly defying their bosses, just found a way to stay under the radar. The invention of the "Momsen Lung" is another example.[30] Charles "Swede" Momsen was a submarine commander in the United States Navy in the 1920s. He stood by while sailors died in a sunken submarine, with no way to help. The pain and frustration prompted Momsen to develop ideas about ways that sailors could escape from sunken submarines. His first proposal for a "rescue bell" that would be attached to subs was endorsed by experienced officers as an idea worth testing, but was rejected by U.S. Navy bureaucrats as "impractical from the standpoint of seamanship."[31]

A couple of years later, when another submarine sank and the crew slowly asphyxiated while they pleaded to be rescued, Momsen couldn't stand by any longer. Although he had no formal technical training, he assembled a group of volunteers and found a bit of money to work on the problem. Some senior navy officials heard rumors that he was working on the problem, but none actually bothered to stop him, or even check into what he was doing. Within a few months, his team had developed and successfully tested a prototype for a device (which looked like a life jacket with a nose plug hanging from it) that enabled sailors to traverse from a sunken submarine to the surface. Momsen demonstrated the device to a newspaper reporter, escaping from a test barrel that was sunk (along with him) 110 feet below the surface. The navy found out about this test the same way the public did—by reading about it in the papers. When Momsen returned to port the next day, he was greeted by the chief of naval operations, who demanded, "Young man, what the hell have you been up to?"[32] But the wave of positive publicity caused the navy to commission more tests, not to punish Momsen. These tests were successful, culminating in Momsen's escape from a submarine that was (intentionally) sunk to 207 feet below the surface. Momsen was given the Distinguished Service Medal, and the navy ordered 7,000 Momsen Lungs for all active navy submarines.

People like these who succeed by defying or ignoring their bosses are fun to read about. And companies sometimes benefit from people with the courage to act on their convictions. But people who defy authority often reap punishments instead of rewards, even when they have great ideas. If a company wanted to officially encourage employees to defy their superiors, I am not quite sure how this policy would be written, implemented, and supported. I've never seen an organization, for example, with guidelines such as "Ignore your boss if you think he or she is wrong," "Defy stupid orders," or "Lie to your boss if you think it will help the company." If you work in a place that actually enforces rules like these, please contact me immediately. I've heard of cases where it is said to happen, but it often turns out to be hollow talk.

I have, however, found some companies that encourage risk taking with the "don't ask, don't tell" technique. Managers provide vague encouragement for employees to work on what they want, but don't ask what they are doing and employees don't tell them. The old idea that "if you ask me no questions, I will tell you no lies" is a quasi-official policy in a surprising number of companies. The "don't ask, don't tell" policy is made explicit at 3M, where technical people are expected to allocate up to 15 percent of their time to working on projects of their own choosing. As William Coyne, 3M's former senior vice president for research and development put it, "They need no approvals. They don't even have to *tell* management what they're working on."[33] Similarly, as mentioned in Chapter 4, Vinton Studios allows artists to use company equipment to work on personal projects during off hours and to take 13-week paid "Walkabouts" to work on their own projects.[34] Founder Will Vinton believes that no matter what he says or what polices he tries to enforce, his best people will find ways to produce their own films, so he makes it harder from them to leave his company by encouraging them to do personal projects on site. Vinton adds, "Every organization values creativity. But creative people need a huge amount of variety in their lives. So why not encourage it? The biggest money makers in any organization are always the people who know how to be different."[35]

The same attitude, and similar practices, are seen at Corning's Sullivan Park research and development lab, which keeps the company furnaces churning out hundreds of kinds of experimental glass each year. Innovations by scientists at Sullivan Park and elsewhere in Corning have meant that 57 percent of the company's sales in 1998 and 78 percent of sales in 1999 came from products less than 4 years old.[36] Scientists are "required" to spend 10 percent of their time on "Friday afternoon experiments," to work on "slightly crazy ideas." This policy not only allows scientists to work on projects that bosses don't know about, it also frees them to work on pet projects that superiors have discontinued. Like everywhere else, authorities at Corning are sometimes wrong: "One whole genomics-technology business is being built on an idea that at one point was killed by the head of research, but which was pursued nonetheless in Friday afternoon experiments."[36] When an innovative company is managed right, leaders recognize they can't be sure which ideas will succeed and which fail, so they have policies that enable employees to sidestep their judgments.

A related approach is to have senior managers who don't hesitate to express negative opinions when they believe people are pursuing a misguided project, but who stop short of insisting that the work be discontinued. Executives who try to persuade people to halt projects that they believe are doomed, but who (at least occasionally) allow people to continue if they feel strongly that a project will succeed, understand what it takes to spur innovation. They realize that most creative people will be inspired to put in extra effort if they are given a chance to prove the boss wrong. They also realize they might be wrong, and if they squash every project where smart people disagree with their judgments, intelligent risks will be stifled. Further, as we saw, some companies are innovative despite—not because of—executives who stop projects that they judge to be misguided. These overbearing executives do not necessarily have more control over their companies; they may simply know less about what is happening because subordinates—especially creative ones—will hide or disguise their work.

If you discover that your employees are doing forbidden things, you should pause to ponder whether stamping out these covert actions will help or hurt your company. Vetoing an unauthorized activity can not only undermine performance, it can also provoke talented people to leave. For example, research by Stanford's Siobhan O'Mahony shows that the open source operating system, Linux, has been used in many companies without the knowledge or support of top management. The chief information officer of one Fortune 500 firm suspected that his staff was using the (forbidden) Linux operating system, but he was not certain. Using someone else's name, he called a Linux user's group meeting to see who would attend. He was shocked when several hundred people showed up, some who reported to him, including several of his managers. But he didn't get upset. Instead, he decided—on the spot—that if so many of his best people were interested in Linux, and willing to attend a voluntary meeting outside of work to learn more, his company should consider supporting the system. Today, they use Linux to run many critical Web applications; it has proven to be less costly and more effective than the propriety solutions it has replaced. This decision was viewed as a triumph by some of the firm's best technical staff, who, rather than searching for jobs elsewhere, are eager to work on open source solutions.[37]

## Managing by Getting out of the Way

Leading innovation can mean doing less rather than more. Hire some smart people, encourage them to ignore and defy you under certain circumstances, get out of the way, and see what happens. After spending a few years studying IDEO Product Development, I was named an IDEO Fellow, which means that I get to hang around, ask annoying questions, and watch how they turn their ideas into new products. I am also sometimes asked to talk to reporters and executives from other firms about IDEO, and the question they ask most is, "Why are the people there so creative?" The short answer is that IDEO understands that, especially in the early stages of the product development process, management oversight can drive out creativity. Once, an executive from a large manufacturing corporation was pressuring me to give him a step-by-step recipe, the precise details, the exact schedule, for transforming his organization into one that is routinely innovative like IDEO. My answer was, "Just do what David Kelley does. Hire a bunch of smart people and stay out of the way until they ask you for help. If you are telling them what to do, you are making it harder for them to do creative work." It was an obnoxious answer to an impossible question, but it was also an accurate answer.

Being wise enough to get out of the way and defer to others is especially important when you manage something that you don't understand. A striking example is the upside-down influence hierarchy at MTV, the music television channel that now reaches 300 million households in 83 countries. The "demo" (the demographic sweet spot that MTV aims to attract) is 18- to 24-year-olds. The result is that "when you are in your early twenties and are working for MTV, you carry in your brain, muscles, and gonads a kind of mystical authority your bosses don't possess." One thirty-something programming manager remarked that, when someone comes to him with an idea, "I may say, O.K., I like it, but I am not in the demo . . . If I'm in love with something then an alarm bell should go off." Producers in their mid-20s, who have just emerged from the demo, have the greatest influence over MTV programming, and by the time they reach their late 20s "a weird career anxiety begins to set in" and they feel the pressure to leave so they can be replaced by younger people who are still in touch with the demo.[38]

This anxiety is evident even among the most senior MTV executives. Right after Judy McGrath took over as the 41-year-old president and creative head of MTV in 1993, she worried aloud, "You know, I sometimes feel that maybe a twenty-year-old person should be doing the creative-director part of my job. Why am I doing it? What do I know about being twenty?"[39] One reason McGrath has been successful, of course, is that she defers to those who still know how it feels to be 20 years old. Indeed, since McGrath took over as president of MTV, it has become one of the top five

---

### *Putting Weird Idea #4 to Work*

*Innovate by Encouraging People to Ignore and Defy Their Bosses*

- If a boss disagrees with something an employee is working on, give the employee the chance to prove the boss wrong.

- Teach managers to tolerate employees who ignore or defy orders to stop work on "pet" projects that might benefit the company.

- Reward, or at least don't punish, employees who "ask for forgiveness later rather than permission in advance."

- Give recognition and rewards to people who have pursued risky but potentially promising projects that their bosses have tried to stop or were never told about. Make sure to provide such recognition and rewards for both successful and unsuccessful projects.

- Encourage—even require—people to spend 15 percent or so of their time on projects that do not require managerial approval.

- Provide space, time, and resources for employees who want to work on "pet" projects, and don't ask how it is being used.

- If you discover that people are doing something unauthorized, or even expressly forbidden, figure out if it is something that could benefit the company before stamping it out.

- Sometimes the best way to spark innovation is to get out of the way; don't ask employees many questions or give them much advice. This is especially true when employees have far more knowledge about the work than you.

---

most profitable networks alongside Fox, HBO, NBC, and ABC, with estimated revenues of over $750 million in 2000.

There are other companies where, even if executives are more intrusive than David Kelley and Judy McGrath, they realize that when their people are pressing hard to develop an idea—even an idea the executives are not sure about—the best thing to do is get out of the way. The team that developed Java, Sun Microsystems' hugely successful programming language for the Internet, reached a critical point when, after working in obscurity for months, team members had a bombastic meeting with senior Sun executives. The group included John Gage, director of Sun's science office, and co-founder Bill Joy. Everyone "screamed at each other for two days."[40] Joy especially pushed the team to develop the language much further. In the end, even though Sun's executives disagreed with many things the team were doing, they "did the best thing they could at the moment. They backed off . . . there was no question of their [the team's] technical brilliance. So the executives backed off, and let them continue to *dork around* and fumble their way to products, a business model, and a strategy."41

Sometimes, the best management is no management at all. Jeffrey Pfeffer likes to say that managers should be required to take something like the physician's oath: "First, do no harm." At least in the case of the Java team, Sun's executives had the wisdom to get out of the way and do no harm. They realized that to breed innovation, sometimes the best thing you can do is relinquish control and give people the chance to prove you wrong.

### CHAPTER 8

# Find Some Happy People and Get Them to Fight

## (Weird Idea #5)

When people agree with me I always feel I must be wrong.

*—Ambrose Bierce, playwright*
*and satirist*

Multiple disciplines in the same studio, fights over what radio station to listen to, divergent perceptions over appropriate work hours, modes of dress, codes of behavior, even what was perceived as quality of work . . . all of this I saw as rich and yeasty opportunity for the kinds of friction I wanted to turn into light rather than heat. The uneasiness in my stomach and the fireworks in my brain told me there was some vital connection between the abrasiveness itself and original thinking.[1]

*—Jerry Hirshberg, founder and president*
*of Nissan Design International*

I don't want any yes-men around me. I want everyone to tell me the truth—even though it costs him his job.

*—Samuel Goldwyn*

IF YOU WANT INNOVATION, you need happy warriors, upbeat people who know the right way to fight. A growing body of research suggests that conflict over ideas is good, especially for groups and organizations that do creative work. Constant argument can mean there is a competition to develop and test as many good ideas as possible, that there is wide variation in knowledge and perspectives. One study, for example, showed that when group members fought over conflicting ideas, it provoked them to weave others' ideas together with their own, to insist that others provide a compelling logical rationale for their ideas, and to contribute still more ideas.[2] The resulting solutions were more comprehensive, integrated, and well-defended.

When everyone in a group always agrees, it may mean they don't have many ideas. Or it may mean that avoiding conflict is more important to them than generating and evaluating new ideas. It may even mean that people who express new ideas are ridiculed, ostracized, and driven out of the group. Regardless of the reasons, lack of conflict and dissent means the group is unlikely to express and develop many valuable new ideas. Groups—and societies—that stifle people with new, untested, ideas undermine both imagination and personal freedom. As Robert F. Kennedy put it, "It is not enough to allow dissent. We must demand it"— which is sound advice for any leader who wants a constant supply of new ideas. Or to paraphrase chewing-gum magnate William Wrigley Jr., "When two people in business always agree, one of them is unnecessary."[3]

When an idea is beyond its infancy, but still unproven, constructive conflict is crucial for developing and testing its value. Conflict is a sign that there is a contest for ideas in the organization, that people are developing and assessing many ideas. Even at this stage, however, not all conflict is constructive. Arguments are crucial to creativity, but people need to learn how and when to fight. In the very earliest stages of idea generation, conflict (and the criticism it entails) is damaging when it causes ideas to be rejected before they can be developed well enough to be evaluated. Worse yet, when conflict rages, fear of ridicule or humiliation causes people to censor themselves before proposing silly or strange, but possibly useful, ideas. This is why idea-generation techniques, such as brainstorming, require participants to "withhold judgment" or "avoid criticism."[4] For example, Peter Skillman is director of product design engineering for Handspring, the maker of personal digital assistants. Skillman trains people not to attack others' ideas in brainstorming groups: "If somebody says that an idea sucks, when somebody says something nasty, I ring a little bell. I make a joke out of it, but it stops them from ripping apart ideas we need to build on and think about more."[5]

Conflict is also destructive once the creative process is over and it is time to implement an idea. Agreement is important once an idea has been developed and tested, and the right path has been chosen; agreement helps ensure that everyone will use the same methods, in the same way, and work toward the same ends. If you were having a simple and proven operation like an appendectomy, you wouldn't want any argument in the operating room about how it should be done.

Research on group effectiveness shows that two kinds of conflict need to be distinguished. The destructive kind is called "emotional," "interpersonal," or "relationship-based" conflict. This is when people fight because they dislike each other and may have a history of trying to harm one another. They are not fighting over what ideas are best, but because they dislike or feel threatened by each other. This kind of conflict upsets and demoralizes people. Groups that fight this way are less effective on both creative and routine tasks. A researcher at the Wharton School of Business described how a group in one company suffered as a result of such personal conflicts:

> The language was harsh (i.e., bitch, asshole, jerk) and behavioral responses were strong (i.e., slamming doors, pouting, crying, or "tearing up"). A member of the communication group told me [the group suffered because of] "Personality conflicts between creative people. So, at that time Trina sat over there, and that's when we first had problems because her radio was too loud and she was a bitch." . . . "Trina and I don't get along, we never will get along. We dislike each other and that is all there is to it."[6]

In contrast, constructive conflict happens when people argue over ideas rather than personality or relationship issues. Researchers call this "task," or "intellectual" conflict. This kind of conflict happens when people "base discussion on current factual information" and "develop multiple alternatives to enrich the debate."[7] These are fights over ideas—about which ones are best, and why—in an atmosphere of mutual respect. Some of the most creative groups and organizations in history had people who respected each other, but fought mightily over ideas. Bob Taylor, a psychologist turned research administrator, encouraged exactly this kind of conflict first among the computer scientists from various universities he funded while at ARPA in the 1960s (the U.S. Defense Department's Advanced Research Projects Agency) and later at Xerox PARC in the 1970s.[8] These scientists and engineers, perhaps more than any others, are responsible for the technologies that made the computer revolution possible, including the personal computer, the Internet, and the laser printer. The computer scientists Taylor funded through ARPA met at an annual series of research conferences.

> The daily discussions unfolded in a pattern that remained peculiar to Taylor's management style throughout his career. Each participant got an hour or so to describe his work. Then he would be thrown to the mercy of the assembled court like a flank steak to a pack of ravenous wolves. "I got them to argue with each other," Taylor recalled with unashamed glee. . . . "These were people who cared about their work. . . . If there were technical weak spots, they would almost always surface under these conditions. It was very, very healthy."[9]

At Xerox PARC, Taylor continued to foster constructive conflict through a weekly meeting called "Dealer," after a popular book at that time called "Beat the Dealer." There was a speaker for the week, called "the dealer," who was responsible for setting both the topic for the week and the rules of debate. The dealer would then propose an idea and try to defend against a group of some of the most critical, motivated, and brilliant engineers and scientists in the world, who were "all lounging improbably on beanbag chairs upholstered in ghastly mustard-yellow fabric."[10] At both the ARPA research conferences and "Dealer" at PARC, Taylor supported only intellectual conflict, and barred relationship- or personality-based conflict. As Taylor put it, "If someone tried to push their personality rather than their argument, they'd find that it wouldn't work."[11] In these "intellectual free-for-alls," he said,

> it was not to be personal. Impugning a man's thinking was acceptable, but never his character. Taylor strived to create a democracy where everyone's ideas were impartially subject to the group's learned demolition, regardless of the proponents' credentials or rank.[12]

There is mounting evidence that groups that avoid interpersonal conflict—and stick to intellectual conflict—are more effective, especially at creative work.[13] But intellectual conflicts are never so free of personal animus, stubbornness, or anger as this distinction implies. Groups that fight over ideas can, all too easily, slip into nasty personal conflict, especially when reputations, careers, and big bucks are riding on the group's performance. People who have their ideas attacked may, perhaps rightly, believe they are facing thinly veiled personal attacks. These negative reactions can make it hard to learn from critical comments. They may also provoke revenge, which can be cloaked as rational arguments against an opponent's position or be unbridled personal attacks against the critic's skill or integrity.

There is much evidence that being upbeat versus unhappy, or optimistic versus pessimistic, is a personality characteristic that is fairly stable throughout one's life.[14] One study that followed people over a 50-year period, for example, showed that having an upbeat personality as an adolescent was a strong predictor of job satisfaction decades later.[15] Hiring such upbeat people is one of the best ways to limit destructive personal attacks, and it has many other benefits as well. Humor, joking, and laughter are among the main tools that effective groups use to keep people focused on facts rather than degenerating into personal conflict. Anthropologists, psychologists, and sociologists have shown that humor can help group dynamics in many ways.[16] The irony in many jokes and funny comments helps people remember not to take life too seriously. The laughter it promotes releases tension. I once watched a bankruptcy attorney defuse tension about charging high fees to creditors (who were already owed millions of dollars by the bankrupt firm he represented) by using a stream of tasteless lawyer jokes.[17] Humor can be damaging when it is used against people who are different, but can be constructive when used to raise sensitive issues and deliver serious messages in less threatening ways, which is especially important for promoting a contest between opposing ideas or choices.

A study of conflict in top management teams of high-technology firms found that the most effective ones consistently used humor, telling jokes during meetings and pulling pranks like decorating the office with plastic flamingos.[18] As the researchers put it, "Speakers can say in jest things that might otherwise give offense because the message is simultaneously serious and not serious. The recipient is allowed to save face by receiving the serious message while appearing not to do so. The result is communication of difficult information in a more tactful and less personally threatening way."[19]

Humor is one of many ways to make people happy. The list is endless: Give them interesting work, treat them with respect, pay them a lot, give them free food, and so on. Some amusing and strange research on emotion suggests less obvious ways. There is now compelling evidence that smiling causes people to feel happy. Requiring people to smile, no matter how they really feel at first, results in increased positive feelings; frowning, conversely, decreases positive feelings. Robert Zajonc and his colleagues show that smiling leads to physiological changes in the brain that cool the blood, which in turn makes people feel happy. The two figures below show that positive emotion and cooler facial temperatures result when people say the letter *e* or the sound "ah" over and over again, apparently because making these sounds requires a smilelike expression. These figures also show that negative emotion (and hotter facial temperatures) result from repeating sounds like the letter *o* or the German vowel *ü*, apparently because making these sounds requires a frownlike expression. This effect was found to be equally strong in both German and American research subjects. These researchers also found direct effects of temperature on emotion, demonstrating that people who have had cold air blown up their noses are happier than those who have had hot air blown up their noses.[20] Hundreds of other studies show that hot temperatures are a powerful and reliable cause of foul moods and interpersonal conflict (especially aggression and violence).[21]

So, if you want to be really weird, try increasing happiness (and thus creativity) by having your people say "ah, ah, ah," "e, e, e, e," or perhaps "cheese" over and over again; or blowing cold air up their noses; or just keeping the buildings cold where creative people work. Or as Jane Dutton at the University of Michigan told me after she heard Robert Zajonc talk

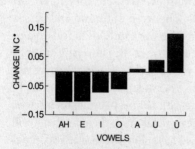

**Changes in facial temperature when uttering different vowels**

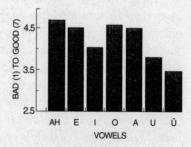

**Reported mood when uttering different vowels**

about these ideas, "When I want to get in a good mood, I'll just go home and stick my head in the refrigerator."

Regardless of how you make your company a happy place, there is a huge literature on the advantages of positive emotion, especially for creative tasks. Psychologists in the United States have devoted an enormous amount of time to studying the virtues of positive emotions, especially during the 1980s. One reason might be that Ronald Reagan was president during this period. This incredibly optimistic fellow was sometimes called the "happy warrior," as was New York State's Governor Al Smith some 60 years earlier. Another explanation is that the U.S. economy during the "go-go 80s" was so vibrant that many people were optimistic about life generally. Who knows, maybe psychologists simply wanted to prove that Bobby McFerrin was right in his hit song, "Don't Worry, Be Happy." Studies examined the differences between happy and unhappy, optimistic and pessimistic people; people with positive affect versus negative affect; happiness versus sadness, and so on. No matter what you call it, there is strong evidence that traveling through life in a good mood is a good thing, especially if you want to be creative.

Many experiments show that when people are put into a good mood (e.g., by giving them candy or showing them a funny movie), they are more creative. For example, they are better at inventing diverse and unusual ways for getting a candle to burn without dripping, or at finding more obscure and remote associations between words and ideas.[22] People in good moods are "more cognitively *flexible*—more able to make associations, to see dimensions, and to see potential relationships among stimuli—than are persons in a neutral state."[23] In other words, they generate more varied ideas and combinations of those ideas, which are crucial aspects of creative work.

These experiments may involve multiple tasks, but they rarely last more than an hour. Research on the link between optimism and persistence is even more pertinent to how creative work unfolds in real organizations. Research by Professor Martin Seligman at the University of Pennsylvania shows that optimists tend to view setbacks as temporary, as not their fault, and as something that won't pervade every aspect of life. In contrast, pessimists have a terrible time with failure, blaming themselves, believing that a single failure means they will fail from then on, that it will pervade every aspect of their lives.[24] As I have shown, innovative companies generate mostly unsuccessful ideas. People who do such work need to be optimistic, for it inoculates them against the loss of energy and effort that follows each failure. Those in innovative companies can't view dead ends, errors, and failures as reasons to give up, or they will never develop the few successful ideas that ultimately result from this potentially disheartening process.

People who are successful at creative work and are involved in other kinds of tasks with high failure rates might need to be more than just optimistic. To keep moving forward and to maintain their mental health, they might benefit by deluding themselves about the probability of success. They might be—and perhaps ought to be—prone to overestimating their chances of success, to deluding themselves into believing that things are and will be better than the evidence suggests at the time. One study compared how managers in large organizations and entrepreneurs made decisions. Entrepreneurs were much more likely to be overconfident in their decisions. Overconfidence may cause problems if it means that firms continue pursuing ideas long after they have proven to be failures. But having more confidence than is warranted by the objective evidence has compensating virtues. Entrepreneurs (and people who do other innovative work) who overestimate their odds of success may work harder and be more persuasive at convincing others to help them succeed, which may increase the (albeit low) chances that any single new idea or company will succeed. An added benefit of such "self-enhancing illusions" is that people who consistently fool themselves into believing that things are wonderful enjoy superior physical and mental health compared with their more realistic (and morose) colleagues.[25]

I don't want to leave you with the impression that negative, grumpy, or nasty people have no role to play in companies. You might hire a few grumpy people because there is evidence that they are less likely to take risks and better at finding things wrong with ideas than upbeat people.[26] One study found that MBAs and engineers with less upbeat personalities were better at unearthing negative information, and took fewer risks, in a simulated decision about whether to race a car given a substantial risk that the engine would fail.[27] This decision had elements of realism because the students used actual data about the link between outside temperature and engine failure that NASA administrators used in their ill-fated decision to launch the Challenger space shuttle, which exploded on January 28, 1986. So in high-risk situations, a few negative people can be especially valuable.

Yet you must be careful before hiring grouchy people. Much research suggests that emotions are contagious, that negative feelings can spread

---

### *Putting Weird Idea #5 to Work*

#### Use "Happy Warriors" to Spark Innovation

- Avoid conflict of any kind during the earliest stages of the creative process, but encourage people to fight over ideas in the intermediate stages.

- Encourage—and teach—people to use tasteful jokes to release tension when arguments over ideas start becoming too tense and personal.

- Teach people how to recognize the differences between interpersonal conflict and intellectual conflict. Use classes and mentoring, and your own actions, to teach them the right (and wrong) way to fight.

- Find examples of how fighting the right way led to more innovation in your company, and tell stories about these successes.

- Senior managers need to set the right example by openly arguing about ideas and avoiding nasty interpersonal conflict.

- If people—including senior managers—continue to engage in nasty personal conflict despite efforts to teach them not to, punish them. If all else fails, fire them.

- Hire upbeat people and do everything possible to keep them that way. Emotions are contagious, so make sure they interact with others in the company.

- Teach people—through classes, mentoring, and setting a good example—to build resistance to rejection and failure.

- Hire a few grumpy people, but keep them away from other people in the company most the time because emotions are so contagious. When you need their expertise and critique, bring them out briefly, and then send them back into isolation.

- If people are upbeat and optimistic, but can't learn how to fight over ideas, they might be better off doing routine rather than creative work.

---

like a disease in a company.[28] One solution to this dilemma is to hire a few grumpy people, but keep them away from everyone else in the company most of the time. I got this idea from a company that had a grumpy engineer who was sometimes nasty and insensitive, but renowned for his ability to uncover errors and problems that others overlooked. Even though everyone else in his building worked in cubicles, they gave him a private office with a door, and brought him out mostly when errors and mistakes needed to be detected. Then he went back into isolation! And since I started talking about this fellow, other executives have told me about at least another half-dozen or so "local grumps" and "resident critics" who are given—or elect to take—a work area that is isolated from others in the company.

### CHAPTER 9

# Reward Success and Failure, Punish Inaction

## (Weird Idea #6)

If you want to succeed, double your failure rate.[1]

> —*Thomas Watson Sr., founder and former CEO of IBM*

Every idea was O.K. Steve Ross had a wonderful philosophy— that people got fired for not making mistakes.[2]

> —*How Steven Ross, chairman of Warner Communications, encouraged wild ideas during MTV's early years*

Creativity is a consequence of sheer productivity. If a creator wants to increase the production of hits, he or she must do it by risking a parallel increase in the production of misses. . . . The most successful creators tend to be those with the most failures![3]

> —*Dean Keith Simonton, researcher, summarizing academic studies on individual creativity*

THERE IS A LOT OF TALK in the business press these days about the wonders of failure. Some stories make it sound as if the more mistakes you make, the richer you get. Management guru Tom Peters quotes everyone from Thomas Edison to Mary Kay Ash (the founder of Mary Kay Cosmetics) to show how people fail their way to success.[4] Benjamin Zander, conductor of the Boston Philharmonic and a frequent speaker on leadership, urges us to celebrate our mistakes. He reacts to his musicians' mistakes by exclaiming, "How fascinating!"[5] At IDEO, David Kelley has argued that the key to innovation is FLOSS: Fail, be Left-handed, get Out there, be Sloppy, be Stupid. And the mantra for innovation at Kelley's company is "Fail early, fail often." American baseball great Babe Ruth probably said it best: "Every strike brings me closer to the next home run."

I don't know about you, but while all this talk about the virtues of failure is convincing and inspiring, I hate when it actually happens to me and mine. I hate my own errors and screw-ups; they annoy and humiliate me. I hate when my family, friends, and colleagues fail; I feel bad for them and always think it is my fault. I don't even like when my enemies fail; I feel sorry for them and have an inexplicable urge to help and comfort them. Failure stinks. Unfortunately, as I showed earlier, every bit of solid theory and evidence demonstrates that it is *impossible* to generate a few good ideas without generating a lot of bad ideas. If you want to eliminate mistakes, avoid dead ends, and succeed most of the time, you will drive out innovation. This chapter is about the reward system that innovative companies need so they will fail enough and in the right ways. My aim is to convince you that if a company wants to encourage people to keep generating new ideas, to test them in unbiased ways, and to avoid reverting to proven ideas and well-honed skills, rewarding success isn't enough; you have to reward failure as well, especially dead ends that teach new lessons and that enable people to have some fun along the way.

A few years back, *Business Week* argued that there were too many new product "flops" and steps could and should be taken to reduce the number of failures from the earliest stages of the development process.[6] This is bad advice. Eliminating flops also eliminates innovation, especially in the early stages of the creative process when generating ideas is crucial. The only way to reduce flops is to avoid unproven ideas and focus on old, proven ideas. *Business Week* would have been wiser to advise firms to fail faster. We all need to be efficient at pulling the plug on ideas that have proven to be bad. If you fail faster, you can get on to (what will probably be) the next bad idea, and learn as much as possible along the way.

This spirit was captured by Soichiro Honda, founder of the Honda Motor Company, when he said, "Many people dream of success. To me success can only be achieved through repeated failure and introspection. In fact, success represents the one percent of your work which results from the 99 percent that is called failure."[7] His remark suggests why the logic of innovation is so different from the logic of exploiting proven knowledge. No one would ever buy a Honda if 99 percent of the parts were defective. From a quality management perspective, variation is the enemy of quality, and any variation from the right way of doing things is correctly called an error. But variation is the friend of innovation. The only way to achieve zero defects in the product development process is to come up with absolutely no new ideas, to use only tried-and-true methods, and to implement that one method perfectly again and again.

Former Warner chairman Steve Ross's philosophy that people who don't make *enough* mistakes should be fired is an anomaly.[8] There are few companies that reward failure, let alone even tolerate it. The belief that successful people deserve to be showered with rewards, and those who fail deserve nothing except perhaps a tongue-lashing, a demotion, or to be fired, is so widely accepted that you may find my idea of rewarding failure to be laughable. I agree that rewarding success alone is *sometimes* right. It is fine if you know the "correct" way of doing things and want to ensure that what people do in the future will be a reasonable replication of past success. It just doesn't make much sense if you want to build a company that is as innovative as possible.

The problem is that rewarding only success discourages people from taking the risks required to import and test new ideas from outside the firm or industry, to find new uses for old ideas, and to try new blends of old knowledge. If you want people to be innovative, then you want them to spend their time dreaming up, refining, and testing unproven—and thus mostly unsuccessful—ideas. Success should be treated like a happy accident, at best an outcome that should worry you if it occurs too often. As a researcher from Duke University put it:

> It is also important to monitor and reward failure, just as a firm monitors and rewards other aspects of an employee's or department's performance. In a firm that is serious about strategic failure, employees who are not producing enough of a "scrap pile" might be viewed as devoting inadequate effort to taking risks, dealing with their failures, and bringing their experiments to resolution.[9]

That old saying "If it ain't broke, don't fix it" is the best reason in the world for staying the course. When things break, or old skills fail in new situations, there is reason to learn and change, to question the status quo and search for new ideas. As Henry Ford put it, "Failure is the opportunity to begin again more intelligently." This notion that failure sparks learning is also captured in a (perhaps apocryphal) story that Warren Bennis tells about IBM's founder and CEO, Thomas Watson Sr. Watson called in a manager who had just made a mistake that cost IBM $10 million. The manager said, "I guess you want my resignation?" Watson replied, "You can't be serious. We just spent $10 million dollars educating you!"[10]

Similarly, Microsoft hired Richard Belluzzo to head its Internet operations. Belluzzo was a high-ranking Hewlett-Packard executive who, after 15 years at HP, then spent almost two years as CEO of Silicon Graphics, where he led a failed effort to turn around the firm. Rather than seeing it as a drawback, however, Microsoft executives apparently viewed Belluzzo's problems at Silicon Graphics as a valuable learning experience that came at another firm's expense. As the *New York Times* reported, "His sometimes difficult experience at Silicon Graphics, which is still losing money and recently shifted strategy once again, is regarded by Microsoft more as a useful learning experience than a black mark on his career."[11]

Companies and other organizations like hospitals and schools, which routinely learn from failures, don't "forgive and forget" when people make mistakes; they "forgive and remember." Forgiveness is crucial when people fail because it enables them to maintain their self-esteem and to continue as useful and respected members of the group, rather than to be ostracized for the "error." Forgiveness is also important because, as a study of surgical errors found, "when a subordinate sees his technical errors are forgiven, he recognizes there is no incentive to hide them. He is less likely, therefore, to compound his problems by attempting to treat problems that are over his head for fear of superordinate reprisal."[12]

Forgiveness isn't enough, however. Organizations that learn from their failures forgive and remember, they don't forgive and forget. As they say at Netscape cofounder Marc Andrerssen's new company, Loudcloud, the goal is to keep making new mistakes, rather than to make the same mistakes over and over again.[13] John Lilly, cofounder of Reactivity (a software firm) is a bit less optimistic about how quickly his or any other company can learn from their mistakes. Lilly told me, "We've learned that, when we don't stop to think and talk about our mistakes, we keep making the same ones over and over. But when we do, we usually make them over a couple of times before we learn not to do it again. I wish we could learn after the first time, but at least we are learning."

Don Hastings, former CEO of Lincoln Electric, showed this ability to forgive both himself and others, to remember what was learned, and to make Lincoln a better company. In a striking *Harvard Business Review* article, he told his readers, as he told Lincoln employees, that the financial losses from the overly aggressive international expansion were top management's fault, and explained what they learned: "The root cause of the crisis was that Lincoln's leaders, including myself, had grown overconfident in the company's abilities and systems. . . . We had been naïve to think that we could instantly become a global company with Lincoln's limited management resources."[14]

I am not saying that your company should reward people who are stupid, lazy, or incompetent. I mean you should reward smart failures, not dumb failures. If you want a creative organization, inaction is the worst kind of failure. Researcher Dean Keith Simonton provides strong evidence that creativity results from action, rather than inaction, more than anything else. In every occupation he studied, including composers, artists, poets, inventors, and scientists, the story is the same: Creativity is a function of the quantity of output.[15] His research shows that "those segments of a creator's career when the most hits emerge will also usually be the same periods that see the most misses as well," and "the quality ratio neither increases nor decreases as the creator gains more experience or maturity."[16]

There are exceptions to this pattern; for example, the botanist and father of genetics Gregor Mendel had a lasting impact with only six publications, and it is often said that mathematicians do their best work before the age of 30. But Edison, da Vinci, Einstein, Newton, and Picasso were more typical "geniuses." All were far more productive than their contemporaries. All had numerous flawed creations. Einstein constructed an elaborate argument against Niels Bohr's work, which failed because he did not take into account his own theory of relativity! Perhaps that is why Einstein said, "A person who has never made a mistake never tried anything new." Isaac Newton spent many hours working at alchemy. Leonardo da Vinci, who is often identified as the smartest person who ever lived, also advocated some crackpot theories. He may have dabbled in human flight by jumping off cliffs armed only with wooden wings. And da Vinci was especially enamored of "physiognomy," the "science" of assessing a person's character through his or her facial features.

In short, research on creative output shows that we can't tell which new ideas will succeed and which will fail at the outset, and that creativity is largely a function of sheer quantity. These findings mean that whether people are doing something—or nothing—is one of the best metrics for assessing people who do creative work, and the evidence indicates that *inaction is the worst failure, perhaps the only kind of failure that deserves to be punished if you want to encourage innovation.* I have, over the years, met people who have tried to convince me to remove the word "punished" from this weird idea. They find the word too harsh. I disagree. If people are not constantly bringing in new ideas, brainstorming about different ways to use old and new ideas, and testing their hunches, there can be no new concepts, products, or services. Use whatever euphemism you want, but if you want innovation, you need to change or get rid of people who fail to act.

Firms should demote, transfer, and even fire people who spend day after day talking about and planning what they are going to do, but never doing it. At a minimum, they should be taught how to actually do something. People who spend their days criticizing their coworkers' ideas but who never have any of their own deserve a similar fate. Likewise, groups that hold meeting after meeting to discuss and write detailed plans about the new products and services they hope to develop but never quite get around to realizing should be disbanded and their leaders removed and retrained. It's probably inaccurate to call "training" a punishment, but believe me, if you pull employees off a job and tell them they can't have it back until they do it differently, they will see it as punishment. It will feel like the time an ice hockey player spends in the penalty box after an infraction.

Jeffrey Pfeffer and I found that many ineffective companies suffer from this disease, which we call the "smart talk trap."[17] This a syndrome where companies hire, reward, and promote people for sounding smart rather than making sure that smart things are done. In such organizations, talking somehow becomes an acceptable—even a preferred—substitute for actually doing anything. Inaction is bad for any company. But it is especially devastating when innovation is the goal, because so many ideas need to be tried to find a few that might work.

Several years ago, I studied a team that was developing an idea for a consumer product. The team members talked endlessly among themselves about whether the product was a good idea. They brought in experts to comment on the product, who all argued about its features. They brought in still more experts to get opinions about whether there was a market for the product. An engineer on the team was trained in the philosophy and methods of rapid prototyping. He kept asking the leader if he could make some prototypes to help the team decide if the product was feasible, what features could be added, and if users might actually want it. He had all the parts at home, and could make a prototype in just a few hours. But his boss kept telling him that it was "too early." After more than a year of talking about the product, not a single prototype had been made, let alone tested. The project was abandoned when an identical (and ultimately successful) product appeared on the market. The company that brought this product to market had also convened a design team about a year earlier, but they did not suffer from the smart talk trap; they quickly started building and testing.[18]

Punishment is not a nice word; it makes people squirm. They don't like being punished, and only a few misguided souls enjoy punishing others. But I believe that the leaders of this ineffective team, or any group that is trying to innovate, deserve to be punished for promoting all talk and no action, for stifling people who actually want to put the team's ideas to the test. Innovation is about much more than having, describing, and criticizing ideas. These first steps are useful, but only if such talk leads to getting the concept, product, or service in a form that it can be tested and refined. Creative companies constantly try new ideas, products, and services under realistic conditions. They use what they learn to decide whether the entire idea is a failure, or short of that, what to change and what to retain. This kind of action needs to be rewarded, and whether a particular idea succeeds or fails doesn't really matter. What matters is that people keep experimenting and learning.

At the SAS Institute, a billion-dollar software company in North Carolina, CEO Jim Goodnight talks openly about the "holes" he and others have dug, and he has an explicit policy of not punishing people who make mistakes. David Russo, SAS's retired vice president for human resources says, "The only smart thing is knowing when to quit digging." The same attitude is seen at Edra, a design house in Milan, Italy, that is renowned throughout the world for its innovative furniture. Head designer Monica Mazzei says that Edra typically starts with 300 renderings, makes about 30 prototypes, and shows perhaps three at Milan's famous Salone Internazionale del Mobile, the largest furniture show in the world.[19] And as I showed in Chapter 1, Skyline, IDEO's toy design company, is successful because of—not in spite of—the fact that they generally develop about 4,000 ideas, turn over 230 into drawings or prototypes, and sell about twelve. Brendan Boyle and his fellow toy designers at Skyline don't cling to ideas or fret about whether they are any good. Instead, they keep talking about more ideas, stopping now and then to turn one into a nice drawing or crude mock-up, and they continue showing their ideas to potential customers. They don't think of themselves as a group that succeeds less than 1 percent of the time; they see themselves as people who never stop thinking up new ideas.

To illustrate, about 10 years ago, when Brendan was fooling around with a CAD (computer-aided design) machine, he drew a prototype of a device that enables people to use at home those "antitheft" coat hangers they have in many hotels, the ones with the little balls on top. Brendan's device is the top half of a hanger, with a slit into which that little ball fits, so if you "borrow" one of those ball-topped hotel hangers, you can use it when you get home. This is a cute and off-the-wall idea. Most audiences giggle when I tell them about it. IDEO never tried to sell this product because they believed the market wasn't big enough and the hotel industry might object to it. Yet this device delights me—and every audience I've ever showed it to—because it is such a charming failure, capturing the playful spirit that keeps an innovation factory humming. Most failed ideas aren't this amusing, but when a company is built for innovation, the passion to keep cranking out ideas is just as strong as it is at Skyline.

Jim Goodnight, Monica Mazzei, and Brendan Boyle don't just talk about the virtues of experimentation and of accepting a high failure rate. They demonstrate such virtues by their actions. This idea of rewarding action, even when it fails, is one that managers like to talk about. They sometimes quarrel with it at first, but typically come to agree with it when they consider the distinction between encouraging people to develop new ideas and using tried-and-true ideas. Yet while they know and may talk about the virtues of a high failure rate, it is harder for many managers to actually reward failed risk taking. In one high-tech company my students studied, new hires were encouraged on their first day to "be risk takers."[20] The CEO was quoted in many company documents as saying he wanted employees to ask "for forgiveness later" for taking risks and trying things that fail, "not for permission in advance." Yet this study showed that when people failed, even when they had instructive failures, senior managers criticized them, withheld stock options, and even fired them. The result was that people at all levels below senior management rarely took risks or experimented. And no one ever admit-

---

### *Putting Weird Idea #6 to Work*

*Innovate by Rewarding Success and Failure, and Punishing Inaction:*

- Promote and hire people who have had intelligent failures, and tell people in the company this is one of the reasons they have been given important jobs.

- Monitor and reward failures, and take time to talk about what was learned.

- If people have a low failure rate, look for signs that they are not taking enough risks or are hiding—rather than helping others learn from— their mistakes.

- Forgive and remember mistakes, don't forgive and forget.

- Encourage new failures but don't reward people who keep making the same mistakes over and over again and never seem to learn from them, no matter how openly they talk about their mistakes.

- Senior managers need to talk about their failures, to signal that it is expected and desirable to do so.

- Use every tool you have—praise, jokes, stories, money, promotions, demotions, even firings—to convey that the failure to act is the greatest failure of all.

- Be wary when people tell you that they don't produce a lot, but when they do, it will be "brilliant." Remember that innovation is largely a function of productivity.

- Remember and learn from the mistakes made by other companies and teams, not just your own. It is cheaper and less painful.

---

ted failure. Despite lip service from trainers and the CEO, it was a place where it was safer to do nothing than to fail.

Finally, although I have focused on learning from your own failures, or failures in your company, it is more efficient and less painful to learn from others' failures. When we think about others' failures rather than our own, we are less likely to get defensive, engage in denial, or try to convince ourselves that the failure was really a success. This is one advantage of the business model used by Hewlett-Packard's Strategic Planning and Modeling Group (SPaM), which was formed about ten years ago to help optimize HP's (often convoluted) supply chains. Many of the HP divisions—over 150 at the time—weren't sharing successes or failures with other divisions, in part because the company was so decentralized. Enter SPaM. They used powerful modeling techniques to save their first clients millions of dollars. Even more important, however, was that each new project taught SPaM new lessons about what worked and what didn't, so that future clients could learn from the mistakes made elsewhere, rather than just from their own setbacks. Corey Billington, who led SpaM for nearly a decade, put it this way: "If an HP division wants to learn about streamlining their supply chain, they can send scouts to every corner of the company or they can talk to us. They might learn some great stuff from talking to the hundreds of people we have worked with inside and outside of HP. But it is a lot faster and cheaper just to work with us."

In short, if you want innovation in your company, you need to reward people for taking intelligent action, not just for talking about the virtues of failure, experimentation, or risk taking. It might not even be enough to give equal rewards for success and intelligent failures. The excessive value that our culture places on success means that people who succeed may still get more kudos than they deserve from peers and outsiders, and those who fail may get more blame than they deserve. To offset this bias, perhaps this weird idea should be "Reward failure even more than success, and punish inaction."

### CHAPTER 10

*Decide to Do Something That
Will Probably Fail,
Then Convince Yourself and
Everyone Else
That Success Is Certain*

*(Weird Idea #7)*

Most deviants end up on the scrap pile of failed mutations, not as heroes or organizational transformation.[1]

—*James March, organizational theorist*

Trust yourself and speak out what you believe. If what you believe is different, dare to be different. Dare to be in a hurry to change things for the better.[2]

—*Geoffrey Ballard, founder of Ballard
Power Systems and coinventor of fuel
cells for powering buses and automobiles*

The self-fulfilling prophecy is, in the beginning, a *false* definition of the situation evoking a new behavior which makes the originally false conception come *true*. The specious validity of the self-fulfilling prophecy perpetuates a reign of error. For the prophet will cite the actual course of events as proof that he was right from the very beginning. Such are the perversities of social logic.[3]

—*Robert Merton, sociologist*

ONE OF THE MAIN REASONS for rewarding both success and failure is that managers, analysts, and other so-called experts (like everyone else) are so bad at predicting which new ideas will succeed that sometimes the only practical thing to do is encourage people to keep trying. I am not saying, as Dilbert cartoons imply, that managers are dumber than their subordinates. Although that is true at times, there are many companies where managers have detailed knowledge of the work they orchestrate. But there is little reason to believe that managers or other authorities will make more accurate predictions than anyone else about which new ideas will succeed and fail. Some executives and experts acknowledge their inability to make accurate predictions. Nokia's CEO Jorma Ollila, for example, reports that, in 1992, his firm predicted mobile phone purchases would grow to 50 million by 2000. These purchases actually grew to 450 million. Ollila emphasized that he has learned to ignore such projections because, although experts often express great confidence in them, they are usually wrong.[4]

After all, authorities rejected Galileo's heretical findings about the shape of the earth, the Wright Brothers' airplane, Xerox's first copier, the television, the microprocessor, the fax machine, and Post-it Notes. Galileo was jailed for asserting that the earth was round.[5] The Wright Brothers were denounced as suicidal maniacs. Everyone who had tried powered flight before had failed, and many had died, so this was a reasonable conclusion at the time.[6] Here is what the head of Twentieth Century-Fox studios, Darryl F. Zanuck, said in 1946 about how American consumers would respond to television: "Video won't be able to hold onto any market it captures after the first six months. People will soon get tired of staring at a plywood box every night."[7] In 1968, an engineer at the Advanced Computing Systems Division of IBM responded to people who asserted that the microprocessor was the wave of the future by saying, "What the hell is it good for?"[8] And engineer Art Fry's idea about Post-it Notes was continually rejected by 3M management, especially marketing.

In hindsight, we know that these "authorities" were wrong to reject these ideas. But the evolutionary perspective suggests that, given the usual fate of new ideas, those who reject new ideas have a far greater chance of being right than wrong. So the problem is not only that you need to hire and fund people who will be wrong most of the time about their weird, wacko, crazy, stupid, and deviant ideas, but also that you won't know when they *aren't* wrong. Organizations try to use all sorts of methods to improve their odds of success. Many firms use "gates" in the product development process, where new ideas are scrutinized by "experts" in marketing, manufacturing, and so on. Hollywood producers hear hundreds of scripts "pitched" to them each year to find a few that might be worth developing into films. Venture capitalists read hundreds of business plans and talk to hundreds of entrepreneurs every year to find a few to fund each year. For example, Heidi Roizen, a venture capitalist at Softbank, screens close to a thousand business plans per year to fund approximately twelve. Producers and venture capitalists both know that the more bad ideas they sift through, the better the chances of finding a few good ones.

These screening practices may reduce the failure rate somewhat (although I can't find evidence to actually support this assertion), but even if they do, the failure rate in domains where innovative work is done remains high even after such careful scrutiny. As one expert on organizational learning put it:

> If it were easy to identify visionary genius, we would embrace it without hesitation. Unfortunately, the difference between visionary genius and delusional madness is much clearer in history books than in experience. . . . The elementary dilemma is that although new, deviant ideas are essential to improvement, most of the dramatically imaginative ideas turn out to be bad ones. . . . The wild ideas of political crackpots, religious heretics, crazy artists, and organizational dreamers are overwhelmingly foolish rather than brilliant. Only a tiny proportion of our heretics will ever be canonized, and we cannot identify the saints ahead of time.[9]

Yet there is one simple, proven, and powerful thing you can do to increase the odds that a risky project will succeed. Once you commit to doing something, a dramatic shift is needed to give it the best possible chance of succeeding. There is overwhelming evidence for the power of positive thinking, that belief can create reality. To increase the chances of success, forget the slim odds. Instead, convince yourself and everyone else that, with determination and persistence, the idea is destined to be a triumph. As Henry Ford put it "If you think you can, or if you think you can't, you are right." Aircraft designer and former test pilot Burt Rutan espoused a similar philosophy to his team when they were developing the Voyager, which became the first airplane to fly non-stop around the world without refueling. Numerous "experts" predicted that the Voyager was doomed to fail, just as they predicted that that other experimental aircraft designed by Rutan wouldn't work. To inspire this feat, Rutan told his engineers that "Confidence in nonsense is required."[10]

The remarkable power of just believing that something (or someone) will be successful, and convincing others to share that belief, has been demonstrated again and again by the voluminous medical literature on placebo effects. Sham operations, sugar pills, and inert vaccines can be as effective as "real medicine," so long as patients expect that the treatment will be effective. In one study, patients who were given fake knee operations (shallow incisions to convince them that they had had an operation, and nothing more) reported the same levels of reduced pain as those who really had their knee joints scraped and rinsed. In drug studies, anywhere from 35 percent to 75 percent of patients improve just from taking fake pills.[11] *The New York Times* reported:

> Last summer, the share price of a British biotech company called Peptide Therapeutics dropped 33 percent after it revealed that its new allergy vaccine was only effective as a placebo. During trials on food-allergy patients, a company spokesman had reported delightedly, 75 percent had improved to the point where they could tolerate foods they'd never been able to before. But when the control group data came in, so, awkwardly enough, had 75 percent of the subjects taking inert tablets.[12]

More than 500 studies have been conducted on the self-fulfilling prophecy. This research doesn't just show that positive expectations can make people feel better, it shows that confidence—even misguided confidence—helps people perform better. Most of this research has been conducted in classrooms, but several dozen studies have been conducted in other organizations as well. These studies find that, independent of other factors, when leaders believe their subordinates will perform well, positive expectations lead to better performance.[13] And the converse holds for poor performance. In nearly all these studies, the researcher misleads the teacher or leader about the virtues of their students or subordinates. In reality, these "high potential" people are randomly selected and have no more or less ability than others.

It can take very little to persuade leaders that subordinates will achieve superior performance. Consider a study in an Israeli boot camp. Drill instructors were told during an interaction lasting just a few minutes that, based on tests on an incoming group of soldiers, it was possible to predict with 95 percent accuracy which one-third had "high command potential." The other soldiers were described as having either average or unknown potential. As in most studies of this kind, the researchers were lying. Soldiers were actually randomly assigned to the "high," "average," or "unknown" groups. No other information was provided to the instructors, and the soldiers were not told what group they were assigned to or even that they were subjects in an experiment. Yet, at the end of 15 weeks in boot camp, compared to soldiers in the "average" and "unknown" groups, soldiers in the "high command potential" group had dramatically superior performance. They excelled at tasks like firing a rifle, navigation, and multiple-choice tests about combat tactics, which were all evaluated by instructors who were not informed about the alleged "command potential" of the soldiers.[14]

This study and related research show that people labeled as "high potential" improve more than their peers because their (deceived) leaders give them more resources and attention, and teach them to believe in themselves. Leaders convince their (randomly anointed) star pupils that setbacks are temporary, not their fault, and won't pervade every aspect of life. And when successes happen, leaders convince their charges that this is the start of a string of successes, that they are responsible for their own success, and that there will be positive ripple effects on many other things they do.

This research also helps explain why successful heretics tend to be so confident and persistent. They believe deeply in what they are doing and are skilled at convincing everyone around them that they are right. Apple cofounder (and, once again, CEO) Steve Jobs does this with his widely ballyhooed "reality distortion field." Insiders recount how he casts a spell on those around him and convinces them that the success of an idea, project, or person is virtually certain. Similarly, Francis Ford Coppola has used his ability to turn belief into reality to drive everything from grand successes like *The Godfather* films and the Niebaum-Coppola Estate Winery, to utter failures like building a television-satellite hub in Belize. Coppola's persuasiveness is demonstrated by what happened when screenwriter John Milius met with Coppola on the chaotic and conflict-ridden set of *Apocalypse Now*. Milius was apprehensive about meeting with Coppola because "I felt like a general going to see Hitler in 1944 to tell him there was no gasoline." Coppola turned the situation around, and got Milius "all excited" by telling him, among other things, that *Apoca-*

*lypse Now* would be the first film to win a Nobel Prize. Coppola reported that, by the time the meeting was over, Milius was saying, "We're going to win the war! We don't need gasoline!"[15]

People like Jobs and Coppola can convince even the most severe critics and skeptics that they are right and that success is certain. But the same fire in the belly that makes them so persuasive to some can also cause them to be intolerant, overbearing, and even mean-spirited toward those who doubt them or stand in their way. Geoffrey Ballard is a perfect example of such a heretic. He and others at Ballard Power Systems (BPS) persisted for 25 years to develop a fuel cell that just might prove to be a power source superior to both batteries and internal combustion engines. There are no toxic by-products from engines powered by these cells, only water pure enough to drink. There is no slow-recharging procedure, just a quick refill of compressed hydrogen. There are already more than a dozen working buses powered by Ballard's cells. Daimler-Chrysler and Ford recently bought large financial stakes in BPS, and DaimlerChrysler announced it intends to sell cars with these cells by 2004 (albeit running on methanol, which is not as clean as hydrogen, but much cleaner than gasoline).[16]

Geoffrey Ballard's belief in the superiority of the fuel cell inspired a skilled, equally persistent, and dedicated team to join him in this long quest, despite numerous technical and financial problems. The same unshakable belief that inspired his team to develop a successful fuel cell caused Ballard to be ridiculed as a crackpot in scientific circles. He realized how overbearing and abrasive he could be, how little tolerance he had for "fools" who did not accept his ideas. This self-knowledge led him to hire, teach, and inspire other people, especially David McLeod, to pitch the fuel cell to government funding sources in Canada. Ballard knew he had made many enemies, and that if he tried to sell the ideas himself he would make even more.

BPS's current top managers are reaping great financial benefit from Ballard's ideas. But they complain that he caused problems for the company by overselling the fuel cell. Mossadiq Umedaly, who was brought on as the chief financial officer at BPS (and who became one of Ballard's main enemies) complained, "The fuel cell . . . has been around a long time. And one of the challenges was that it had no credibility as a technology. Frankly, none! . . . because all these cuckoo clocks had been talking about fuel cells so long. And Ballard was one of those cuckoo clocks."[17] I would add that without "cuckoo clocks" like Ballard, far fewer ideas would have been developed in human history. In the case of Ballard Power Systems, the firm could not have achieved its multibillion-dollar market capitalization.

"Swede" Momsen, the inventor of devices for escaping from sunken submarines mentioned earlier, had the same persistence and intolerance for critics. Momsen was first told by so-called experts that his ideas were certain to fail. Undaunted, he persuaded people with deeper technical knowledge to work with him to develop and test ideas for the Momsen Lung. Later, he used the same determination—and bypassed more procedures and authority lines—to develop a diving bell for rescuing sailors trapped in submarines that had sunk too deep for the Momsen Lung. Like Ballard, he "stepped on too many toes, and reddened too many faces" because he was so dogmatic and overbearing in the process. The result was that, although he conceived the bell, personally directed its development, and nearly died while testing it, the Navy named it after another member of the project who played a smaller role, calling it the McCann Rescue Chamber. In 1939, this diving bell was used to rescue 33 sailors from the *U.S.S. Squalus* who were trapped 247 feet below the surface; it has been called the greatest submarine rescue in history. And it was Momsen, not McCann, whom the Navy asked to direct the rescue.[18]

Taken together, these studies and cases imply that, if you can't decide which new projects or ideas to bet on based on their objective merits, pick those that will be developed by the most committed and persuasive heretics you can find. You should also be aware, however, that their persistence, combativeness, and refusal to compromise can make them difficult and frustrating to manage. They are likely to ignore or insult you if you question what they are doing or why. And their intolerance for skeptics and critics may generate enemies who attack their ideas with guile.

There are other hazards to this weird idea as well. When the prophet is convincing, he or she can inspire people and companies to devote enormous energy to ideas whether they are good or bad. Consider former Motorola CEO and current chairman Bob Galvin, who is credited with making Motorola the great company it is today. He boldly pushed the company to get out of the television business and to focus its energy on microprocessors and other computer technologies, insisting these were the paths to future growth. He was right. Galvin was vehement and persuasive in his arguments that Motorola meet the challenge of Japanese competition by increasing the quality of its products. Many people at Motorola thought Galvin was "crazy" when he insisted that the company spend 1.5 percent of employees' base salaries on training to bolster the skills of people who made their product. He was right again. Motorola saved over $2 billion between 1986 and 1991 and won the prestigious Malcolm Baldrige Quality Award.

In the mid-1990s, Galvin was just as confident and insistent that Motorola should devote enormous resources to the Iridium global communications project. This was a system of small satellites that allowed people with portable phones to make and receive calls from anywhere in the world.[19] The Motorola spin-off company that developed this technology, called Iridium, had a working network for just 474 days and suffered huge financial losses. They projected having 1.6 million users by the year 2000, but they never exceeded 30,000. Iridium filed for bankruptcy in August of 1999 and discontinued the service in March 2000. The confidence that people in Motorola had in Bob Galvin's decisions, and have to this day, helped the company remain innovative for decades. Yet, although Motorola and its shareholders are better off overall since he began his long tenure there, this optimism has a cost: Motorola wrote off $2.5 billion on its investment in Iridium, and the failed start-up lost a total of $5 billion. The rest of us are also at a (very slight) risk as well because the Satellite Network Operations Center, which is operated by Motorola, will spend the next few years "deorbiting" Iridium's 88 satellites. Experts expect some of this space junk to fall to Earth, rather than to be burned up by the atmosphere, because these are such large satellites.[20]

At least Motorola finally had the sense to stop wasting money on the Iridium project. Some believers don't know when to quit no matter how much evidence there is that an idea is hopeless. Engineer Paul Moeller has devoted all of his money and most of his time during the past 32 years to developing the Skycar.[21] This flying car "is capable in theory of lifting straight up past rooftops and then zooming over hill, dale, and traffic jams."[22] Moeller's unwavering confidence and passion have helped him extract millions of dollars from investors. He has also poured millions of dollars of his own money into the project. Moeller had developed a successful $5 million-a-year business called Supertrapp that made aftermarket mufflers for motorcycles. He sold the business and poured the money into the Skycar, explaining, "Anything I did besides working on the flying car was to raise money for the car."[23]

As of this writing, Moeller claims to be close to a working prototype (although he keeps pushing back the test date) and has accepted $5,000 deposits from 100 people. But he admits that even if the prototype works,

---

## Putting Weird Idea #7 to Work

### Innovate by Backing Risky Projects, Then Convince Everyone That Success Is Certain

- Support a few crackpots, heretics, and dreamers, especially if they are wildly optimistic about their ideas.

- Once you decide to support a risky project, convince yourself that success is certain. If you can't, replace yourself with someone who is more optimistic.

- Hire people who are genuinely optimistic about the success of the project or company, and are skilled at instilling such hope in others.

- Optimism does *not* mean ignoring or denying setbacks; it means viewing them as temporary events that can teach crucial lessons, which, if followed, ensure success.

- Focus on "pulling the plug" on failed ideas more quickly, not on reducing your failure rate.

---

he will need at least $45 million before the Skycar can go into production, and at the moment he has no investors. Moeller's persistence is impressive, but the Skycar has been a financial failure for 32 years and there is no hint that it will succeed in the foreseeable future. That is the problem with persuasive and overconfident leaders and inventors: They can convince a lot of people—including themselves—to waste a lot of time and money even when there is little or no hope that their ideas will succeed.

There is also another troubling problem with this weird idea. It implies that hypocritical and even dishonest actions can spark innovation. I have shown that after picking a person or project that is likely to fail, the best thing a leader can do to increase a company's innovation rate is to express complete confidence that it will succeed. And when people have setbacks, it is best to tell them that the problems are only temporary and that success is ultimately certain if they keep trying. This kind of optimism is routinely applauded and glorified, as when John Gardner proclaimed that "the prime function of a leader is to keep hope alive." But keeping hope alive can mean deluding yourself and others, recruiting some optimists, some true believers, and enticing them to join you down a path that is most likely to lead to a failed end.

Leaders who want innovation face a nasty dilemma. They can tell people whom they have selected to work on a risky project that it will probably fail, which will help ensure failure and lead to negative consequences for both the company and the person. Or they can deceive people who work on these projects (and themselves) into believing that success is nearly certain, which reduces the (albeit still high) odds of failure but increases the sunk costs involved in each project. I am not advocating that leaders ought to routinely lie to people to spark more creativity. While lying is a sleazy thing to do, the fact remains that all creative work entails risky projects. If deception helps reduce that risk, a case can be made that it is the right thing to do at times. Indeed, dilemmas like these have caused ethicists and philosophers to assert that deception is sometimes more ethical than telling the truth, the whole truth, and nothing but truth.[24]

### CHAPTER 11

# Think of Some Ridiculous or Impractical Things to Do, Then Plan to Do Them

## (Weird Idea #8)

One Dozen Long Stem DEAD & BLACK Roses. Same as DEAD Roses but sprayed BLACK for added effect. Direct shipped to the recipient home or (recommended) OFFICE in a long rose box with dead greens and filler. Price: $55.00.

> —*A popular item sold by Revenge Unlimited, which asks potential customers, "Have you been wronged, mistreated, annoyed or ignored? Are you ready for some PAYBACK?"*

When Marcy said he was looking for other planets, the others looked at each other, wondering if he might be joking.[1]

> —*Reactions of fellow astronomers to Geoffrey Marcy's (ultimately path-breaking) search for planets orbiting around distant suns*

"You're mad."[2] "You're a megalomaniac, Richard."[3] "You'll have to a have lot of [Virgin Records] hits on the *Top of the Pops* to keep the airline going."[4]

> —*Advice from friends, investors, and other experts to Richard Branson when he proposed starting Virgin Atlantic Airways*

The ideas that people think are the stupidest are the most pro-
tectable. . . . I think this is especially true with new business
models. People are especially likely to say they are stupid and to
be afraid to copy them.

—*Bill Gross, founder and CEO of idealab!,
which incubates new companies*

GETTING STUPID CAN BE a mighty smart thing to do if you want to build
an innovative company. Thinking up the dumbest, most ridiculous, and
most impractical things you can do is a powerful way to explore your
assumptions about the world. It helps elicit what you know and believe
but may have a hard time articulating, perhaps because it is so obvious
you don't even notice it. It also helps you imagine what might happen if
your dearest beliefs turn out to be dead wrong. And thinking up the most
ridiculous things you can do—and then thinking about why you might
do them—creates a broader palette of options. This weird idea works
because it sparks two essential forces for constant innovation: variance
and *vu ja de.*

This weird idea was inspired by Justin Kitch, the CEO and founder
of Homestead, an Internet company that bills itself as "The easiest way
to build a free Web site."[5] Right after he graduated from Stanford,
Justin went to work for Microsoft in a group that developed educational software for young children. One day, he led a brainstorming
session, on "What would be the worst product we could possibly
build?" His idea was to do just that, and then to think opposite. "Think
about what's the worst characteristics it could have. What's the least
educational thing we could do?" The result was "a talking Barney doll,
called Barney 1, 2, 3. It was a Barney doll that talked to you and taught
you numbers. I still have the drawing. I made it as a total joke and I
gave it to my boss."[6]

To Justin's dismay, Microsoft came out with pretty much the same
product a couple of years later. He said, "I couldn't believe it. They
built exactly what we brainstormed would be the worst possible product." Justin seems confident that "my team's little chuckle over Barney
had nothing to do with the eventual project." Although he refuses to
accept any credit—or blame—for Microsoft's ActiMates Interactive

Barney, I think he is onto something important, something that more companies ought to do if they want to make innovation a way of life.

The hazards of failing to identify and then test "dumb" or "obvious" assumptions are illustrated by the technology ultimately found to be superior to the Momsen Lung for escaping from sunken submarines—no technology at all! An interesting footnote to Momsen's work is that although his devices saved some lives, only about 5 percent of the men trapped in disabled submarines during World War II survived, and there were only five documented cases of submariners who were saved by the Momsen Lung. Research ultimately showed that free ascent—filling one's lungs with air and slowly exhaling on the way to the surface—is the most effective way to escape from a submarine at any depth up to 300 feet. The air in the lungs expands as the pressure increases, so a person never runs out of oxygen. The pressure is slowly released during the ascent. So high pressure in the lungs, which causes "the bends" or decompression illness, is avoided. Momsen, and thousands of submariners who died in trapped submarines, made the assumption that escape was impossible without some kind of technology. In retrospect, we know that for those trapped at depths less than 300 feet, many would have survived if they had swum to the surface and slowly exhaled as they rose. So, even one of the boldest and most persistent innovators in American history might have developed better ideas if he had generated and tested a list of ridiculous and impractical ways to solve the problem at hand.[7]

Brainstorming is just one way that companies can generate absurd ideas, but it remains one of the best tools for generating new ideas. Brainstorming sessions are the only gatherings I know of where people are required to generate wild ideas, at least when the official rules are followed. Advertising executive Alex Osborn popularized brainstorming during the 1950s in his best-seller *Applied Imagination*.[8] Osborn believed that "idea-producing conferences are relatively fruitless unless certain rules are understood by all present and are faithfully followed."[9] His basic brainstorming rules are (1) *criticism is ruled out;* (2) *free-wheeling is welcomed* ("the wilder the ideas the better; it is easier to tame down than to think up";)[10] (3) *quantity is wanted;* and (4) *combination and improvement are sought.*

Brainstorming is not a panacea, but when groups follow these rules, they generate larger numbers of novel ideas than groups that are just asked to "develop some ideas," especially when a trained facilitator leads the session.[11] This technique has been used to spark new ideas in many companies, to develop product ideas at Apple Computer and Xerox PARC, to build better companies at Reactivity, to design advertising campaigns at McCann-Erickson and eBay, and to identify new business strategies at law firms like Pillsbury Winthrop.

Yet, despite the power of brainstorming to generate new ideas, people often hesitate to say really wild things or suggest ideas that clash with what the company has always done or believed to be true. This happens because, as Chapter 1 showed, people have automatic and unconscious negative emotional reactions to things that are unfamiliar or run counter to their beliefs. People also censor themselves because even though the stated rule is to defer judgment, some suggestions are received with silence, and others with enthusiastic comments like, "Wow, that's cool." And when an idea is built upon by others, it is treated as a sign that the person had an especially "smart" idea. The result is that people see brainstormers as status competitions. The meetings may seem fun, even giddy, on the surface, but they are also gatherings where winners gain respect from their peers and losers do not. In companies that use them as part of the work, people in brainstormers have good reason to worry that saying something dumb (or saying nothing at all) could damage their reputations.[12]

Peter Skillman, the director of product design engineering at Handspring, is unusually skilled at leading brainstorms. Handspring makes the Visor, a personal digital assistant that uses the Palm operating system. Skillman tries to counteract pressures for self-censorship by insisting that people come up with ridiculous ideas. He tells them, "Delaying judgment isn't enough. I think it's very important to enthusiastically embrace stupidity." Justin Kitch's method is even more explicit: You just ask people to list the worst ideas they can imagine.

Regardless of exactly how it is accomplished, the aim is to get people to list those products, services, business models, or business practices they believe are destructive, misguided, dumb, or impractical. There are three main reasons that talking about dumb things is a smart thing for companies that want to be hotbeds of innovation.

## Making Clear What Ought to Be Done

This method can be used to make explicit what the company *should* be doing, or at least what people *believe* it should be doing. By listing ideas that people believe are wrong or misguided, and then reversing them, people follow a different cognitive path than usual to reveal beliefs, theories, and evidence about what the company ought to do. This different point of view can help crystallize widespread and shared beliefs that have never been articulated before, and in doing so, people may notice gaps between what they believe is right and what they actually do. This is why Justin Kitch used this technique during the "Barney brainstorm." He thought that by listing all the features of the least desirable product possible, and then reversing them, a more complete and powerful set of design principles could be developed than if he had just used the more common practice of asking brainstormers to generate good ideas.

I use a similar method in my consulting work. I was working with a newly formed professional services firm a few years ago. To help them think about the kind of company they wanted to be, we developed a list of what they believed were the worst characteristics of several key competitors. These undesirable—but common—attributes included selling clients only PowerPoint presentations instead of helping them implement ideas, relying primarily on young and inexperienced consultants to do most of the work, requiring long hours and excessive travel, and developing a "star system" where a tiny percentage of the consultants reaped the lion's share of the profits. This exercise helped them realize that their own company was already using some of these same practices (especially excessive travel and long hours) and that some practices they were about to discard were important to their success (e.g., they used a pay system that did not breed superstars). A senior manager commented that this exercise made them realize that their success resulted from being different from their competitors, and that they were—unwittingly—on the verge of implementing practices that would make them just like their competitors. They decided that they needed to focus on enhancing, not narrowing, these differences.

You can take this weird idea a step further and convince people to try the dumb ideas for a while. This is similar to what some writing teachers do to help their students distinguish between weak and strong writing styles, and to improve their prose. John Vorhaus has taught writing in 17 countries, to everyone from novelists to scriptwriters for television sitcoms.[13] He instructs students to write badly, for example, to *"write a run-on sentence,* and the plan is simply to *put off the period as long as possible."*[14] He also asks them to "write nonsense," "wallow in lame analogies," and to "be repetitious."[15] Vorhaus says that such "stretching exercises" teach people to write better prose because it helps them learn the difference between good and bad writing, and teaches them they can learn more from doing bad writing than no writing at all.

I use a similar practice in my management classes. I ask for volunteers to come in front of the class, and to perform as poorly as possible in a mock job interview, negotiation, or brainstorming session. In one executive education class, a manager in a mock brainstorming session responded to every idea by saying, "That's too expensive," "That won't work," or "We tried that already, it was a disaster." We then discussed what was wrong—and what might be right—about this constant criticism and why. These exercises might be contrived, but they are still enlightening, in part, because people mimic bad practices that are used in their own companies. In the destructive brainstorming technique I just described, for example, the manager who did it told the class, "I am not making this up. This is exactly what my boss does in what he calls brainstorming meetings." People see others (and themselves) in these exercises, so they start thinking more deeply about what ought to be done (and not done) in their company.

Many companies fail to be innovative because they fail to act on their knowledge, not because their leaders are ignorant about how to boost innovation. As Jeffrey Pfeffer and I show in *The Knowing-Doing Gap*, there are many times when managers, teams, and businesses do things that clash with or undermine their knowledge about which work practices or business models they ought to use.[16] Applying this weird idea gives people a vantage point that helps them see what they are doing right, what they are (unwittingly) doing wrong, and what they ought to do differently as they move forward.

## Challenging Assumptions About What Ought to Be Done

The second reason to use this technique is nearly the opposite of the first: to question rather than to crystallize what a company knows and does. First, you need to identify the most ridiculous, the dumbest, or most impractical things your company could do. Then, you need to pretend these are brilliant and profitable things to do, to think up good reasons why your most fervent beliefs might be 100 percent wrong. This is *almost* what Justin Kitch did in the Barney brainstorm at Microsoft. His team just needed to take his method one step further, and to pretend that what they thought was *wrong* was actually *right*.

Perhaps this is what happened elsewhere in Microsoft. Whether or not it happened, the ActiMates Barney was the right thing for Microsoft to do. The "input-output gizmo you could hug" was a moderate commercial success; several hundred thousand were sold. Microsoft claimed sales were about 20 percent above projections. The toy was acclaimed by various consumer publications. A panel of children picked the ActiMate as toy of the year for *Disney's Family Fun* magazine, *Consumer Reports* called it the "breakout hit" of 1997, and *Parents* magazine named it the top toy of 1997.[17] Even researchers at MIT's renowned industry-funded Media Lab admired the talking Barney. Professor Bruce Blumberg said, "My sense on Interactive Barney is that it's really an interesting first step." He went on to say that Microsoft was "absolutely right" in developing the technology because "it's worth spending the money now to control the standard." The Barney doll has been discontinued, but following Blumberg's prediction, Microsoft has come out with new talking Arthur and Teletubby dolls.[18] So, whether or not Kitch's technique sparked this creative idea, the success of the Barney doll he despises suggests that if this technique were used intentionally, it could produce commercially successful ideas that clash with accepted dogma.

An article in *Forbes* magazine called "Dumb and Dumber" on "the most idiotic business ideas of 1999" provides further hints that this technique just might be effective.[19] The article identified ideas including music for lonely pets; the "Netwanga magic bag," which uses Haitian voodoo to protect computers from breaking; a service called Finalthoughts.com, which sends final messages from people who die to their loved ones on the occasion of their death; and Revenge Unlimited, which helps you get back at your enemies by sending them things like dead roses, rotten fish, and melted chocolates. These "idiotic ideas" are especially interesting because several turned out to be profitable. Journalist Rob Wherry reports:

> It seems 40% of all pets go through separation anxiety after a stay at the kennel. Not to worry: You can arrange to calm the pooch when you return—and save your furniture from being the object of your pet's pent-up anxiety—by playing selections from a $20 three-CD pack called *Pet Music,* featuring "Sunday in the Park," "Natural Rhythms," and "Peaceful Playground." We'd like to laugh, but who gets the last bark? According to Incentive partner Andrew Borislow, 50,000 people have ordered the set since the summer.[20]

What could be a dumber idea than selling Pet Rocks? Perhaps not selling them, since they became of one of the most successful fads of all time. The little rocks came with a *Pet Rock Training Manual,* "a step-by-step guide to having a happy relationship with your geological pet." More than a million Pet Rocks were sold in just a few months, at $3.95 each.[21]

Research by psychologists suggests two sound reasons for generating allegedly dumb and impractical ideas (and then imagining they are smart): To jolt people into questioning the existing dogma and to generate counterintuitive ideas. As I mentioned earlier, most of what human beings do is "mindless behavior," acting on taken-for-granted assumptions without paying attention to what they are doing.[22] Psychologist Ellen Langer's research shows that "the individual becomes mindlessly trapped by categories that were previously created when the person was in a mindful mode."[23] When people engage in mindless acts, they are unable to even consider whether what they are doing is constructive or destructive. If people state their assumptions and beliefs, and then reverse them, they are forced to become mindful about thoughts that are usually buried in their company's collective unconscious, and to think about the drawbacks of these mindless actions.

This technique is also promising because it helps overcome the ingrained human tendency to reject the unfamiliar. Once any human being notices something, he or she can't stop from evaluating it, from having a positive or negative emotional reaction to it. These quick judgments can hamper creativity, because most people react to new things with negative feelings. As I showed in Chapter 1, a substantial body of research on "mere exposure effects" shows that, even though they don't usually realize it is happening, people have consistently negative reactions to "unfamiliar stimuli."[24] Most creativity experts implore people to withhold judgment during the idea-generation phase, to avoid squashing new and young ideas. But it turns out that this is impossible for human beings to do. This weird idea works, in part, because it forces people to list ideas that they find unfamiliar and strange, but that leaves the ideas out there so they can be used, perhaps by others who don't find them so odd or repugnant.

There are two other related ways to surface and challenge a group's ingrained beliefs. The first is to assign one or more members to the devil's advocate role: Give them the job of pointing out flaws in the assumptions, beliefs, facts, and decisions made by the group. The second is called "dialectical inquiry," and it goes a step further (and is closer to what I recommend here). In dialectical inquiry, anointed critics not only challenge the group's beliefs and assumptions, they develop contrasting (and plausible) assumptions that are contrary to the group's beliefs. They then use these new assumptions to construct different, even opposite, recommendations.[25]

Groups that use these methods make better decisions, including better creative decisions like constructing corporate strategy. In particular, groups can use devil's advocates and dialectical inquiry to avoid groupthink, a syndrome identified by Irving Janis, where members pressure each other to express the same opinions and to "discount warnings or other information that might lead members to reconsider their assumptions."[26] Janis also suggests that, if you use such techniques, they work best when you assign at least two team members at a time to these "contrary" roles and they are rotated out of the roles. Otherwise, the task done by these "naysayers" will be seen as a personality characteristic, something they do because they are "difficult people" who are always looking on the dark side of things. These contrarians—even though they are just doing their jobs—will then suffer the usual fate of deviants in most societies; they will be discounted, shunned, and ignored for questioning the prevailing wisdom.

A related technique is to identify assumptions, business practices, business models, or products that are viewed as especially silly in your industry, rather than in your company. This might be less threatening to colleagues, as their most precious beliefs and assumptions are not being attacked head-on, but the company still benefits from *vu ja de,* that ability to see the same things others see but in a different way. The success of Southwest Airlines is due, in part, to the revelation that other carriers were focusing on the wrong competitors: Southwest sees ground transportation as its primary competition in many markets, not other airlines.[27]

### Developing Ideas That Others Won't Copy—At Least for a While

The lack of competition might just be the biggest advantage of using this technique. As the quote from Bill Gross that opens this chapter suggests, if you do come up with an idea that is contrary to the conventional wisdom in your industry, and it is a good idea, you will be able to get far ahead of your competitors because they will think it suicide to copy you. The Palm Pilot is a good example of this advantage in the computer industry. One reason that the Palm hand-held devices are among the best-selling electronics devices of all time is that when they first came out, the prevailing wisdom was that the product category was doomed to failure. After all, some of the greatest corporations, including Apple and

Microsoft, and the smartest engineers in the world had failed to develop a successful hand-held computer. So when CEO Jeff Hawkins and president Donna Dubinsky went to find funding, they were turned down by every venture capitalist they approached, who feared losing even more money on this dumb idea. The venture capitalists said, "Please, no more pen-based computers. We've already lost enough of our investors' money on this failed concept." But the skepticism and lack of competition proved, in the end, to be a huge advantage, because major competitors did not believe that the success of the Palm Pilot was real, and by the time they did, the Palm Pilot and its operating system had been accepted as the industry standard.

Another example of this advantage is Geoffrey Marcy's pathbreaking research on the possible existence of planets orbiting around other suns.[28] Fellow astronomers assumed he was joking when he told them what he was studying. Marcy's hopes of finding planets that orbited around distant suns were based on two assumptions that most astronomers found laughable. The first was that it was possible to detect a tiny wobble in the distant suns, which was caused by the gravitational pull of a large planet on its sun. This wobble was so small that a planet the size of Jupiter would cause the light waves in its sun to cyclically lengthen and compress at a magnitude of about 1 part per 10 million. The second assumption that needed to hold (at least at the start of his research) was that huge planets at least five times larger than Jupiter existed. This was because, even with the powerful telescopes he was using, the planets needed to be that large to detect the tiny wobble in their suns. These assumptions—and the whole idea that planets could be detected from Earth—were viewed as so absurd (especially in the United States) that he couldn't even admit that he was looking for planets when asking for the most modest of research grants, just $20,000 or $30,000 to support his undergraduate research assistant. So he asked for funds to look for "brown dwarfs, stars not quite big enough to become full-fledged stars, but too big to become planets."[29]

The fact that Marcy's research was viewed as a joke, that his assumptions were thought to be absurd and impractical, ultimately gave him a huge advantage. He had few competitors in the United States, especially during the early years of his research. So, once he (and European) astronomers started uncovering evidence that these huge planets did exist and could be detected, he had a rapid ascent, moving from the very bottom to the very top of prestige in his field. His work made him a media celebrity and enabled him to get a prestigious post at the University of

California at Berkeley. It also helped cause fundamental changes in the space probes that NASA developed, and it led to predictions that the first "blue water" Earth-like planet will be seen within the decade. There are other reasons that Marcy was so successful, including the fact that he was detached from other scientists and worked with young people who didn't know they were working on an impossible task. But having so few competitors proved a huge advantage for Marcy and his team when it turned out they were right.

### Protecting People Who Think "Different"

An assumption runs throughout much of this chapter—indeed, throughout much of this book—that many new ideas are generated by people who are seen as deviants within their companies, industries, and societies. Apple Computer's simple slogan, "Think Different," captures this perspective well. Unfortunately, thinking and acting differently is given lipservice in most companies, but when people actually do it, they are ignored, humiliated, and fired. If you really do want to encourage people to develop ideas that will be seen as dumb and impractical, I have one more piece of advice: Outlaw even light-hearted ridicule and put-downs when people suggest these wacky ideas.

Humor and laughter can be wonderful things, as I have demonstrated, but they have a dark side. Research on humor shows that when we joke and tease, we let each other get away with meaner and nastier comments than when we are "serious."[30] The ridicule and put-downs that many people are subjected to because they are "different" are good examples. Such humiliation not only damages souls and spirits, it also stifles and silences people who have the courage to try something new, or to do anything at all.

The damage that seemingly light-hearted ridicule and put-downs can cause is illustrated by a story told by Gordon MacKenzie, who gives workshops on maintaining creativity in big companies and who had the title of Creative Paradox during his years at Hallmark Cards.[31] MacKenzie taught a workshop at Hallmark where "with a bashful eagerness" a woman began a sketch that showed how she felt about herself, the Management of Information Systems group she was part of, and Hallmark. Her coworkers reacted with a "rowdy taunting" about her lack of drawing skills. She quickly changed from looking eager to looking hurt, and then "after an apologetic explanation of her

---

## *Putting Weird Idea #8 to Work*

### Innovate by Thinking and Doing Ridiculous and Impractical Things

- Brainstorm a list of absurd things to do, reverse the ideas, and talk about why you should or shouldn't do these things.

- Brainstorm a list of ridiculous and impractical things to do, and then develop the best arguments you can about why they are actually smart things to do.

- To remind people about the dangers of taken-for-granted assumptions, review ideas that were proposed in your company and elsewhere that were once thought to be absurd, but are now commonplace.

- Imagine several different contradictory versions of the company's future that could happen given what is known now.

- Identify the most sensible things that some of your competitors are doing (or have done), and develop arguments about why your company *shouldn't* do them.

- Identify the most absurd things that companies in other industries are doing (or have done), and develop arguments about why your company *ought to* do them.

- Use a devil's advocate and dialectical inquiry: Assign people to challenge your group's assumptions and decisions, and to develop arguments that the opposite assumptions and decisions are actually superior.

- Don't allow even (seemingly) light-hearted ridicule and put-downs when people suggest ridiculous or impractical ideas

---

drawing, she scurried, eyes down, back to her seat." MacKenzie confronted the group with their behavior:

> Teasing is a disguised form of shaming . . . I suspect that when you teased this woman, it was an unconscious effort to throw her off balance—to stop her from risking, which she was most clearly beginning to do. Why would you want to do that? . . . [B]ecause we don't want to admit to others or ourselves that we are trying to stop growth, we disguise our shaming as teasing–"all in the spirit of good fun."[32]

MacKenzie is right. Although disguised as light-hearted teasing, ridicule and put-downs can stop people from thinking and acting differently, even though the tormentors who do it rarely are aware of the damage their words have done. If you want people to come up with dumb and impractical ideas that, later on, just might bring joy and riches to your company, praise them or try to come up with even more absurd ideas of your own. If you hear others taunting people who propose outrageous or silly ideas, take it upon yourself to stop them. And realize that if you and others in your company taunt people about their silly ideas, even in a light-hearted way, chances are that creative people will start hiding what they know. They will just go along with the crowd, at least for while, until they go to work for one of your competitors or start their own companies.

# Avoid, Distract, and Bore Customers, Critics, and Anyone Who Just Wants to Talk About Money

## (Weird Idea #9)

I can't ask my customers what they want. They haven't been born yet.[1]

—*An engineer from Xerox PARC*

After you plant a seed in the ground, you don't dig it up every week to see how it is doing.[2]

—*William Coyne, former 3M senior vice president for Research and Development*

I could see that his views would be crushed at Sony Headquarters . . . So I took Kutaragi and nine of his team to Sony Music, cleared the former office of Epic Sony at Aoyama, and set up an environment where Kutaragi's team could develop the CD-ROM with software staff. Although many people complained at Sony about this decision, I went ahead with it regardless. I can say with confidence that one of the factors that led to the success of the Sony PlayStation was removing the genius Kutaragi from Sony.[3]

—*Norio Ohga, former president (currently chairman) of Sony*

SHAKESPEARE SAID THAT ALL THE WORLD IS A STAGE. But if you want a company that puts on stunning performances for adoring audiences, your people also need to spend time backstage, out of the spotlight, to craft new wares. This chapter shows how and why companies do some strange things to keep innovative work from being transparent to others, especially from interactions with the wrong customers, critics, and money mongers at the wrong times.

The notion that innovators should avoid outside scrutiny stems from something that humans share with ants, cockroaches, chickens, greenfinches, mice, rats, and monkeys: Research shows that when others are present, we are better at doing old things and worse at doing new things. In contrast to when working alone, being around other "species mates" causes us to perform familiar actions faster and better, but to learn new responses more slowly and perform them less well. There are parallels in nature: In an experiment with cockroaches, after three learning trials, solitary bugs ran an E-shaped maze in an average of 2 minutes, bugs in pairs took 6 minutes, and bugs in groups of three took 9 minutes.[4] One reason these so-called audience or social-facilitation effects occur is that, for both people and animals, being around others increases physiological arousal. This increases energy, but leads to a narrow focus on ingrained actions and away from new or less-familiar actions.

In people, the sights and sounds of others can trigger a kind of tunnel vision, where their heightened energy is devoted to what they already do best because they fear failure and want to impress others. People are especially hesitant to try new things in front of "evaluative others," like critics and bosses, because they want to protect their reputations. The desire to make a good impression causes people to cling to tried-and-true ways, which are more likely to succeed than new and unproven ways. Even if a trusted way fails, it can be defended as a "standard practice that has always worked well." Finally, when nosy clients, bosses, coworkers, or reporters keep interrupting to ask for performance updates or additional justification, or just out of pure curiosity, it slows the work. People badgered by intruders may focus on routine tasks simply because they have less time for (more time-consuming) innovative tasks.

Most research on "audience effects" focuses on individuals, but experiments on brainstorming groups and case studies show that both welcome guests and unwanted intruders can hamper group and organizational innovation too, especially when they are nosy, distracting, and judgmental.[5] The virtues of doing innovative work in isolation are demonstrated by well-known cases. Tracy Kidder's Pulitzer Prize–winning book *The Soul of a New Machine* describes an engineering team that was sequestered in spartan basement offices. Kidder shows how the resulting lack of attention helped the "Microkids" on this "Eagle Team" do a better (and faster) job of designing a new microcomputer for Data General.[6] Similarly, in 1978, then president Kiyoshi Kawashima was concerned that Honda was losing its vitality because senior managers couldn't understand what kinds of cars young people wanted. Kawashima assembled the youngest members of his staff (average age 27) to design a new car that would appeal to younger customers and promised that senior managers would not interfere with the team's operation. The result was the hot-selling Honda City car.[7]

The team that designed the first Macintosh computer was isolated from others at Apple Computer in a separate building. Rather than being basement-quality, however, this building had a grand piano in the lobby and team members were offered a massage at their desks twice a week. The team's leader, Apple cofounder Steve Jobs, protected them from interruption and evaluation, especially from other Apple engineers and managers.[8] Finally, the scientists who invented the first working atomic bomb are perhaps the most famous group to do creative work in isolation. This "Manhattan Project" was sequestered in Los Alamos, New Mexico, ostensibly "for the quarantine of a talkative and unpredictable scientific community."[9] This isolation not only helped maintain secrecy, the absence of intrusions and distractions is often used to explain why the team built the bomb so quickly, despite difficult technical challenges.

The hazards of opening up innovative work to outsiders, no matter how well-meaning, are demonstrated by the fate of the Wallace Pipe Company. Wallace developed and implemented numerous innovations in its manufacturing and sales process during the late 1980s. These innovations were so successful that, in 1990, it became the first small manufacturing company to win the prestigious Malcolm Baldrige National Quality Award. After the company won the Baldrige, managers from other companies visited for "benchmarking," Wallace executives gave numerous speeches at conferences and to other companies, and they were interviewed by a stream of reporters. These flattering distractions helped drive the company into bankruptcy.[10] An executive from the company that acquired Wallace put it this way:

> When you do win the Baldrige, there is also an obligation, if not a contractual commitment, to go out and spread the gospel. It takes a lot of time from work for the key people to give talks and spread the gospel. You also have to open up your business to others who want to see your systems and your procedures. That

is good, but if you are in the business of trying to survive, it can become a financial problem and defeat your original purpose of being in business.[11]

These diverse writings suggest that, to innovate, people, teams, and companies sometimes need to avoid nosy, opinionated, and intrusive outsiders—or anyone who is interesting enough to distract them from their work. Part of the problem is that well-meaning managers or investors who insist on close oversight and frequent explanations can unwittingly kill innovation, because people will respond by doing what *appears best* in the short term rather than what they believe will *be* best in the long term. Another part of the problem is that irrelevant distractions, whether they are nice or nasty, drain precious time and resources that are needed to do innovative work.

I don't want to leave you with the impression, however, that all aspects of innovative work are best done in isolation. This isn't just an oversimplification, it is downright wrong. There are numerous junctures in the innovation process when people and teams desperately need outsiders. To name just a few, they need to hire diverse outsiders to keep bringing in new ideas. They need to keep talking to outsiders to learn about new technologies, services, and business models. They need outsiders to shake things up when a company or team is stuck in the past. And, ultimately, without support from senior managers, powerful critics, and customers, most projects are doomed. The fact remains, however, that bringing in outsiders is destructive when people or teams first try to learn something that is new to them and when they are trying to imagine, develop, and do initial tests of some incomplete but promising ideas. In particular, if you want to shield a promising idea from being nipped in the bud or pummeled into a tepid imitation of the original, you need to be wary of exposing innovative work to three kinds people: The wrong customers, managers, and money mongers.

## OUTSIDERS WHO (UNWITTINGLY) SQUELCH INNOVATION, AND WHAT TO DO IF YOU ARE ONE OF THEM

### The Wrong Customers, or the Right Customers at the Wrong Time

Be wary of opinions from clients or customers who use your company's current products or services, along with colleagues in marketing and sales who represent their views. Special caution is needed when dealing with marketing researchers who want to test customer reactions to a new concept at every juncture in its development. Research on "mere exposure" introduced in Chapter 1 suggests that when you ask people what they want, they will be drawn to the familiar and repelled by the unfamiliar. Also, when you ask customers about what they want, they focus on what they need right now, not what they will need and want in the future. Most of the mainframe computer users that IBM surveyed in the 1970s couldn't imagine why they would ever want a small computer on their desks. Many of the consumers that 3M's marketers surveyed couldn't imagine why they would ever want to use the adhesive on the back of a Post-it Note in place of paper clips or staples.

The stifling effects of listening too closely to customers are magnified when there is pressure for short-term sales and profits, because the safest path is to find something that works in your industry *right now* and try to imitate it or improve it slightly. This happens in the film industry "when creative teams are 'brought to heel' by the marketing team."12 The filmmaker Cameron Crowe, who worked on hits such as *Fast Times at Ridgemont High, Jerry Maguire,* and *Almost Famous,* explains how working with marketers, especially those focused on maximizing short-term financial returns, stifles imaginative ideas in Hollywood:

> You have more and more people coming into the tent with the creative guys. You have marketing and concept testers, advertising people. What you find gets the high numbers is easily appealing subjects: a baby, a big, broad joke, a high concept. Everything is tested. The effect is to lessen the gamble, but in fact you destroy a writer's confidence and creativity once so many people are invited into the tent.13

Michael Eisner, CEO of Disney, voices a similar complaint: "Most audience—or customer—research is useless."14 Eisner admits that customers provide useful reactions to current movies, which are helpful for fine-tuning marketing messages, but says such information is useless for deciding what to do next. He argues that just because everyone loved *Titanic* does not mean they want another movie "about a love affair and sinking ship." This inability to use current preferences to predict future ones is why the engineer from Xerox PARC half-joked that he couldn't ask customers what they wanted because they weren't born yet. It is also why Bob Metcalfe, founder of 3Com, asserts that the financial success of

3Com's Etherlink, a high-speed way to connect computers, happened because he ignored reports from 3Com salespeople that customers were clamoring for a slight improvement in a hot-selling product.[15] Some salespeople even quit in disgust after the decision not to develop an improved version of the existing product because 3Com was "not listening to our customers." Metcalfe said 3Com had to ignore these salespeople because the product their customers wanted would soon be made obsolete by the Etherlink:

> The real lesson is that you have to choose which customers to listen to very carefully. And even then, you can't necessarily give them what they want. You have to develop products that your customers will need by the time you are able to deliver them. If you don't, when the development cycle is finished, and you're ready to ship, you will be offering what the customer said he wanted last year.[16]

This doesn't mean that people in marketing, sales, and product testing should *always* stay out of the way. Metcalfe ignored his salespeople in the prior example, but tells envious engineers that he is rich because someone sold the technologies he developed, "not because of any flowery flash of genius in some academic hothouse." In addition, people in marketing can spark innovation by bringing back ideas from customers who are not buying the company's products, either because they aren't old enough yet, can't afford them, or don't find them appealing. When marketers in Ford's European operation wanted to get some advice from "brand conscious teens, so-called echo boomers," they didn't use focus groups to figure out what these future customers wanted. They went to watch and talk to these "echo boomers" where they hung out, including a London hair salon featuring experimental techno-pop and London's hottest clubs. As Ford's European Consumer Marketing Insights manager, 27-year-old Andrew Grant, put it, "It was a deliberate shock tactic. . . . Suddenly, our customers were no longer statistics on a page or a clever write-up by an ad agency. They were flesh and blood—and standing right in front of us." Ford not only asked the echo boomers what they wanted, they used computer-aided design tools to get their reactions to design ideas, and implemented suggestions from these teens on the spot. "The kids would suggest a line here or there and, with the designers, came up with a sketch of a car that's simple and relatively inexpensive to buy."[17]

An even more powerful approach is to give future customers primary responsibility for developing what they will buy. The development of the Palm V is a splendid example. IDEO did much of the work on this product. Earlier Palm hand-held computers were hugely successful, but over 95 percent of users were men. Project leader Dennis Boyle not only held sessions with 15 female IDEO workers to critique the product, he assigned two female design engineers—Amy Han and Trae Niest—as project leaders. These engineers helped overcome design challenges like how to attach the stylus, provide enough power, and design a strong and thin casing. And the concerns raised by all the women at IDEO had a profound effect on the product. The way it was ultimately designed and sold is an outgrowth of questions such as "Why does it have to be square? Why not curved, tapered and graceful?" and concerns about why it had to be sold in a "guy place" like an electronics store instead of Nordstrom. The resulting sleek and beautiful product has been a huge success, and both men and women have bought millions. Supermodel Claudia Schiffer has even partnered with Palm to sell her own edition of the Palm V in a brushed metallic aqua color.[18]

## The Wrong Managers

A nosy boss can hamper innovation just by constantly interrupting people or teams to ask for progress reports. These are, to paraphrase 3M's William Coyne, the managers who dig up the seed every week to see how it is doing. A manufacturing company that I worked with a few years back illustrates this syndrome. There was so much pressure from top management to do "high-quality" product demonstrations with fancy prototypes, well-crafted PowerPoint presentations, and slick videos during the development processes that an exasperated engineer said, "We spend so much time getting ready for these dog-and-pony shows that we don't have much time to work on the product line itself."

This problem is magnified when work is subjected to a minute inquiry by leaders who have lot of power, *but who know little or nothing about the technology, product, or market.* Such managers provide endless material for Scott Adams's Dilbert cartoons. Overbearing managers who overestimate their knowledge and taste not only can waste employee's precious time, they often reject or ruin good ideas, and leave a destructive stench of cynicism in their path. A few years back, a Stanford student told my class that she had a boss like this at Hewlett-Packard. "He stuck his nose in everyone's business, and gave us awful advice. He told us that he was following the HP Way, and doing MBWA [managing by wandering around]. But he should have stayed in his office." There is a happy ending to this story, however, because after complaints filtered up to senior executives, this manager was reassigned to a job that better matched his skills.

Following my earlier suggestion, if you are a manager, a useful guiding principle is "First, do no harm." If you don't have a deep understanding of something, stay out of the way and trust that more knowledgeable employees will make fewer mistakes than you. One hallmark of wisdom is having enough humility to defer to others who have greater knowledge, instead of arrogantly assuming that you will be right just because you have more power or prestige. Dennis Bakke provides an extreme example of such wisdom in action. Bakke is CEO and cofounder of AES, an enormously successful company that designs, builds, and manages over 110 electric power plants in 16 countries. Bakke doesn't just talk about letting people who know a market best make local decisions. On November 3, 2000, regional AES managers made a surprise bid of over $1 billion for a huge Chilean power company. It wasn't just a surprise to AES's competitors, it was a surprise to Bakke as well. The *Wall Street Journal* reported:

> But its chief executive wasn't losing any sleep over the billion dollar bid, which would soon send the stocks of both companies into a frenzy. "I learned about it after the fact," says CEO Dennis Bakke, who was told by one of AES's regional managers that the tender offer had finally been made. "He called me up and said, "We did it."[19]

Bakke was consulted about this decision, but delegated the authority and responsibility for making it to executives in South America. This is a standard practice at AES, where senior managers see themselves as coaches rather than decision makers. Few senior executives trust their people this much, and some might say that AES delegates too much. But it is hard to argue with the results. AES consistently moves more quickly than its competitors, which is one reason that the firm had a total return to shareholders of approximately 1,000 percent between 1995 and 2000, over ten times the industry average.

## The Wrong Money Mongers at the Wrong Time

There is no innovation without money. Projects that lack resources suffer because they don't have the time, people, and materials required to gather diverse ideas, to try them in new combinations, reach a lot of dead ends, and refine and perfect good ideas. An intensive study of creativity in 26 product development teams shows that a primary difference between the top six teams and the bottom six teams was that less-creative teams talked much more about money and resources, in large part because they didn't have enough to do their work right.[20]

Thinking and talking about money can also stifle innovation even when there is enough money around to do the work right. A huge body of research shows that when people and teams focus on the money (and recognition) too much, rather than on the work itself, the quality and creativity of the work suffers. This happens because people who focus on the "extrinsic" rewards rather the "intrinsic" aspects of the work itself shift attention from the joys and challenges of doing the work to the money and praise the work will (or will not) bring them. Teresa Amabile, a leading creativity researcher, calls this the Intrinsic Motivation Principle of Creativity: "People will be most creative when they feel motivated primarily by the interest, satisfaction, and challenge of the work itself—and not by external pressures."[21]

The evidence supporting Amabile's Intrinsic Motivation Principle is compelling, but it is difficult to implement because so many forces in organizations, even nonprofit organizations and universities, turn members' attention to money. It is easier to reduce the focus on extrinsic rewards in some settings; for example, showing parents compelling evidence that paying their children to get good grades ultimately undermines learning, interest in school, and academic performance. But it is much harder in the workplace. After all, pay is one of the main reasons, perhaps *the* main reason, that most people work in the first place. Social standing in organizations and societies is closely tied to how much one is paid. And pay, benefits, and stock options are among the main rewards used to entice people to join companies in the first place. So convincing people to stop thinking about money and just think about their work may not always be realistic.

Even in those rare companies where the pay system is seen as fair and most people have interesting work, senior management can have a hard time shifting their own focus away from financial matters because, if the company is publicly held, they will be hounded by investment analysts about the firm's short-term financial performance. When employees own stock, they will have a similar focus away from the work. I remember a visit to British Petroleum's offices in Cleveland a few years back, where the television set in the stark lobby displayed one thing at all times: BP's current stock price. The same thing happens at companies like Intel and Microsoft, where the stock price is displayed on the computer screen savers used by many employees, who talk about it constantly.

It is difficult to reduce the focus on extrinsic aspects of work, especially among people who specialize in financial matters like accountants, controllers, stock analysts, and investors. But people in such jobs should realize that too much emphasis on money, especially on short-term financial performance, can kill innovation. An excessive focus on the financial aspects of work can be reduced by using certain recruitment and hiring practices. For example, early 1999 was a time when many Internet start-ups were luring new employees with high pay, and especially stock options. Justin Kitch, the CEO of Homestead, wanted assurance that people weren't joining the company just to get rich, that they were interested in the company and the work. Homestead screened out arrogant people who were looking for a fast buck. Although they could afford to pay market salaries, Homestead chose to pay about 85 percent of market. Kitch explained, "If people come because of the money, they will leave because of the money. The kinds of people we want aren't focused on shallow rewards."22

Senior managers who focus their attention on the work itself, rather than on extrinsic parts, can inspire others in a company to do so as well. Most senior executives of public companies that are listed on stock exchanges focus on pleasing stock analysts, who play a large role in determining a firm's valuation. A consultant I know, for example, tells me that the CEO of a large chemical company he works with is "depressed when the analysts beat him up and ebullient when they give him positive feedback, which sends the wrong message to everyone in the company." But if the CEO can convey that a focus on short-term stock price isn't especially wise, and not take the analysts opinions too seriously, the quality and imagination of the work done by the management team and other employees might be better because the focus turns to doing what is right in the long run instead of what looks best in the short run. This is exactly what CEO Dennis Bakke of AES has done. He attributes the firm's long-term performance partly to a focus on building a great business instead of on maximizing short-term earnings or taking others steps that please investment analysts.

The way that senior managers talk about their own compensation can have a marked effect as well. Yahoo!'s former CEO Tim Koogle was the highest paid CEO in the world in 1999. Largely because of the rise in Yahoo!'s stock price, his compensation was over $100 million. Koogle didn't like to talk about his wealth when he was CEO. When asked about all of the millionaires Yahoo! created, Koogle pointed out that he lived in a modest two-bedroom house. Koogle repeatedly emphasized that one of the main reasons Yahoo! became such a great company was that he, along with its founders Jerry Yang and Jeff Filo, had always focused on building a great company, not on getting rich. Koogle always said and acted as if building and sustaining a great company gives him more joy than his riches ever could.[23] Koogle's philosophy is reminiscent of Herrigel's classic *Zen in the Art of Archery,* where he says that if you focus on the pleasures of attaching the string, setting the arrow in the bow, drawing it back, and releasing it, rather than on hitting the target, you will be rewarded in two ways: You will take greater pleasure in doing the tasks and be more likely to hit the target as well.[24]

## Tactics for Avoiding and Dampening the Wrong Kind of Attention

Innovative work can suffer when it is done in a goldfish bowl, where everything that is imagined, said, and done is rendered transparent to all comers. It isn't enough to hope that customers, critics, and money mongers will know when it is best to avoid intruding, or just hanging around. *Fortune* columnist Michael Schrage writes that if companies really managed innovation right, there would be no need for skunk works and other means of isolating anointed innovators.[25] Schrage also described how such "innovation apartheid" creates resentment from those who feel excluded. I agree with Schrage that it is best to avoid creating elite and separate groups, and that companies can be more innovative when everyone contributes ideas. Schrage's vision is correct, but there are few companies that seem to be able to innovate without using teams that are removed and protected from the mainstream. In most companies, there are just too many forces that can derail and undermine innovative work, from executives who use the logic of routine work to manage it, to political enemies who have an interest in undermining a team's work, to well-meaning customers who demand things now that they won't want later.

So, to make innovation happen, skilled managers need to protect—and sometimes insulate—innovators from outsiders. I offer a menu of six, often intertwined, tactics that can be used and blended to suit your needs. It is no accident that these tactics are meant primarily for team leaders or senior managers. Anyone who does innovative work can use these tactics, but dealing with outsiders usually is and should be management's job. As Henry Mintzberg put it, "Someone, only half in jest, once described the manager as that person who sees visitors so that everyone else can get their work done."[26]

### Tell Them to Go Away

If you have the power, and the courage, an effective strategy for dealing with unwanted attention is to tell people to go away, that you do not have the time, interest, or energy to deal with them. For example, Nobel Prize winners often find that, after working in obscurity for decades, all the public accolades distract them from intellectual efforts. Some winners fight against these distractions and interruptions. Nobel Prize–winner Francis Crick used this form letter to respond to many requests:[27]

Dr. Crick thanks you for your letter but regrets that he is unable to accept your kind invitation to:

Send an autograph
provide a photograph
cure your disease
be interviewed
talk on the radio
appear on TV
speak after dinner
give a testimonial
help you in your project
read your manuscript
deliver a lecture
attend a conference
act as a chairman
become an editor
write a book

This tactic is one that can only be used when a person or team has the clout to do so. It worked for Apple founder Steve Jobs when he protected Apple's Macintosh development team; indeed, he was delighted when they raised a pirate flag over their building to broadcast the team's defiance to the rest of the company. And, although he was less dramatic about it, President Norio Ohga was just as vehement in instructing others at Sony to avoid interfering with the team that developed the Sony PlayStation.

## Learn to Ignore Them

When you don't have the power to chase outsiders away, or prefer not to exercise it, another strategy is to delude yourself a bit, to pretend that they aren't watching you or talking about you. If you can do it in a civilized way, this strategy helps you avoid attention, criticism, or advice that can distract your team from more important tasks, or worse yet, upset everyone if they find that what is said about them is inaccurate, unfair, or even downright mean. As the plight of Wallace Pipe shows, even when the attention is flattering and comes from people with the best of motives, if it causes you to neglect more important things, then you need to ignore it. The psychologist Richard Lazarus points out that that there are times when denial of reality facilitates well-being and decision making. Denial of facts is sometimes destructive, as when a cancer victim delays treatment. But Lazarus shows that denial is healthy when it diverts attention away from a source of distress a person cannot change; the attention and associated worrying only sap a person's ability to cope with things he or she *can* change.[28] This means that managers may benefit from using denial-like defense-mechanisms to avoid thinking about irrelevant or uncontrollable threats, or even complementary people and fun things that will cause their attention to stray from their work.

For example, John Reed was CEO of Citibank (now Citigroup) for more than 15 years, and during his controversial reign he led innovative changes at the bank, including the national marketing of credit cards, installing automatic teller machines throughout the world, and extending Citibank's services to emerging Asian and Latin American markets. When Reed was CEO, he told me that he didn't read, listen to, or view media reports about himself or the bank. He said that CEOs who focused on press reports were thinking about the wrong things, that it was more effective to please key constituencies directly rather than through the mass media. Reed asserted that he couldn't learn useful new information about the bank from the media because the issues they focused on were different from those he needed to work on, and because such reports contained so many errors.

A similar method was used by the late Carnegie Mellon psychology professor Herbert Simon. He won the Nobel Prize in economics, was one of the founders of the field of artificial intelligence, and is widely regarded as among the most imaginative and productive behavioral scientists of all time. Simon didn't read newspapers or watch television to get news. He said that when something important happened, people always told him, so it was a waste of time. Simon even made this point in a speech he gave to the National Association of Newspaper Editors, who were not amused. "I've saved an enormous amount of time since 1934, when I cast my first vote," Simon told them, and he went on to say, it had left him more time to focus on his research.[29]

### Avoid Them—But If You Can't, Don't Talk About Your Work

A related strategy is to avoid outsiders. It is easy to ignore people if you never see them. Avoiding people is more polite and less likely to annoy potential intruders than telling them to go away. This is one of the main reasons that the "Microkids" at Data General worked in isolation on the Eagle, as did scientists on the Manhattan Project and the engineers who developed the Sony PlayStation. And so did the teams led by Lockheed's Kelly Johnson, who is credited with coining the term *skunk works* to describe the elite and isolated teams that designed the U-2 and SR-71 Blackbird high-altitude spy planes. If you can't avoid interaction completely, the next best thing is not to mention what you are doing. The Microkids were told, "Don't even mention the name Eagle outside the group." "Don't talk outside the group."[30] Of course, not everyone outside the group needs to be avoided—only those who do more harm than good. I am advocating selective exposure to outsiders, not complete isolation. Michael Schrage's book *Serious Play* shows how such selective exposure is accomplished in one high-technology company:

> [P]eople are happy to show their bench prototypes—until the audience reaches the vice-presidential level. Then the unspoken but widely understood edict "never show fools unfinished work" kicks in. Top management finds it too difficult to see beyond prototype roughness to the ultimate product, and good

ideas are often rejected for what is seen as an inadequate execution of the prototype. As a result, many engineers conceal their more provocative prototypes from senior management until they have been appropriately polished.[31]

The challenge, following Schrage's advice, is to figure out who the "fools" are at any given moment in the innovation process. But it is just as important to remember that without the fools you need to avoid today, there might be no success tomorrow. In Schrage's example, without support from senior management for "appropriately polished" prototypes, no product can succeed in this company.

## Distract Them with Intriguing Diversions

This tactic involves raising interesting subjects, even creating exciting events, that distract outsiders from the innovative work. Skilled politicians use the tactic to distract reporters from raising difficult questions. President Ronald Reagan sometimes told jokes and interesting stories about when he worked as an actor or a sports announcer in an apparent effort to distract reporters from asking, or following up on, tough or intrusive questions.[32] Managers who are trying to protect innovative work from senior managers and reporters sometimes do the same thing.

Charles Galunic, a professor at INSEAD University in Fontainebleau France, interviewed an R&D manager who was concerned that attention from senior executives would distract and constrain a team in his division that was designing a computer peripheral. This manager believed that if senior managers got interested in the project, they would ask for more reports, want to see demonstrations and prototypes, and would want to give (misguided) advice, which would undermine the speed, creativity, and quality of the development process for this crucial product. This had happened many times in the past, to both him and other R&D managers. He defended his team by distracting upper management with more visible but far less important projects. To reduce "hype" about the key project, he always began presentations to top management by talking about other projects and didn't leave much time to talk about the one he believed was most crucial. This R&D manager told Galunic that by the time discussion turned to this less visible product, top managers didn't have much time left to talk about it and were too distracted and tired to offer strong opinions. Top managers usually just conveyed a bit of tepid pessimism about the (eventually very successful) product before turning to other matters.[33]

## Be Vague

Clarity in organizational communication is overrated, at least that is what some researchers claim.[34] They say that ambiguity is a useful compromise between total silence, which is interpreted as sign that there is something to hide, and complete clarity, which can lead people who disagree with the decision or who are rendered powerless by it to feel excluded. Clear and specific information about what will be done next also creates obstacles to flexibility and change, as it suggests a rigid course of action. These researchers point out that strategic ambiguity allows flexibility.

Political leaders are infamous for their excruciatingly obvious vagueness, which allows them plenty of "wiggle room" later. Although lambasted in the press for their inability to take a clear stand, their vagueness can actually serve the public (and themselves) well when it becomes necessary to alter a failing course of action. In contrast, when there is a lack of vagueness, change becomes more difficult and potentially damaging when attempted. Consider former U.S. president George Bush's tax increases leading up to the 1992 presidential elections. These measures were necessitated by falling government revenues in the wake of the 1989–93 recession and the desire to stem the growth in government debt. Although tax increases seemed prudent, Bush's prior lack of vagueness (i.e., "read my lips, no new taxes") made this decision not only more difficult to make and implement than it might have been but also damaging to the president's credibility as he entered the 1992 race.

Strategic ambiguity is one of the tools that managers can use to protect innovative work. It may reduce social facilitation effects because if purveyors of scrutiny do not know exactly what organization members are thinking, planning, and doing, they can't offer much more than broad and ill-considered advice, which is easily ignored.

## Be Boring

Companies, teams, and people are often subjected to attention because people find them intriguing. It follows that leaders can dim the spotlight by becoming less interesting to others. If done effectively, others will pay less attention to a boring leader or company, and then devote less energy to monitoring performance, asking about minute details, and making one (perhaps misguided) suggestion after another. So while the virtues of engaging communication are widely recognized as crucial managerial skills, there are times when being dull is the best thing for the company or team. You already know how it is done. Think of the most boring teachers you ever had. Speak in vague terms. Talk slowly. Never vary your pitch. Use long and winding sentences. Avoid eye contact with your audience. Talk about minute details. Use colorless language. Talk about dull topics and use convoluted examples to illustrate your points.

The result just might be that even if people want to listen to what you are saying, it may be impossible for them to hear your words. And if they have the chance to talk with you—and by extension the people you are trying to protect—they just might wander off and bother someone who is more engaging. There are probably some people and teams who benefit from being boring but who don't know it. Certainly, some of the most productive and imaginative researchers I know are quite dull in person. I suspect that one reason they can be so productive is that they are not besieged by visitors or speaking invitations. Although some people and teams benefit from leaders who are unintentionally boring, I got this idea from the CEO of a Fortune 50 company who I interviewed years ago. He gave a boring speech *on purpose* to protect his company from excessive scrutiny. The wisdom and humility of his actions made me realize that the ability to be boring is an important, and overlooked, skill for managing innovation.

This CEO told me he was invited to address a prestigious gathering of the national press right after he took over the company. His initial reaction was to refuse the request because this firm was in deep financial trouble and was selling products that the CEO believed were deeply flawed. Once he and his head of public relations talked about the request in more detail, however, they decided that this was a good opportunity to reduce the intense interest that the press had in this corporation and in him. They believed that past CEOs had been scrutinized too closely by the press. They wanted the company to be ignored as much as possible for a year or so until it brought out some exciting new products that were under development. So this CEO and head of PR decided that the best strategy, rather than refusing the chance to speak, was to give a talk on a boring topic and in a boring manner (with a dry delivery, filled with facts and figures, and sentences written in the passive voice). The CEO told me that the national press seemed to lose interest immediately, which helped him and other senior managers focus on developing products instead of sparring with reporters as much as in the past.

## Striking a Healthy Balance Between Being Open and Being Closed

I suggested at the outset of this chapter that just because innovation needs to be shielded from certain people at certain times, that does not mean it should be done in complete isolation. In fact, as a general rule, being open supports innovation and being closed stifles it. I can't draw you a comforting linear diagram to specify exactly when and to whom innovation

TABLE 3  **Times When Innovative Work Is Best Left Closed vs. Opened to Outsiders**

| Times to Banish or Avoid Outsiders | Times to Invite Attention from Outsiders |
| --- | --- |
| • When team members are learning to do something they have never done before | • When scouting for varied knowledge to use in new ways and combinations |
| • When outsiders interrupt so much that it slows the work | • When a team needs more resources to start or complete the work, to convince people to support the work |
| • When outsiders repeat the same advice over and over | • When a team can't solve some problem, and needs ideas about how to get unstuck |
| • When people are spending too much time working on ways to present innovative ideas, and not enough time developing ideas | • When team members talk about the same things over and over, especially when they seem to use the same set of solutions to solve every new problem |
| • When outsiders focus only on maximizing short-term financial gains | |
| • When team members spend too much time talking about the money and recognition their ideas will generate, and not enough time talking about the ideas | • When the team is making incremental improvements in a product or service that is widely used by existing customers |
| • When the team is developing a brand-new product, solution, or service, not making incremental improvements in existing ones | • When a product or service needs to be tailored to the immediate needs of a specific group of customers |
| • When outsiders keep insisting that things should be done as they have always been done | • When a team uses familiar, deeply ingrained work practices to produce innovative results |
| • When outsiders' enthusiasm about one or more of the team's ideas prematurely halts generating and testing new ideas | |
| • When there is intellectual property that must be protected | • When it is time to "sell" the team's finished ideas |

should be open versus closed. This process is too messy. But it is possible to identify times when innovative work is best left opened versus kept closed to outsiders. I have done so throughout the book and have summarized these instances in the attached table. One of these times requires additional explanation: My suggestion that teams invite more outside attention when they use familiar, especially deeply ingrained, work practices to produce innovative results.

This advice may seem to clash with the research on audience effects introduced at the outset of this chapter. But working in front of an audience only interferes with the learning and performance of unfamiliar actions. If a person or team uses familiar methods to achieve innovation, then the increased energy and focus on ingrained routines will spark, rather than stifle, innovation. This is precisely what happens at IDEO, where experienced designers use variations of the same work practices—observing users, brainstorming, rapid prototyping—to produce original designs. An engineer's comment that "brainstorming is our culture, and rapid prototyping is our religion" tells you that these work practices are used again and again. So experienced IDEO designers ought to perform them at least as well in front of audiences—even judgmental audiences—as when they work alone. This is why IDEO could invite ABC's *Nightline* to film over an entire week every action they took while designing a shopping cart, why they could do brainstorming and rapid prototyping to develop a bicycle cup holder for a *San Jose Mercury* reporter, and why they routinely invite clients backstage to join brainstorming sessions. The notion that being around "evaluative others" stifles innovation is an oversimplification; it only holds when you have to learn something new.

IDEO's willingness to invite outsiders backstage is important not just because it suggests that innovative work can be done without sealing off the team from outsiders; it implies that some teams and companies are excessively paranoid about hiding themselves and their ideas from outsiders, that there are times when they might be able to learn more, get more resources, and gain more political support by being more open. A good example is the team at Sun Microsystems that developed Java (originally called "Oak"). When the first limited release of the product occurred, team members waited in fear that top management would veto the product. "Everybody on the team was nursing a little Dilbert doomsday scenario." But "no such ogre ever really appeared."[35]

# Don't Try to Learn Anything from People Who Say They Have Solved the Problems You Face

## (Weird Idea #10)

I never would have conceived my theory, let alone have made a great deal of effort to verify it, if I had been more familiar with the major developments in physics that were taking place. Moreover, my initial ignorance of the powerful false objections that were raised against my ideas protected those ideas from being nipped in the bud.[1]

> —Michael Polyani on how he developed his theory of molecular adsorption, which was initially rejected but then became a widely accepted scientific axiom.

When Daniel Ng, an American trained engineer, opened Hong Kong's first McDonald's in 1975, his local food industry competitors dismissed the venture as a non-starter: "Selling hamburgers to the Cantonese? You must be joking!" Ng credits his boldness to the fact that he did not have an M.B.A. and had never taken a business course.[2]

> —James Watson, professor of Chinese studies, reporting that McDonald's now has 158 thriving restaurants in Hong Kong

We isolate ourselves to stay *away* from ordinary thought or the state of the art as it currently exists.[3]

> —Jim Jannard, reclusive founder and chair of Oakley, manufacturer of premium and futuristic sunglasses

IN THE CREATIVE PROCESS, ignorance is bliss, especially in the early stages. People who don't know how things are "supposed to be" aren't blinded by existing beliefs. They can see things that others have failed to notice, and imagine new ideas and perspectives that would never occur to people who develop deep, but narrow, expertise in an area. Ignorant people don't know what they are supposed to see or ignore, so they can see old things in new ways that so-called experts have rejected, or never thought about.

I first got this idea by reading about Nobel Prize winners who had done exceptionally creative work. The virtues of ignorance and detachment are evident in the accomplishments of many winners, including James Watson and Francis Crick's discovery of the DNA structure, Cary Mullis's invention of polymerase chain reaction, and Richard Feynman's work in physics. These scientists, and many others, attribute their great breakthroughs to their detachment from what other people in their fields were doing. They didn't know how things were done in the past, how things ought to be done, and what was believed to be impossible or absurd. So they did what they thought was logical and right.

Richard Feynman refused "to read the current literature, and he chided graduate students who would begin their work in the normal way, by checking what had already been done. That way, he told them, they would give up the chances of finding something original."[4] At one point in Feynman's life, he was discouraged because he felt less creative than in past years. He had a chance meeting with fellow Nobel Prize–winner James Watson at the University of Chicago faculty club, who gave him a manuscript (eventually published as *The Double Helix*) that described the process Watson and Crick used to discover the structure of DNA. When Feynman gave Watson's manuscript to a fellow physicist to read, his colleague commented, "You know, it's amazing that Watson made this great discovery even though he was out of touch with what everyone in his field was doing." To that, Feynman wrote: "DISREGARD. That is what I've forgotten."[5]

There are two main ways to capitalize on naiveté. The first is to find novices, young or naive people who not only lack expertise about the problem or question, but who also lack expertise about related areas. Jane Goodall's groundbreaking research on chimpanzees is a good example. It started when anthropologist Louis Leakey hired Goodall to do two years of intensive observations of these apes in Africa. Goodall hesitated to take the job because she had no scientific training. Leakey insisted that not only was university training unnecessary, it had serious drawbacks.

Goodall realized that "he wanted someone with a mind uncluttered and unbiased by theory who would make the study for no other reason than a real desire for knowledge."[6] Ultimately, Goodall and Leakey both believed that if she had not been so ignorant of existing theories, she never would have been able to observe and explain so many new chimp behaviors.

A milder form of this approach is to hire people who have formal training in some area, but are not jaded by the historical, and perhaps arbitrary and outdated, customs in the industry. This is what they do at Dyson Appliances, which makes the hottest-selling vacuum cleaner in the United Kingdom. The "Dual Cyclone" has a powerful and groundbreaking vacuum technology, and requires no bag. The machine has a striking, colorful design and a see-through chamber that lets you see the cyclone inside as it spins at nearly 1,000 miles per hour. Founder and CEO James Dyson believes that one reason the firm invents successful products is that they employ graduates straight from the university: "The basic reason for this is that they are unsullied. They have not been strapped into a suit and taught to think by a company with nothing on its mind but short-term profit and early retirement. We are trying to do things differently than everyone else. . . . our marketing has been done by Rebecca Trentham, from a standing start as a languages graduate from Oxford, and all of our products have been designed by and engineered by new graduates."[7] Similarly, the first Sony PlayStation succeeded partly because the young engineers who invented it were new to the video game industry. "We were fortunate because we were amateurs when it came to games and we naively went about doing what we thought would be sure to work. . . . We were not preoccupied with established industry practices—we started from square one and let the ideas flow freely and without reservation," says Shigeo Maruyama, vice chairman of Sony Computer Entertainment Incorporated.[8]

The second way to capitalize on naiveté is to find people who aren't working in the same industry or occupation, but have expertise in another area that allows them to see your problems—and possibly solve them—from a new perspective. People with different technical skills and different backgrounds not only broaden the range of possible solutions to a problem, they also don't suffer from the same narrowness that people who have been working on a problem for a long time do. An additional advantage is that people who are well versed in different knowledge can operate efficiently, as they are simply applying something they know how to do well to a different problem. For example, engineers have been working for years to improve the battery life of laptop computers, focusing on the development of longer-lasting batteries and various software solutions to dim and shut off power-hungry displays. The approach used by 3M's Microreplication Technology Center was to reframe the problem; to make a display that uses less power. Microreplication is a three-dimensional surface composed of microscopic pyramids, first developed by 3M in the 1950s to focus light and increase the brightness of overhead projectors. Rick Dryer and Sandy Cobb adopted microreplication technology to develop Brightness Enhancement Film, which magnifies the brightness of backlit flat panel displays and extends battery life substantially; it is now being used by numerous laptop manufacturers.[9]

A similar approach was used during the early days of Ballard Power Systems. In 1974, founder and then CEO Geoffrey Ballard hired young chemistry professor Keith Prater as a consultant. At that time, Ballard's emphasis was on developing longer-lasting batteries. Prater warned Ballard that he had no experience working on batteries. "That's fine," said Ballard, "I don't want someone who knows batteries. They know what won't work. I want someone who is bright and creative and willing to try things that others might not try. That's where the breakthroughs come from."[10] And, indeed, Prater played a key role in developing innovative batteries during the company's early days, and later, in making breakthroughs to help make fuel cells a technology for powering buses and cars that just might lead to a revolution in this industry.

Keith Prater knew a lot about chemical theories. What he didn't know was which assumptions and beliefs were taken for granted by people working on batteries and fuel cells, so he wasn't constrained by industry dogma. It is often wise to seek advice from people who face challenges that—though they appear different on the surface—are actually similar to those faced by you or your company. Hiring such people can be an efficient way to import fresh solutions to old problems. For example, the tiny stents developed by the Guidant Corporation to prop open obstructed heart vessels are a lot different from the planes and missiles developed by defense contractors. Yet Ginger Graham, group chairman, reports that Guidant's research and development efforts on stents have been bolstered by hiring engineers from the defense industry. Engineers who worked in places including NASA, Hughes, Lockheed, Ford Aerospace, Raychem, and General Dynamics have brought materials and design solutions that are new to the company and industry, and that have helped Guidant design better stents and other medical products. Former Raychem engi-

---

### *Putting Weird Idea #10 to Work*

#### Innovate by Ignoring Work on the Same Task or Problem

- During the early stages of a project, don't study how the task has been approached in the company, industry, field, or region where you are working.

- If you know a lot about a problem and how it has been solved in the past, ask people who are ignorant of it to study it and help solve it. Young people, including children, can be especially valuable for this task.

- Ask new hires (especially those fresh out of school) to solve problems or do tasks that you "know" the answer to or you can't resolve. Get out of the way for a while to see if they generate some good ideas.

- Find analogous problems in different industries, and study how they are solved.

- Find people working on analogous issues in different companies, fields, regions, fields, and industries, and ask them how they would solve the problem or do the job.

- If people who have the *right* skills keep failing to solve some problem, try assigning some people with the *wrong* skills to solve it.

- If you are a novice, seek experts to help you, but don't assume they are right, *especially if they tell you they are right.*

---

neers used their extensive knowledge of polymeric materials to design improved catheters, which surgeons use to insert and position stents in heart vessels.

A less drastic form of this practice is to assemble teams or companies with people who have worked on the same problem, but in different groups, industries, or places. This is what Ray Evernham did when he assembled a crew to support stock-car racer Jeff Gordon, who rose from obscurity to unprecedented success in the Winston Cup Series in the mid- and late 1990s. As Evernham put it:

> One reason we got off to such a fast start when the Rainbow
> Warrior team was assembled five years ago was that, right from
> the beginning, we dared to be different. I didn't hire anybody for
> the team who had Winston Cup experience.... We were also the
> first team to hire a coach specifically to train and rehearse the pit

crew. People laughed at the way we trained: rope climbing, wind sprints, guys carrying each other on their backs. People said, "What in the world are you guys doing?" I am sure it looked funny, but it worked. Typically, we pit in 17 seconds or less— about a second faster than other teams do. In one second, a car going 200 mph travels 300 feet. So right there, we gain 300 feet on the competition.[11]

Another variation of this theme is, if people who have the "right" skills and experience for a task keep failing at it, see if people with the "wrong" skills can solve the problem. The fresh perspective they bring might enable them to see solutions that narrow experts are blind to, or they may have "irrelevant" knowledge that ultimately solves the problem. When the inventors in Thomas Edison's lab repeatedly failed to produce a satisfactory chemical substance to insulate wires, he assigned an electrician, Reginald Fessenden, to the job. Fessenden complained that he knew nothing about chemistry. Edison responded, "Then I want you to be a chemist. I've had a lot of chemists . . . but none of them can get results."[12] Edison was so impressed with Fessenden's work that he eventually was assigned to lead the insulation project. When the project ended, Edison wrote a strong letter of recommendation for Fessenden as a chemical (not an electrical) experimenter.

Knowledge about effective ways of doing things can stifle creativity. Sometimes being ignorant, but curious, playful, and persistent, is better than knowing the way things are supposed to be done and the way that others have done them. The rule of thumb is that if you know a lot about a subject, seek advice from people who are naive, either because they lack bias or because they are experts with biases that are drastically different from people in your industry or company. And, of course, if you are ignorant about a subject, find someone who is knowledgeable. The relationship between the renowned anthropologist Louis Leakey and the young and unschooled Jane Goodall is a great example; Leakey needed Goodall's ignorance, and Goodall needed Leakey's knowledge.

### CHAPTER 14

# Forget the Past, Especially Your Company's Successes

## (Weird Idea #11)

In graduate school, Venter was told there were no questions left in biology; it would be hard to find a doctoral thesis worth writing about.[1]

> —The bad advice given to Craig Venter, whose pathbreaking work in "shotgun genomics" has been crucial to spelling out the human genetic code

I asked, "If we got kicked out and the board brought in a new CEO, what do you think he would do?" Gordon answered without hesitation, "He would get us out of memories." I stared at him, numb, then said, "Why shouldn't you and I walk out the door, come back and do it ourselves."[2]

> —Andrew Grove on how he and (then) CEO of Intel Gordon Moore in 1985 decided to get out of the memory chip business and focus on microprocessors

When you come to work at St. Luke's in the morning, you never know where you are going to be sitting. There is completely open space here. It is terribly destabilizing not to have your little desk or space where you can put your photographs up. . . . But we decided collectively to do this because we want to defeat habit. Creativity is the defeat of habit by imposing originality and change.[3]

> —Andy Law, cofounder of St. Luke's Communications, advertising agency of the year in Britain in 1998

GEORGE SANTAYANA'S FAMOUS WORDS that "those who cannot remember the past are condemned to repeat it" is bad advice if you want constant innovation. At least it is bad advice when it comes to memories of what *your company* has done in the past. People and organizations do learn from studying *others'* successes and failures. Although it isn't always easy to turn such knowledge into action, studying other companies can help managers learn which new practices to adopt and which to avoid. For example, the "Committee of 99" that designed the blueprint for General Motors' (then) revolutionary new Saturn plant in Springhill, Tennessee, traveled throughout the world to learn about the best practices used for designing, building, and selling new cars, many of which were adopted by the new GM division. In contrast, learning from *one's own past* is far more problematic. At least for organizational life, Santayana's saying would be more accurate if it were something like: "Those who *can* remember their company's past are condemned to repeat it."

As mentioned earlier, research by psychologists such as Harvard's Ellen Langer show that the way the human brain operates makes us prone to repeating what we have done in the past, especially if it was successful. Controlled experiments show that when a person does something even once, and has no reason to question what was done or why, the action becomes automatically, or "mindlessly," repeated again and again. This ability to make a behavior "automatic" is one of the main reasons that human beings can accomplish so much. The problem, however, is that such "mindless behavior" has been shown to persist even when it undermines performance. If a person did not learn the right way to do something in the first place, or if circumstances change, people need to engage in active, or "mindful," analysis to perform well. It is impossible to invent new uses for old ideas and new combinations of old ideas without switching cognitive gears from automatic to active thinking.[4]

Another reason so many companies rely on obsolete methods and technologies is that the people who defend and use them are often more powerful than those who advocate new and superior ways. The past successes of the old guard helps them gain powerful positions and control precious resources, which they use to undermine people who come along with better ways that will help the company, but threaten their dominance. This is what happened to Ken Kutaragi, the father of the Sony PlayStation. His work on the digital technologies that the PlayStation (eventually) used was stalled and stigmatized because so many powerful executives and engineers defended and benefited from Sony's deeply ingrained (and successful) analog tradition. He struggled to get the people and resources he needed, but his work was slowed, and sometimes stopped, by powerful rivals in Sony. Kutaragi was warned by a powerful Sony executive: "I hear that you want to develop digital technology; you must never say that at Sony. You will be transferred immediately. . . . That's out of the question. That's taboo at Sony."[5]

Another reason obsolete ways persist is that people become so skilled at doing things in old ways. Their deep competence at old ways and lack of skill at the new can mean that they perform worse when trying new (but ultimately superior) concepts, methods, and technologies. James March calls this a "success trap" or a "competence trap."

> As a result of success, it [a company] repeats the action that appears to have produced the success. As a result of repeating actions, it becomes more proficient at the technology involved. . . . This process leads to an endless cycle of success, increased competency, and exploitation. New ideas are not tried, or if tried, do not do as well as the existing technology (because of the disparity in competence with the two).[6]

This "paradox of success," where "core competencies often turn into core rigidities," has been studied in depth, especially by Michael Tushman and Charles O'Reilly in *Winning Through Innovation* and Clayton Christensen in his best-seller *The Innovator's Dilemma*.[7] This research shows how success traps undermine once-successful companies, even entire industries, that were unable to switch from outmoded technologies and business models to superior "disruptive innovations." These researchers use cases including Kodak's success in chemical-based film, Smith-Corona's typewriter business, Swiss watchmaking consortium SSIH's dominance in mechanical watches, and the computer disk-drive industry to show how once-successful technological innovations often lead companies to buy equipment, develop cultures, hire and train people, and implement policies that are "stultifying," "innovation numbing," and lead to "continuous, incremental improvement [that] actually traps the organization in its distinguished past."[8]

### Common Ways to Forget Past Successes

There are a variety of ways that companies can avoid such success traps. I

will first talk about the proven and frequently repeated remedies for success traps advocated in these writings. Then, following the spirit of this
book, I suggest some stranger remedies.

The most common suggestion about how to break free from an organization's successful past, and the main one suggested in Christensen's
*Innovator's Dilemma,* is to start a new company, or at least a new business
unit. Many companies have broken free from established technologies,
business practices, and business models by setting up new divisions, freestanding companies, and joint ventures in ways and places that aren't held
hostage by their company's past successes. This is why Wal-Mart.com was
formed in Palo Alto, California, in January 2000 with Silicon Valley venture capital firm Accel Partners. Wal-Mart had first tried to sell products
on the Internet by working within the confines of company headquarters
in Bentonville, Arkansas. After lagging behind competitors that only sell
products online like Amazon.com, and missing a planned deadline to
update the Web site for the 1999 Christmas season, they created a new
company. This was done to avoid the cultural and financial conflicts that
occurred when Wal-Mart tried to launch an Internet business in the face
of the firm's revered and successful traditions in their "bricks and mortar"
business, and to be closer to skilled employees in Silicon Valley.

A related strategy is to start a new business unit, and to do everything possible to get people in it to ignore, defy, and rebel against the
organizational code. This is easier to accomplish when a business unit is
formed away from the center of power and influence in the company, so
that defenders of the corporate code have fewer chances to impose old
ways of doing things on the new business. This was one reason that General Motors' first Saturn plant was built in Springhill, Tennessee, over a
thousand miles from GM headquarters in Detroit. Partly as a result of
the distance, and partly because of unprecedented cooperation between
CEO Roger Smith and United Auto Workers official Donald Ephlin, the
new plant was able to free itself from GM's traditional adversarial relationship with the UAW.[9] Indeed, Saturn became the model of union-
management cooperation in the United States auto industry for many
years. To give you just one example, Gary High, Saturn's director of
Human Resource Development, was interviewed for the job by four
people, two GM managers and two hourly GM employees who were
UAW members. High couldn't tell who was "management" and who was
"union" because all four seemed concerned only about the success of the
Saturn plant as a whole.[10]

Hewlett-Packard's Richard Hackborn led the firm's efforts to develop and sell printers for personal computers by moving far from HP's headquarters in Palo Alto. When Hackborn first tried to convince HP traditionalists to sell printers, they resisted the low profit margins associated with consumer products. At one point, several senior managers insisted that they only sell printers that were compatible with HP personal computers, even though HP had only a tiny percentage of the PC market share. So Hackborn and a crew of managers known as "Dick's Cowboys" set up shop in Boise, Idaho, far from corporate headquarters. They broke away from a slew of long-standing HP practices. "Dick was successful by leaving the system. He never got permission for anything. He'd rather ask forgiveness after the fact," says Network Appliances' CEO Dan Warmenhoven, who worked with Hackborn for five years in the 1980s.[11] As of this writing, these printers (and especially the replaceable ink cartridges inside) account for approximately 50 percent of HP's sales and 75 percent of their profits.

The logic for locating a new company or business unit far away from headquarters is that by being far from purveyors of the corporate code, and near people and companies that use technologies, business models, and business practices that clash with the traditional code, the new business will be able to break from the company's past. These practices can make it easier for companies to do two things: Create a new future and make it impossible to go back to the past. This one-two punch is facilitated by giving employees who join the new company or business unit "one-way tickets," where once they join the new business unit or company, they aren't allowed to go back to the old. This practice was used when Saturn was formed. General Motors employees who moved to the Saturn plant—both unionized and nonunionized—were told that they couldn't have their old jobs back if things didn't work out at Saturn. The same practice was used when Proctor & Gamble and several Silicon Valley venture capital firms formed Reflect.com, a new, high-end Internet cosmetics company. Proctor & Gamble employees were not assured a job if they wanted to go back to the mother company. One-way tickets help ensure that people who join the new business want to break from the past—may even have some disdain for it—and that they are bold enough to join a new business. Like Saturn and Wal-Mart.com, Reflect.com is located in San Francisco, far from Proctor & Gamble headquarters in Cincinnati, Ohio.

Forming a new business far from headquarters does not, however, guarantee that innovative ideas will be discovered and developed. If ties to headquarters or managerial oversight remain too strong, the result can be the worst of both worlds, where people at the distant outpost follow the company code closely, but have the burden of being a distant and often powerless entity. This is what happened when German-based Daimler-Benz (now DaimlerChrysler) opened the Research & Technology Center in Silicon Valley in 1995. The center was formed to harvest ideas from Silicon Valley about new technologies and services to help Daimler-Benz make more innovative products. A study by Stanford graduate students reported that the center had surprisingly weak connections to people and companies in Silicon Valley, and that researchers were told what to work on by superiors in Germany. Furthermore, when a center employee did come up with a good new idea, it was rarely implemented because the center was powerless compared to research units in Germany. My recent conversations with managers at the Research & Technology Center suggest that many of these problems have been resolved, but they admit that during its early years, the center struggled to be autonomous and innovative.

If you can't start a new company or business, another common "suggestion" is to lead or join a revolution. Management guru Gary Hamel has developed guidelines for revolutionaries who want to start insurrections that overturn old, outmoded ways and replace them with superior business practices, business models, and technologies.[12] Hamel's perspective is reminiscent of work on how to start political movements like Saul Alinsky's famous handbook *Rules for Radicals*.[13] Both corporate and political revolutions are started by people, or groups, who have a strong point of view about what needs to change and why. Successful revolutionaries articulate their goals in a clear and exciting way, build a coalition of powerful allies, and study closely the behavior of the old guard they are trying to topple. They also convince former enemies to join them or, failing that, neutralize their power. Finally, they stage small victories to demonstrate that their new ways are superior to old, ingrained ways of thinking and acting. Hamel's compelling case study of IBM shows how David Grossman and John Patrick, who were among the first people at IBM to recognize the importance of the Internet, used many of these tactics (and the Internet itself to implement them) to start an "insurrection." Despite much initial resistance from top management, these actions ultimately transformed IBM into an "e-business powerhouse."[14] As Hamel put it, "Like dissidents using a purloined duplicator in the old Soviet Union, Patrick and Grossman used the Web to build a community of Web fans that would ultimately transform IBM."[15]

Successful corporate revolutions need not always occur on such a grand scale. My favorite small-scale revolution was led by Annette Kyle among the 55 employees at the Bayport Terminal in Seabrook, Texas. The terminal was part of the chemical group of Hoechst Celanese Corporation.[16] It loaded nearly three billion pounds of chemicals per year from railcars onto trucks, barges, and ships. When Kyle took over in 1994, she discovered that most practices had not changed since it had opened in 1974, even though the volume handled had tripled. The operation was grossly inefficient as a result. For example, when a ship arrived to be loaded and had to wait because operators were running late, Celanese was charged waiting fees called "demurrage charges," often $10,000 per hour. In 1994, the terminal paid about $2.5 million in these charges. It also took operators an average of three hours to load a truck, even though the industry average was under an hour. The terminal had a traditional structure where supervisors closely oversaw the operators who loaded the chemicals. The supervisors clung to old ways, even though it hampered the speed and quality of the work.

Kyle spent over a year bringing in new tools, training supervisors and operators in better work methods, and trying to implement dozens of small improvements. By late 1995, however, Kyle and her management staff had decided that incremental changes were not working. Inspired by a "WOW" seminar they attended from management guru Tom Peters, she and her staff started planning a revolution. On the morning of January 3, 1996, the terminal was closed and all employees attended a meeting. Kyle announced and immediately implemented sweeping changes. Operators were now self-managing and worked without immediate bosses; supervisors were now "marine planners," responsible for planning the flow of materials; and schedules and information about how well goals were being met were displayed on a large board that everyone could check at any time. She also brought in a coffin where she put various items to symbolize that the past was dead, like a "Ships Happen" sign from the supervisors' office, which reflected the destructive old attitude that preparing in advance to load a ship wasn't always possible.

The positive effects of Kyle's revolution were evident almost immediately. Demurrage fees dropped from over $1 million in the first half of 1995 to less than $10,000 in the first half of 1996. More than 90 percent of the trucks were loaded within an hour of their arrival. Supervisors and operators were shocked at first, but soon developed positive reactions to the new ways. An evaluation by independent researchers from the University of Southern California indicated that employees were satisfied with and motivated by the changes. Kyle accomplished these changes by relying more on her authority (and courage) and less on building a coalition than her fellow revolutionaries at IBM, but she also used many tried-and-true tactics of successful revolutionaries. She had a strong point of view about what needed to change and why, and she articulated her goals in clear and exciting ways. Kyle worked alongside the supervisors and operators for almost a year before changing their jobs. They knew she understood their work, so they quickly became strong allies. She also neutralized the power of senior managers who might stop the revolution by *not telling them* it was going to happen; only her immediate boss knew of the plan. And she used the early successes to convince people throughout the company that the new ways were superior to old, ingrained habits at Bayport.

Finally, to complete the line-up of conventional approaches, while the revolutions at IBM and Bayport illustrate dramatic ways to break from the past, organizations can and do change all the time through less dramatic and incremental ways. There are many well-known and effective techniques that firms use to make people aware that ingrained, mindless practices are standing in the way of innovation, and to provoke people to use better ways. In some companies, for example, people mindfully hunt down and eliminate "sacred cows," which are ineffective ways of thinking and acting that have outlived their usefulness, but that people either don't think about or are afraid to stop or change. One company I know used an amusing and inexpensive program to attack its sacred cows. The CEO bought all the managers Beanie Babies, specifically Daisy the Black and White Cow, and told everyone to "throw them at people when they defend sacred cows." A manager at the firm told me, "We giggled about the Beanie Babies a lot, but it helped us get rid of some really dumb procedures."

Pillsbury, Madison and Sutro LLP (now called Pillsbury Winthrop LLP) used a more serious and sweeping program to unearth and eliminate sacred cows. The 125-year-old San Francisco-based law firm was clinging to old practices and business models that, although once effective, had been rendered obsolete by the information revolution. As part of their effort to break from the past, firm chair Mary Cranston and managing partner Marina Park established a "sacred cow task force" in early 1999, which was charged with identifying and eliminating ingrained habits that were slowing change and wasting money. Task-force members identified over 100 sacred cows, and specific attorneys and administrators were charged with eliminating them and reporting progress on specific dates.

The importance of this program was reinforced at an offsite where one speaker was Robert Kriegel, author of *Sacred Cows Make the Best Burgers*.

Many sacred cows were found in the complex and varied processes that local offices used to bill clients and to collect overdue payments. Several senior partners insisted that local autonomy was crucial because clients who received impersonal bills would be offended. Over these objections, the task force developed and implemented a simpler and more centralized system for doing these routine tasks. But it still maintained the personal touch because each bill was still sent with a personal letter from the responsible partner, as had always been done. The new system decreased the average time that clients paid their bills from 4.5 to 3.2 months and reduced related labor costs by over 25 percent (adding several million dollars to the firm's bottom line). Some partners who voiced the strongest opposition now agree that the new system is superior because clients' queries about bills are resolved more quickly and overdue payments are collected more efficiently—not to mention the fact that partners pocket their share of the increased profit. Much like the role of brainstorming in the Toyota Production system, this task force generated varied new ideas and viewed old problems in new ways to improve routine tasks. As a result of the changes in the billing system, and dozens of other incremental changes, the *American Lawyer's* annual rankings of the top 100 law firms for 1999 indicated that Pillsbury's profits-per-partner increased 44.2 percent, the fourth-largest percentage increase among the 100 law firms in the survey.

---

### Putting Weird Idea #11 to Work
#### Common Ways to Forget Past Successes

- Start a new company.
- Start a new business unit, preferably in a new place.
- Give people who join new companies or business units "one way tickets."
- Make "revolutionary changes" in the company.
- Use task forces, workshops, and companywide meetings to make extensive incremental changes.
- Encourage people to be agnostic about the best business models, business practices, and technologies.

## Uncommon Ways to Forget Past Successes

The methods I have suggested so far for breaking from the past are based on sound theory and evidence. These techniques are also widely known and accepted. But this is a book about weird ideas that work, not common ideas that work. So let me also suggest some unusual ideas for building companies with diverse knowledge, where people keep seeing new things in old ways. Some of the weird ideas I've already suggested can help companies avoid getting trapped in an unsuccessful past. As I showed in Chapter 3, for example, if you want people who are unaffected by the past, you need to hire and protect some slow learners, people who don't want to learn and don't care about the organization's or industry's past. You need to look for people like Nobel Prize winner Cary Mullis, who "was screaming for a year and a half about how important PCR was and no one was listening." They don't care about the past, only about what they believe is right. You also don't want people who all insist on the same thing because, as I showed in Chapter 8, you want people who fight like crazy over ideas. In particular, you want conflict over whether current ways of doing things are obsolete to keep everyone mindful about what they are doing and why. You want people like futurist George Gilder, who worries that when everyone agrees with him, he isn't thinking far enough ahead.[17]

There are other unusual, but effective, things that companies can do to avoid getting stuck in the past. One of the most powerful is to routinely take people out of jobs where they are competent and comfortable, and assign them to jobs where they don't have the right skills and that make them feel uncomfortable. Companies that do this routinely are forcing constant mindfulness, forcing people to keep learning new things and putting people in positions where they will see the same old tasks in new ways. This idea can, however, be taken too far; for example, I wouldn't want the first heart operation done by an inexperienced nurse. This technique also isn't very efficient because people have to keep learning new things, which takes time and leads to higher failure rates in the early stages. But there are some companies whose leaders have demonstrated that playing a game of musical chairs is a potent way to spark innovation.

One example is the Lend Lease Corporation, which is over 40 years old and is Australia's leading real estate development company. People at Lend Lease are constantly shifted among diverse positions to keep them learning, keep them uncomfortable, and to keep teaching senior management about what people can—and cannot—do well. One day in 1997, manager Peter Scott was called to a meeting where the chairman, Stuart Horney, radically reorganized the management structure. Just about every senior manager was given a new role because, as Horney put it, "We need to refocus, so I thought we'd just stir the place up." Scott was shifted from head of one major project to a job that involved him in all major projects. He was moved into yet another job less than a year later. Lend Lease does this deliberately; they call it "careening careers." Scott says, "It's invigorating—and it's also intimidating because you're constantly being pushed outside your comfort zone." Susan McDonald is a 28-year-old employee who has already held seven different jobs at the company. She adds, "The basic operating procedure here is that people don't stand on titles. They don't stand on position, and they don't stand on precedent. It's all about ideas. . . . It's incredibly energizing—and brutal. People either love to work for Lend Lease or absolutely hate it."[18]

Similar practices are used by AES, a global independent power producer mentioned earlier.[19] The company consciously uses management practices to ensure that people are constantly mindful about what they are doing and why. It is radically decentralized and has no human resources or environmental compliance department. Cofounder and CEO Dennis Bakke believes that one reason the firm is so innovative and financially successful is that it constantly gives people new jobs to do, even tasks that they are not trained to do and have never done. Veterans at AES are routinely rotated among different functions, and newcomers are given jobs that they have never done before. When engineer Paul Burdick first joined the company, for example, his first job was to "sign up a billion dollars worth of coal," even though he didn't know anything about the task before he started. He spent weeks on the phone talking to people inside and outside the firm to learn the best way to do it. Because AES is so decentralized, people are constantly forced to learn and do new things on the job. They don't complain about their lack of training or that it isn't their job; people like that don't get hired in the first place. They just figure out how to do it. They can't consult the human resources department (there is none) and there is no AES University. If a group of employees want to learn something, they find someone to teach it and organize the class themselves. Many tasks might be done faster by someone who does them over and over, but Burdick asserts that giving people new things to do is crucial to the company's success because "the minute you systematize something, you suck the life out of it. You impose a set of rules or procedures for doing something, and nobody asks questions any more—questions such as, Why is it done this way?"[20]

A related technique is not just to move employees around a lot, but to constantly disband and reform work groups. Longstanding teams are especially prone to getting trapped in the past. Members can become so fond of each other and talk among themselves so much that they start ignoring outsiders. A study of 50 research and development teams by Ralph Katz and his colleagues found that during the first couple of years of life, the number of ideas produced by the R&D teams went up, but after about three or four years, the creative output of these teams peaked and declined thereafter.[21]

> It is almost as if some demon were at work, selecting the most useful form of communication in each instance and causing it to decay most with increasing mean tenure of project members. Development team members isolate themselves from organizational colleagues, research teams from external colleagues, and technical service teams from each other.

Katz and his colleagues suggest that this drop in innovation happens because, over time, team members focus more strongly on the virtues of their own ideas, and begin to dismiss the ideas of outside groups and competitors as inferior. This is called the "Not-Invented-Here Syndrome." Research introduced in Chapter 1 explains how this syndrome develops. Recall that it is hard to change behavior when it becomes ingrained and mindless. Also recall that "mere exposure" research shows that people will have positive reactions to anything familiar and negative reactions to anything unfamiliar. The longer a group has been together, the stronger these forces become. What happens inside the group becomes increasingly familiar to members, while what outsiders do seems less familiar or interesting. As time passes, motivation, experimentation, and learning may diminish so gradually that no one on the team realizes that these changes are actually taking place.[22] To make matters worse, I've noticed that after a group of people have been together for a long time, they spend more and more time talking about things outside of work—their families, sports, hobbies, and so on—and less and less time talking about their work. After all, they don't really think about the work; they have decided who in the group is good at what, and they don't feel compelled to waste time talking with outsiders, so they have plenty of time to talk with their pals about other things! Katz recommends that long-standing groups play musical chairs, just like they do at Lend Lease and AES. He argues that bringing in new people and ideas forces the group to see old problems in new ways. He proposes that a surefire way to avoid a drop in creative output by long-standing groups is to disband them on a regular basis, to make them die before they get old. This is exactly the lesson learned by Denmark's Oticon Corporation, one of the leading makers of hearing aids in the world.[23] The company was in deep financial trouble in the late 1980s when Lars Kolind took charge of the company. Competitors were coming out with superior products at a far faster rate than Oticon and the company was losing money. In changes reminiscent of the revolution led by Annette Kyle at Bayport, Kolind released a memo announcing that drastic changes were to be made at once. Kolind believed that one of the main problems was—as Katz's research would predict—that people had worked in the same groups for so long that they had stopped thinking about what they were doing, so creativity had stalled. One of the key changes that Kolind made was that projects, not departments, became the key work unit and were disbanded and reformed constantly.

Even with these radical changes, Kolind found that product development teams sometimes fell back on old habits. In December of 1995, for example, he noticed that people in the company had spent a full year obsessed with developing a line of digital hearing aids, but "the downside to this productive focus was a sense that long-standing project teams were hardening into something dangerously close to departments."[24] Kolind's response: "I exploded the organization." All the teams were disbanded and new teams were formed and relocated on the basis of time horizon rather than function. Kolind says, "It was total chaos. . . . Within three hours, over a hundred people had moved. To keep the company alive, one of the jobs of top management is to keep it disorganized."[25]

My next suggestion for breaking from the past is perhaps the strangest: Use a random process to generate and select decision alternatives. Sometimes it is better to ignore the traditional decision-making process, where people spend a great deal of time comparing the pros and cons of each alternative. Writers from Benjamin Franklin to modern decision theorists have shown how, by decomposing a complex problem into simpler elements, the problem as a whole can be better understood, and better decisions can be made. As one team of researchers put it, "the terms *decision theory* and *decision analysis* describe a myriad of theoretical formulations; an assumption made by most of these approaches is that decisions are best made deliberately, objectively, and with reflection."[26] But these methods, while effective, have a troubling limitation: No matter how hard people try *not to think* about their past experiences, irrational prejudices, and personal preferences, much research shows that these and a host of other biases have powerful effects. These biases shape—in often suboptimal ways—which decision alternatives are generated, which decision criteria are applied, and which decisions are ultimately made and implemented.

The logic behind using a random process is that it will not be biased by knowledge of past successes. Evidence that random acts can generate important innovations is found in the long list of scientific breakthroughs made through serendipity and "mistakes." The discovery and isolation of penicillin is the most famous example: It resulted from a series of chance observations that spanned a 50-year period. Alexander Fleming is usually credited with being the first to notice in 1928 that a certain kind of mold inhibits bacterial growth. But the role of chance in this scientific breakthrough goes back much further, at least to 1874, when William Roberts observed that cultures of the mold Penicillin glaucum did not show signs of bacterial contamination.[27] Chance continues to play a role in scientific breakthroughs. The events that led to the 2000 Nobel Prize in chemistry started in the early 1970s when a researcher in Dr. Hideki Shirakawa's lab in Japan "misheard his instructions and added 1000 times too much catalyst to the chemical reaction. The result was a silvery film composed of a different form of polyacetylene."[28] This mistake helped inspire Hideki Shirakawa, along with Alan MacDiarmid and Alan Heeger, to create a plastic that conducts electricity, which opened up the important new field of carbon-based electronics.

In these cases, chance events broadened the palette of ideas available to scientists, but the randomness was not intentional. I suggest that companies go a step further. In addition to having people observant enough to learn from chance events, they can *intentionally* use a random process to generate broader and better lists of new possibilities to explore. I got this idea from Karl Weick of The University of Michigan:[29]

My favorite example of wisdom in groups is the use of Caribou shoulder bones, by the Naskapi Indians, to locate game. They hold bones over the fire until they crack and then they hunt in the directions to which the cracks point. This ritual is effective because the outcome is not influenced by the outcomes of past hunts.[30]

Pretty much the same logic is used by some companies to generate ideas about what paths they might take. Reactivity, the software firm mentioned earlier, has regular brainstorming sessions where they talk about ideas for new technologies, products, and companies. In the summer of 2000, software designers Jeremy Henrickson, Graham Miller, and Bill Walker were concerned that the ideas discussed at the lunches were getting too narrow, particularly because everyone was talking about Napster too much. So they invented a random selection process reminiscent of the Naskapi Indians. Bill Walker led the meeting at which process was first used. While the 30 or so people at the meeting were getting their pizza, he asked them to write the name of either a technology or an industry on an index card, which were then sorted into two piles with about 15 cards in each. One pile contained industry cards (e.g., shipping, shipbuilding, in-home nursing care, vacation cruises, funerals, mental health, and homemaking), and the other contained technology cards (e.g., wireless communication devices, global positioning systems, risk analysis, artificial intelligence, and collaborative filtering). Walker shuffled each deck and created random pairings by picking cards from the top of each deck. The group then brainstormed about how to build products and companies that were inspired by random pairs: in-home nursing, and wireless communication devices, shipbuilding and risk analysis, shipping and artificial intelligence, mental health and video processing. Brainstorming was limited to five minutes per pair.

The process used at Reactivity was like that used by the Nasakapi Indians for another reason. The Nasakapi Indians generated directions to hunt through a random process, but decisions about *which* of the randomly generated paths to pursue further were shaped by hunters' past experience. Weick contends that this approach reflects the proper attitude.

> [P]ast experience is discounted when a new set of cracks forms a crude map for the hunt. But the past is also given some weight because a seasoned hunter "reads" the cracks and injects his own past experience into an interpretation of what the cracks mean. The reader is crucial. If the reader's hunches dominate, than randomization is lost. If the cracks dominate, then the experience base is discarded.[31]

In the same way, Bill Walker and other experienced software engineers decided that some pairs they drew were so absurd that they weren't worth brainstorming about (e.g., the funeral industry and XML, a computer programming language for keeping track of structured information) and that some were worth researching in more detail. Those ideas that were most promising became homework for several small subgroups, which reported what they learned at the next meeting. For example, the pairing of shipbuilding and risk management inspired some promising ideas about doing dynamic risk management in real time, a method that could be quite valuable for helping companies price insurance of all kinds, not just for ships. Graham Miller emphasized that, to make this process work, "You had to have a lot of discipline to get through the groans" provoked by how silly some of the pairings seemed at first. Once they started brainstorming, however, they were surprised by how many promising ideas were generated about pairs that seemed utterly ridiculous a couple minutes earlier. Indeed, after the meeting, people even had second thoughts about ideas that were rejected on the spot as too ridiculous to brainstorm about. Carmela Krantz, the vice president for people, pointed out that the XML and funeral industry pairing wasn't so absurd after all. She noted that hundreds of thousands of bodies are shipped each year because many people die in one place and are buried in another, so XML could be used to help track the location and progress of this precious cargo.

Graham Miller said this process "helped us get out of the rut we were in" and "it taught us that there were a lot of industries that we didn't know much about that we needed to learn about." Bill Walker added, "We didn't talk about Napster at all for a few weeks." Even if none of the ideas from the brainstorm actually result in any new Reactivity products, client services, or companies, the random pairings met Walker's immediate goal of "creating the right climate in the room" and of "getting people excited about some new ideas." Jeremy Henrickson noted that it helped people develop a longer-term perspective on the kinds of things that Reactivity does and should do.

People at Reactivity again used the power of randomness a few months later to help avoid the hazards of mindless actions. They decided that the 55 or so people in their Silicon Valley office were spending too much time talking with people who sat nearby, and not enough time talking with people who sat elsewhere. To encourage people to mix up their ideas, to get them to break out of old patterns, they randomly reshuffled people into four different neighborhoods. Unlike the technique used by Lars Kolind at Oticon, project teams were left intact; they just moved to their new spot as a group. Each of the four neighborhoods had room for two project teams and two or three individual contributors. People drew numbers from 1 to 30, either as a representative of a project team that would all move together or as an individual contributor who would move alone. Those who drew lower numbers won the right to pick which of the four areas they or their group moved to, but as areas filled, choices diminished. So, by giving people some choice over where they sat and by keeping project teams together (but introducing a large random element in the decision process), a balance was again struck between the virtues of randomization and past experience.

Perhaps the most astounding part of this story is that it took just about an hour to draw the numbers and form the new neighborhoods, even though nearly every person moved. It took only another day or so to get the phone numbers switched to all the right desks. This rapid move was possible because people at Reactivity work in an open office, have desks and chairs with wheels, work on laptop computers with high-speed wireless modems, and don't have many books or papers. People were apprehensive when the process started. But there was so much excitement about all the new communication and ideas that resulted from this "huge win" that they plan to reshuffle desks every six months or so. As Bill Walker put it, "Both applications of randomness help make everyone here more comfortable with change."

Further evidence for the virtues of making random decisions comes from a pair of experiments in Australia by S. Alexander Haslam and his colleagues.[32] Their experiments compared the performance of small problem-solving groups (three to five people) that were asked to select their own leaders, with groups that were randomly assigned a leader (i.e., a person whose name appeared either first or last in the alphabet). These experiments involved 91 groups that worked on one of three closely related group decision-making exercises: the "winter survival task," the "desert survival task," or the "fallout survival task." Each of these small groups of college students developed a strategy for ranking potentially useful items for the particular task, and their decisions were scored relative to expert ratings. Both experiments showed that *groups that had randomly assigned leaders performed significantly better than those that had selected their own leaders*. Random assignment was shown to be superior to groups that had used either an informal process where they selected leaders by "whatever means you see fit," or a formal process where each group member completed 10 self-report questions on a leadership skills inventory that had been shown to predict managerial success in prior studies. Leaders who scored the highest on the inventory were assigned to lead groups that used the formal process. There were no significant differences between groups that used an informal or a formal process. Both had inferior performance to groups with randomly selected leaders.

Haslam and his colleagues believe that the process of selecting a leader in these experiments focused attention on differences between group members, which undermined the group's sense of shared identity and purpose, which in turn undermined performance. Instead of thinking about how to solve the problem together, of having a "united we stand, divided we fall" mentality, they thought about differences among themselves that were unrelated to the task, like who had more prestige in the group and why. My interpretation is similar. I would add that the leaders who are given a mandate to be in charge of a group often—without realizing it—start imposing their individual will too strongly, which can stifle the range of ideas that are seriously considered by the group. The researchers admit that they have suggested only one possible explanation for these findings, and acknowledge that a random process of selecting a leader is probably inferior to a systematic process for groups that do other tasks. But these findings are intriguing because they force many of us—both practitioners and researchers—to see an old problem in a new way. They spark the *vu ja de* mentality and suggest that our assumptions about how to select a leader may, at times, be flawed.

I don't know of any teams or companies in the real world that, at least intentionally, make decisions about which paths to pursue or which leaders to select *purely* on the basis of a random process. But there is strong evidence that a random decision process is as good—and might be superior—in another decision-making process: stock market investments. Princeton economist Burton Malkiel has infuriated analysts and others who believe they can pick winning and losing stocks by arguing that a "random walk" through Wall Street is typically as good, and often better than, relying on expert advice about which stocks to buy and sell:[33]

> A random walk is one in which future steps or directions cannot be predicted on the basis of past actions. When the term is applied to the stock market, it means that short-run changes in stock prices cannot be predicted. Investment advisory services, earnings predictions, and complicated chart patterns are useless. On Wall Street, the term "random walk" is an obscenity. It

is an epithet coined by the academic world and hurled insultingly at the professional soothsayers. Taken to its logical extreme, it means that a blindfolded monkey throwing darts at a newspaper's financial pages could select a portfolio that would do just as well as one carefully selected by the experts.[34]

Malkiel has numerous critics on Wall Street and in academia. But it has been nearly 30 years since the first edition of his book was published, and his argument that investors do best over time by investing in index funds is supported by a great deal of research. His assertion that professional stock pickers rarely do better than a "random walk" through the market as a whole, and often do significantly worse, continues to receive much support. Malkiel suggests one explanation for his findings: Stock-picking strategies that were successful in the past become obsolete so quickly that past success at picking stocks is rarely useful for guiding current actions. For example, any investment adviser who predicted that the dramatic rise of NASDAQ stocks in 1999 would continue in 2000 was sorely mistaken.

The final way to break from a successful past, especially the recent past, is the "back-to-the-future" method, a technique for getting the company to do new things by exhorting people to do old things. Rather than encouraging people to look ahead or copy competitors, you encourage people to go back to the company's glory days. It is a powerful technique because old-timers aren't being asked to ignore or devalue their history, identity, or skills; on the contrary, they are being asked to return to a bygone era and take what worked best. This is a smart strategy because many companies have lost their way, and if they do go back to the business practices and models that made them successful in the early days, they might prosper once again. The back-to-the-future method is also smart because, although the past can't be changed, interpretations of what happened and what it means for present actions are infinitely flexible.

Interpreting events is an important part of any leader's job. Karl Weick asserts that skilled leaders "wade into the swarm of events that constitute and surround the organization and actively try to impose some order on them."[35] Weick claims, in fact, that the most important part of a leader's job is not making decisions, but interpreting events in ways that inspire opinions and actions that are favorable to the organization. Leadership guru Warren Bennis puts it this way:

The leader's goal is not mere explanation or clarification but the creation of meaning. My favorite baseball joke is exemplary: In the ninth inning of a key playoff game, with a three-and-two count on the batter, the umpire hesitates a split second in calling the pitch. The batter whirls around angrily and says, "Well what was that?" The umpire snarls back, "It ain't *nothing* until I call it!"[36]

The back-to-the-future technique is especially useful to leaders who want change because they have so much leeway in how history is interpreted. With all the turnover and hiring that happens in any company, many people who are the targets of such interpretations weren't around in the good old days. For example, Hewlett-Packard's 2000 Annual Report to shareholders states that 50% its 89,000 employees had joined within the prior five years. And those who were around at HP (or any other firm) during the "good old days" probably can't remember them very well. Human memory is notoriously poor; no matter how confident people are in their memories, all of us forget and have grossly distorted recollections of events, facts, figures, and feelings. The so-called Pollyanna effect is particularly well documented: People remember positive experiences and positive material more easily than negative experiences and material. They remember the past as a far happier time than it ever was.[37] This tendency toward rosy retrospection can make it easy to persuade old-timers to go back to old ways. It can also make it easy to convince them to help persuade people who weren't around in those days that going back to the future would be a wonderful thing, since that's the way they remember it.

Not only that, because human memory is so selective and so poor, persuasive leaders can selectively focus on elements of company history that reflect where they want the company to go, and ignore (or even denigrate) elements that clash with the future they hope to create. Leaders' recollections are just as biased as anyone else's, and they might not be completely honest when reinterpreting the past, so there is no reason to expect their interpretations to be accurate. In fact, accuracy is not usually what is most important to leaders and their companies. For better or worse, leaders are hired to do what is in the best interests of the company, and the quirks of human memory can mean that it is easier to convince people to return to a past that never happened than to convince them to try things that they find new and unfamiliar.

The back-to-the-future method has been used extensively by CEO

---

### Putting Weird Idea #11 to Work

#### Uncommon Ways to Forget Past Successes

- Hire and retain slow learners of the organizational code.

- Learn to forget by discarding records of old ways and bringing in people who never knew about the good old days.

- Recall the past in your own company and others, but interpret it as a cautionary tale about all the blunders and failures suffered by those who become snared in success traps.

- Encourage people to keep fighting over whether established practices are obsolete.

- Assign people to jobs they don't know how to do.

- Disband long-standing work groups, especially when people talk to each other too much and are too fond of each other.

- Use a random process to generate and select decision alternatives rather than the traditional method of analyzing the pros and cons of each alternative.

- Change the physical setting on a regular basis, including where people work, who they work next to, and what they see.

- Use the "back-to-the-future" strategy: Get people to do new things by convincing them they are really returning to older, better ways.

---

Carly Fiorina to invigorate Hewlett-Packard, which was on the verge of turning into "a stodgy hardware has-been, unable to keep up in the Internet age" when she took over as CEO in July 1999. I first saw the term *back-to-the-future strategy* in an *Economist* article about Carly Fiorina. HP is famous for being founded in a garage in Palo Alto, by Bill Hewlett and David Packard in 1940.[38] The company was innovative and entrepreneurial for years, but had been slowed in recent years by a time-consuming consensus decision-making process, red tape, in-fighting, and the lack of a unifying philosophy or strategy. One former HP general manager described how, at its lowest point, people bragged about engaging in "malicious compliance" rather than the traditional "enlightened defiance." In contrast to the days when Chuck House was given an "award of defiance" because he did what was best for HP even though it meant ignoring David Packard's orders, by the mid-1990s some of HP's most skilled managers did precisely what they were told, *especially* when they believed it was bad for HP. They called this "malicious compliance" because their aim was to show how badly things would turn out when poor decisions or dysfunctional procedures were implemented.

During her first year as CEO, Fiorina worked hard to keep her promise to "preserve the best" and "reinvent the rest." She reminded people at HP that founders Bill Hewlett and David Packard made and implemented decisions very quickly. Fiorina was one of the main authors of the new "Rules of the Garage," which she says are based on how HP operated in its early days. These 10 rules include "Radical ideas are not bad ideas," "Work quickly, keep the tools unlocked, and work whenever," and "No politics, no bureaucracy (these are ridiculous in a garage)," and the last rule is a one-word slogan that is displayed everywhere at HP these days: Invent. This back-to-the-future theme is also part of HP's recruiting efforts. One HP poster had a photograph of Bill and Dave standing in the original garage, and asked prospective candidates: "Do you have what Bill Hewlett and Dave Packard had? Are you, in short, an inventor? Inventing the new HP. Want to come along?"[39] Frankly, I don't think it matters to HP very much whether the "Rules of the Garage" were actually followed in the company's early days. Regardless of where they came from, these rules are things that Fiorina believed the company needed to do when she and other senior managers wrote them. What really matters is whether these interpretations inspire people at HP to break from the dysfunctions of the company's more recent past.

The transformation of Gillette's razor business in the late 1980s was also accomplished with the back-to-the-future strategy, with the added twist being that the turnaround was done entirely with Gillette lifers.[40] They got no help from consultants, new executives, or a wave of new hires. Gillette had long been the profit and sales leader in the industry by developing technologically superior razors that consumers were willing to pay high prices for, but by the late 1980s they were focusing on disposable razors. Gillette had entered "commodity hell," where the product was "essentially interchangeable with all its competitors," so the only way to get market share was to keep cutting the price.

The return to the past, where the new Gillette became the old Gillette, was punctuated in 1987 by John Symons, then head of Gillette's North American Group. Symons lost his temper during a presentation by a fellow executive on the blue Good News disposables: "He had barely started speaking when Symons took the bag of disposables from him, threw it on the floor, and crushed it beneath his heal." Symons growled, "That's what I think about disposables."[41] Gillette returned to using intensive research to develop innovative products with high profit margins, beginning with the hugely successful Sensor razor. More recently, their research and development lab in Reading, England, led a seven-year, $750 million effort to develop the Mach3, which debuted in July of 1999. The Mach3 is a hugely successful product, with sales topping a $1 billion in 2000. But Gillette isn't satisfied. They already have a successor in the pipeline.

# PART III

# PUTTING THE WEIRD IDEAS TO WORK

### CHAPTER 15

# Building Companies Where
# Innovation is a Way of Life

Most managers are quick to *say* that drastically different practices are needed for innovation, as opposed to routine work. You might even react to my weird ideas by saying, "Sure, they're not weird." Yet many managers don't act as if they mean it. They see practices that spark innovation as strange, even downright wrong. And they act as if practices suited only for routine work are generically good for running all businesses all the time. So they end up stifling innovation instinctively.

This happens to the best managers and companies. Start-ups are as vulnerable as established companies. A typical scenario is that a young company generates some great ideas. Once successful, the company reaches a point where it needs "discipline," or as some venture capitalists say, "It's time for some adult supervision." This means that part of the company—sometimes most of it—is organized for routine work. Tasks like accounting, sales, and human resource management can be done in innovative ways. But when "professional management" is brought into a start-up, routinization takes hold. After all, experimenting with unproven accounting practices can increase the chances a young company will stumble. The trouble starts, however, when the "adult" practices spread to innovative work. Although these managers have the best of intentions, they may unwittingly destroy what made the company vibrant in the first place.

Consider what happened at the Lotus Development Corporation in the mid-1980s. Lotus (which is now part of IBM) was founded in 1982 by Mitchell Kapor and Jonathan Sachs. The company's first product was Kapor and Sachs's Lotus 1-2-3, a business productivity tool. Industry observers give this "killer app" much credit for the success of the IBM personal computer in the mid-1980s. Lotus 1-2-3 sales grew from 53 million in 1982 to 156 million in 1984, which led to an urgent need for experienced professional managers. McKinsey consultant James Manzi was brought in as president in 1984 and became CEO in 1985. Manzi built enormously profitable marketing and sales operations, focusing on building operations modeled after Fortune 500 companies. The head of sales was from IBM, as was most of his sales force. Many early employees were resentful of the compensation and other perks granted to the sales force. They saw these salespeople as merely order-takers, because Lotus 1-2-3 was flying off the shelves.

Revenues continued to grow. But Lotus started having trouble developing successful new products. Part of the problem was that techniques suitable only for managing routine work were being used throughout the company. By 1985 or so, around the time the company had grown to over 1,000 employees, many original members felt they no longer fit in at Lotus. Some were simply not competent, but most were creative people who couldn't find a place in the company and found that their skills were no longer valued. Most of the new hires were cut out of the "big company mold," having worked for such firms as Coca-Cola and Procter & Gamble and then going on to get MBA degrees. One disenchanted early hire described them as "boring people who had never created a product or a company spirit."

In 1985, Mitchell Kapor (then chairman of the board) and Freada Klein (then head of organizational development and training) tried an experiment. With Kapor's approval, Klein pulled together the résumés of the first 40 people to join the company. She changed each résumé slightly, usually just disguising the employee's name. Kapor's was changed a bit more because he was known for working as a disk jockey and teaching transcendental meditation. Some of these people had the right technical and managerial skills for the jobs they applied for, but they also had done a lot of "wacko and risky things." They had been community organizers, clinical psychologists, and transcendental meditation teachers (not just Kapor), and several had lived at an ashram.

Not one of the 40 applicants was called back for an interview. Kapor and Klein viewed this as a sign that Lotus was unwittingly screening out innovative people. All signs are that they were correct. The only hit product invented by the company after Lotus 1-2-3, Lotus Notes, was developed 20 miles from headquarters, as Klein put it, "so the team could work unfettered by the narrow Lotus culture." Lotus did need great marketing and sales organizations to cash in on its innovative ideas. The narrowness that came along with these changes, however, was a double-edged sword. It is hard to generate new ideas when practices are used that screen out (and drive out) people with varied ideas and who see things in disparate ways. Kapor and Klein's experiment shows that every company, even a great one like Lotus, needs to be mindful about what it takes to spark innovation. Otherwise, it will be filled with replicants who think alike and act as if the future will be a perfect imitation of the past.[1]

## Putting the Weird Ideas to Work

I end with nine guidelines that can help you apply the weird ideas or, better yet, provoke you to invent your own weird—and not so weird—ideas for sustaining innovation. You can use them to build a team or company that keeps developing new ideas and cashing in on its creativity. Or, if your team is charged with doing routine work, you can use them every now and then to shake things up, to get people to imagine and try new ways of thinking and acting.

## The Best Management Is Sometimes No Management

Leading innovation can require a soft touch, or getting out of the way completely. We have seen how leaders of some of the most innovative companies expect and encourage their so-called subordinates to ignore and defy them. They institute policies like 3M's 15 percent rule or Corning's "Friday Afternoon Experiments" to make sure that employees can follow their hunches, even when their bosses believe those hunches are wrong.[2] Yet some managers still have a hard time bringing themselves to "manage by getting out of the way." After all, everything from Hollywood movies to an MBA. education teaches us that management is about overseeing people, giving them orders, goading them on, and inspiring them to perform. As we have also seen, managers can have huge positive effects by creating self-fulfilling prophecies or allocating critical resources to a project. But managers can be oblivious to the harm they cause. Rather than following Pfeffer's advice that, like physicians, managers should "first, do no harm," they take ignorant actions that make things worse. William Coyne, former head of research and development at 3M, tells how a human resource manager once threatened to fire a scientist who was asleep under his bench. Coyne took the HR manager to 3M's "Wall of Patents" to show him that the sleeping scientist had developed some of 3M's most profitable products. Coyne advised, "Next time you see him asleep, get him a pillow."[3] Unfortunately, not all executives are so wise.

Why do so many managers delude themselves into believing they are helping their companies even though they have no effect, or are even hampering innovation? One reason is that managers overestimate their value. Gordon MacKenzie, the former "Creative Paradox" from Hallmark, shows how this happens in a fantasy about how Hallmark's "Prince of Profit" would manage a herd of cows: "Outside the zigzag of the fence stands a rotund gentleman in a $700 powder-blue pinstripe suit . . . shaking a stern finger at the cows." As the cows peacefully chewed their cud, the "Prince" would holler, "*You slackers, get to work or I will have you butchered.*"[4] The "Prince" could not understand "that his shouting will not cause cows to produce more milk."[5]

MacKenzie's fantasy is backed by an experiment at Stanford. MBAs in the "experimental group" were duped into believing they were supervising a subordinate who was sketching a wristwatch advertisement in the next room. "Supervision" ranged from low (only seeing the work at the end), to medium (seeing it once in the middle, but giving no feedback), to high (seeing it once in the middle and giving feedback). When the drawing was allegedly completed, the "supervisor" rated its quality and the worker's ability. These evaluations were compared to ratings by M.B.A.'s in the control group who were not duped into believing that they had supervised the work. The same drawing was shown to all subjects, so it was impossible for the "supervisors" to influence it. Yet the students who believed they were "supervisors" rated the drawing far more favorably than the ones in the control group. And those who believed that they had engaged in closer supervision rated the drawing and worker more favorably than those who believed they had used lighter supervision.[6] As in Gordon MacKenzie's fantasy about the "Prince of Profit" hollering at the cows, these "supervisors" believed they had enhanced the output even though it was impossible for them to have done so.

This delusion, called the self-enhancement bias, helps explain why so many companies hesitate to delegate authority despite strong evidence that it enhances productivity and employee commitment. Yet when managers can bring themselves to get out of the way, good things can happen. Basketball coach Phil Jackson, who won numerous championships with the Chicago Bulls during the Michael Jordan era, and more recently with the Los Angeles Lakers, is a great example. Jackson is renowned for his light touch, for sitting quietly and not calling time-outs during slumps and crucial junctures in the game.[7] Most coaches shout out numerous plays during a game, but "Jackson almost never calls plays; he thinks play-calling makes players feel as if they are on a string (his)."[8] The key to Jackson's success, like David Kelley at IDEO and managers at Corning's lab, is that he has the humility to lead skilled people by giving them what they need to do their jobs and then to leave them alone. When Jackson arrived in Los Angeles, he was ballyhooed as the team's savior, the one person who could lead the underachieving Lakers to a championship. He responded, "I'm no savior. . . . They have to be the savior of themselves."[9] Ironically, he *was* the Laker's savior because he made it clear that winning was up to the players, not him.

## Innovation Means Selling, Not Just Inventing, New Ideas

Creativity is in the eye of the beholder. As cases from the Beatles' music to Ballard's fuel cell show, no matter how wonderful something new is, it will only be accepted if the right people can be persuaded of its value. Ralph Waldo Emerson was wrong when he said, "If you build a better mousetrap, the world will beat a path to your door." Too many innovations succeed because they are sold better, not because they are objectively superior to those of competitions.

The competition between gas and electric lighting in the 1880s is a good illustration.[10] Researchers Andrew Hargadon and Yellowless Douglas show there was little difference in the illumination provided by gas lamps and the 12-watt light bulbs Thomas Edison sold at the time. Early electric lighting was plagued by black-outs, unreliable lamps and light bulbs, and fires from short circuits and poor wiring. It was more expensive than gas, and "the Welsbach mantle, introduced in 1885 as a response to the incandescent bulb, provided a sixfold increase in the candlepower of gas lamps, changing the flickering of the faint, yellow glow into a clean, white light."[11] Even though electric lighting was not clearly superior, gas lighting was nearly extinct in the United States by 1903. Hargadon and Douglas show how this innovation triumphed largely through Edison's marketing skill and design decisions that, rather than making it as technologically advanced and inexpensive as possible, made electric lighting systems, lamps, and the language used to describe them as similar to gas lighting as possible. Remember, familiarity is comforting.

Selling a completed new product or service is crucial for cashing in on any idea. That is why Bob Metcalfe, who invented the Ethernet and founded 3Com, said, "Most engineers don't understand that selling matters. They think that on the food chain of life, salespeople are below green slime. They don't understand that nothing happens until *something gets sold*."[12] As we have seen, selling starts inside companies long before an innovation is brought to market. Disney employees are invited to pitch ideas for new "attractions" at monthly open forums. At 3M, inventors write proposals for $50,000 "Genesis Grants" to develop prototypes and market tests. The innovation process in every big organization—from Ford, to NASA, to McDonald's, to Virgin Airlines, to Siemens—is punctuated with formal and informal gatherings where innovators try to sell their ideas to peers and bosses. A hallmark of successful innovations in big companies is that they are promoted by persistent and politically skilled champions.[13]

Similarly, all but the wealthiest entrepreneurs must convince investors to support their start-ups. Experienced entrepreneurs and investors Audrey McLean and Mike Lyons teach Stanford students how to do so with an "elevator pitch" exercise. Class that day is conducted *inside* two elevators in a five-story building. Aspiring entrepreneurs are graded on how well they sell their product, market opportunity, and management team to McLean and Lyons during a two-minute elevator ride. McLean and Lyons believe that if you can't create investor excitement in two minutes, you won't get funding for your company. Indeed, a small industry of "venture packagers" has emerged to help entrepreneurs sell their ideas. Carryer Consulting in Pittsburgh, for example, writes convincing business plans, develops PowerPoint presentations, and critiques pitches for entrepreneurs. Babs Carryer (who runs the firm with her husband, Tim) also uses her theatrical background to teach entrepreneurs how to tell stories that excite investors.[14]

This book is about innovation, not persuasion. But if an innovator can't sell an idea, or find a representative to do it, then it rarely travels beyond the inventor's mind. This is why so many people practice selling their ideas, study how others do it, seek coaching, and read books such as Robert Cialdini's *Influence*.[15] Innovators especially need to know that judgments of them and their ideas are intertwined, perhaps inseparable. As Arthur Rock, the pioneer venture capitalist who funded Intel and Apple Computer, emphasizes, "I generally pay more attention to the people who prepare a business plan than to the proposal itself." When Rock meets entrepreneurs, he looks for those who "believe so firmly in the idea that everything else pales in comparison," and he claims, "I can usually tell the difference between people who have that fire in their stomachs and those who see their ideas primarily as a way to get rich."[16]

Similarly, Kimberly Elsbach and Roderick Kramer's research on how scripts are pitched to Hollywood producers suggests that, if you want people to believe your ideas are creative, persuading them that *you* are imaginative is more important than the ideas themselves.[17] Being slick isn't always important, and it can backfire if one is boring, stiff, recites a list of facts, or come across as "just a guy in a suit." Such "pitchers" are seen as insincere and passionless, as dull people who lack imagination. Conversely, being naive or quirky can convince others that a "pitcher" has fresh ideas and rejects conventional thinking. People also shouldn't pitch a laundry list of ideas. One producer noted, "There's not a buyer in the world you can convince that you have the same passion for five different projects. What you're selling is your passion. You're rarely selling your idea. You are selling *you*. You're selling your commitment, your point of view." The best pitchers spark creative thoughts in "catchers," who join them as "creative collaborators" rather than passive listeners. The filmmaker Oliver Stone told Elsbach: "I think that magic is perhaps the most important part of the pitch. And in a sense . . . it's a seduction, a promise of what lies ahead. At a certain point the writer needs to pull back and let the producer project himself as the creator of the story. And let him project what he needs onto your idea that makes the story whole for him."

Oliver Stone's point is crucial for selling any idea. Once buyers become excited enough to add their own creative touches, it means they are infected by the pitcher's passion and commitment. Elsbach and Kramer emphasize that people who make *others* feel more creative will be seen as people with more imaginative ideas. It is important to remember, however, that it is easier to sell good ideas. As Babs Carryer puts it, "A great idea with a crappy business plan will still get funded, but a crappy idea with a great business plan won't," which is why her ideal client is an "inarticulate engineer with a great idea."[18]

## Innovation Requires Both Flexibility and Rigidity

Innovation requires flexibility. Generating different ideas and seeing old things in new ways can only be accomplished by people who can revise their beliefs easily. But recall how much rigidity, how much downright stubbornness, was required for Geoffrey Ballard to develop those fuel cells and for the team at Sun to develop the Java language. Some rigidity is necessary for developing successful innovations. It helps to define problems narrowly enough so they can be talked about in a constructive way, so people know what to focus attention on and what to ignore, and so ideas can be developed and tested in sufficient depth to see if they are any good.

A useful guideline for striking a healthy balance between rigidity and flexibility is to hold either the solution *or* the problem constant, and to let the other vary. The most common strategy is to find a problem and then to search for and evaluate alternative solutions, to *keep the problem rigid and the possible solutions flexible.* Efforts in the eighteenth century to develop an accurate method for calculating longitude illustrate such a "problem-driven search." Dava Sobel writes in *Longitude* that so many ships and people were lost from navigational errors that "the governments of the great maritime nations—including Spain, the Netherlands, and certain city-states of Italy—periodically roiled the fervor by offering jackpot purses for a workable method. The British Parliament, in its famed Longitude Act of 1714, set the highest bounty of all, naming a prize equal to a king's ransom (several million dollars in today's currency) for a 'Practicable and Useful' means of determining longitude."[19] The prize required a navigational tool that could provide longitude to within half a degree (two minutes of time), that would be tested on a ship that sailed "over the ocean, from Great Britain to any such Port in the West Indies as those Commissioners Choose ... without losing their Longitude beyond the limits before mentioned."[20] Hundreds of ways to calculate longitude were tried until the English clockmaker John Harrison came up with an ingenous mechanical solution.

Much innovation in modern times is also problem driven. McDonald's has tried thousands of solutions to the problem of getting more people to visit their restaurants. Disney's Imagineers constantly tinker with solutions to the intertwined problems of making the long lines of "guests" in their parks *actually* move quickly and *seem* to move quickly. Gillette's research and development laboratory in Reading, England, will test virtually any material or design if it might lead to a fashionable product that works. The lab's ultimate goal is crystal clear: A closer and more comfortable shave, "The Holy Grail as far as shaving techies are concerned."[21]

The other way to balance rigidity and flexibility is to *hold the solution constant and let the problems vary,* or a "solution-driven search." This is what a two-year-old does with a hammer: hit everything in sight to see what happens. It happens when some new or old technology, product, theory, or service is treated as the possible solution to many as-yet-unknown problems. I mentioned earlier that 3M's Microreplication Technology Center used a three-dimensional surface composed of tiny pyramids to develop a display for laptop computers that used less power than conventional displays. Microreplication was developed in the 1950s to increase the brightness of overhead projectors. 3M managers believed that the microscopic pyramids could be used in many other applications, but did not know exactly how or where. They opened the center to find ways to put Microreplication in as many products as possible. It is now used in dozens of 3M products including recording tape, sandpaper, traffic lights, grinders, and mouse pads.

The Freeplay Group in Cape Town, South Africa, also innovates via a solution-driven search. They invent and sell "self-powered" devices that generate electricity when the user cranks the handle on a 2-inch-wide, 20-foot-long ribbon of carbonized steel flashlight. As the spring unwinds, it produces enough electricity to power a radio (the firm's first product) for 30 minutes. This radio is not just a cool gadget that attracted computer geeks at the Consumer Electronics Show in Las Vegas. It is changing the lives of the world's poorest people, who can now have working radios without using (unattainable) electricity or expensive batteries. Co-CEO Rory Stear says, "We are not just in the radio business. We are in the energy business. We always ask ourselves, what else can we do with this technology?" This solution-driven thinking has led them to develop, or start developing, self-powered products including a flashlight, global-positioning system, land-mine detector, water purifier, and a mechanism for a toy monster truck.[22]

## Incite and Uncover Discomfort

As should be obvious by now, discomfort is an inevitable and desirable part of innovation. The weird idea to hire people who make you uncomfortable makes this point directly. Discomfort can also be generated by hiring people you don't need, when employees defy bosses, when people imagine dumb things and try to do them, and when people argue over their precious ideas. Discomfort isn't much fun, but it helps people to avoid and break out of mindless action.

Unfamiliar ideas and things generate negative feelings like irritation, anxiety, and disapproval, as do interruptions of routine action and challenges to taken-for-granted assumptions. If everyone always likes your ideas, it probably means that you are not doing many original things.

When Howard Schulz, founder of Starbucks, wanted to partner with former basketball star Magic Johnson to build seven coffee houses in low-income African-American neighborhoods in Los Angeles, other Starbucks executives objected because it was risky. They had built many Starbucks overseas but never in an inner-city neighborhood. These executives also reacted with discomfort when, to appeal to African-American tastes, Johnson wanted to sell food like sweet potato pie and play music like Miles Davis and Stevie Wonder. Schulz and other Starbucks executives ultimately decided to build these stores and to tailor them to the inner city. This decision to overcome their discomfort proved to be wise: The initial agreement with Johnson was expanded after the first stores posted spectacular sales and profits, and executives' fears that crime would be rampant in and around the stores proved unfounded.[23]

The belief that new ideas provoke discomfort helped Herman Miller develop Resolve, a furniture system that "re-solves" the uniform "squaresville" of the traditional office cubicle environment.[24] "Instead of muted-gray walls and severe right angles, it features lightweight, translucent screens and generous 120-degree angles." Resolve also is said to revel "in bright colors and personal touches."[25] Lead designer Jim Long says, "My metaphor is a screen door.... It offers openness but not complete openness, not total visibility." During the early phases of development, Long showed a prototype to 200 information technology managers, designers, and facility managers. He was pleased that most didn't like it because, if the reaction had been more positive, it "would have meant that the ideas were too ordinary."[26] At Sempra Energy Information Solutions, a test site, the first reaction was "culture shock." As employees became accustomed to Resolve, their enthusiasm grew; they found that communication improved and the office was quieter. Herman Miller isn't ready to pronounce that Resolve is the office of the future. But whatever the office of the future is, their designers anticipate that the first reactions to it will be negative.

Discomfort plays another role. Many successful ideas were invented because someone got upset about something and then did something about it. Inventor David Levy uses "The Curse Method."[27] Levy says, "Whenever I hear someone curse, it's a sign to invent something."[28] Levy designed the Wedgie lock after he heard a coworker cursing because a thief had stolen his bicycle seat. Levy noticed that the streets near his lab in Cambridge, Massachusetts, were filled with abandoned bikes without seats, suggesting there was a market for a good bicycle seat lock. Being uncomfortable or downright unhappy isn't much fun, but it can be an innovator's inspiration. Says Levy, "When I lie in bed, I try to think of things that suck."[29]

## Treat Everything Like a Temporary Condition

The organizing principles for routine work reflect the assumption that everything is a permanent condition; the organizing principles for innovative work reflect the opposite assumption. Both are useful fictions. After all, exploiting existing knowledge is only wise if what worked in the past will keep working. And bringing in varied ideas—seeing things in new ways, and, of course, breaking from the past—only makes sense when, even if old ways still work, they will soon be obsolete. Leaders of innovative companies constantly create alarm and warn that just because things are working well now does not mean that they will work later. Andrew Grove of Intel is famous for being paranoid that a "disruptive" change—a new technology that makes their technology or business model obsolete—will appear. John Chambers of Cisco does pretty much the same thing, as does Jorma Ollila, CEO of the Finnish telephone giant Nokia:

> The chairman and chief executive of Nokia Corp. said Monday that one of his biggest concerns is that 'we are not as quick we were six years ago,' when the company had half the 56,000 employees it has today. 'You start to believe that what you created three years ago is so good, because it was good two years ago and 18 months ago, and you continue to make money.... And then there's someone in Israel and Silicon Valley just loving to kill you with a totally new technology.'[30]

Sustaining innovation requires treating everything from procedures and product lines to teams and organizations as things that might be useful now but will need to be discontinued. It can also mean forming temporary companies, not just temporary projects and teams like AES and Lend Lease. The goal at birth would be a planned and graceful death, with disbanding done once the company had completed a project or intertwined set of projects. The argument for temporary organizations is that constant disbanding and reforming keeps variance and *vu ja de* high in a company, and makes it difficult for people to engage in mindless action.

This is why some traditional companies, including a team at General

Motors Research and Development Center in Warren, Michigan, have examined the film industry to get ideas about sparking innovation. The "Hollywood model" is intriguing because these days a temporary production company is formed to make most films. After the film is completed, any money made by these single-project organizations is distributed, the team is disbanded, and the life-of-project workers go on to their next job. Hollywood was once dominated by large studios like MGM, Warner Brothers, and Paramount, which employed all workers, including directors, writers, and actors. In contrast, contemporary Hollywood producers rely on brokers to supply "packages" of people and to help build the temporary companies that make films. Talent agencies like William Morris and the Creative Artists Agency are among the enduring hubs in a complex network of formal and informal relationships, which explains why, although film production companies are temporary, there is much stability and predictability in the industry.

There are intriguing parallels between Hollywood and new-economy industries. There has been a great rise in contract work—especially by skilled professionals with technical skills—and an associated set of agencies to supply companies with temporary help to meet short-term demands in high-tech industries. Although there is much rhetoric about forming "built-to-last" companies in Silicon Valley, most start-ups in this region are temporary. Those that endure as freestanding firms are rare; far more are acquired by large firms, and demise is even more likely. Regardless of whether employees are classified as temporary or permanent, there is enormous turnover in Silicon Valley. This didn't start in the Internet age: Turnover has averaged over 20 percent per year in high-technology companies since the early 1980s. In both Hollywood and Silicon Valley, people constantly take new roles, work with an ever-changing cast of characters, and new companies are constantly formed with new combinations of existing talent.

I don't mean to imply that temporary organizations are the only path to sustained innovation; enduring companies like 3M, Motorola, Hewlett-Packard, Home Depot, and Virgin suggest that other paths are possible. But if you think about the three principles for organizing innovation, building and constantly disbanding temporary organizations helps ensure that variance, *vu ja de,* and breaking from the past are ways of life. Big companies that treat products and projects as temporary conditions can accomplish the same thing, as when CEO Bob Galvin decided to market Motorola's color televisions under the Quasar brand in 1967.

He did so because, looking ahead, he realized it would be easier to sell their television business if its brand name was distinct from the Motorola brand. This move set the stage for Motorola to sell the Quasar television trademark and production facilities to Matsushita in 1974, when televisions had become inexpensive commodities with slim profit margins, just as Galvin had predicted a decade earlier.

## Make the Process as Simple as Possible

A hallmark of innovative companies and teams is that they follow the law of parsimony: Make everything as simple as possible (but no simpler). They use work practices that help people focus on what matters and ignore the rest. Needless complexity arises when companies consider every contingency and involve anyone who could possibly improve, support, or be opposed to an idea. These misguided efforts to inject order and control, and to achieve perfection, can tangle aspiring innovators in red tape and condemn them to meeting after meeting with people who barely understand their work (but don't hesitate to give them advice about how to do it). These complex and dysfunctional processes can also require innovators to devote too much time to selling ideas and playing organizational politics, and not enough to developing ideas.

Consider a consumer-products firm I studied a few years ago. Senior executives believed that nearly every step in the development process could be specified and applied to every product. I can't name the company, but I can tell you that executives insisted that ideas for new products travel through an 8-step process comprising over 30 more specific milestones. There were 8 formal reviews along the way, each with more than 100 time-consuming tasks (e.g., "financial plan" and "trademarks") that had to be completed before it could pass to the next stage. The process specified when each of 25 groups should and should not be involved (from senior management to marketing) and when each of 35 or so questions should be asked (e.g., What are the features? Are all plans complete?). The designers of this process had great faith in it, boasting it would speed innovation, increase consensus, and reduce mistakes. Although it was at least five years old at the time, not one of the managers I interviewed at this company could recall a single product that actually made it through this gauntlet, even though all the managers had devoted many hours to trying to push products through it. This does not mean that this company failed to develop new products. Quite a few successful products had been developed, but all by teams that had enough power or political skill to work outside the official process.[31]

Innovation is easier to sustain in companies that follow the law of parsimony. General Electric's Jack Welch says, "Bureaucracy hates simplicity. . . . Simple messages travel faster, simpler designs reach market faster, and the elimination of clutter allows faster decision making."[32] A simpler structure and incentive system helped one of Guidant's biggest businesses, the Vascular Intervention Group, push Johnson & Johnson aside to become the market leader in coronary stents (tiny metal tubes that prop open blocked arteries). Conflict and communication problems between R&D and manufacturing were hampering the group's ability to bring new stents to market. President Ginger Graham and her team simplified the structure by making the same executive head of both R&D and manufacturing. They also simplified the incentive system so that people in both R&D and manufacturing had the same large stake in the success of development efforts. This shift to a simple, fast-moving development process has been crucial to maintaining Guidant's market dominance, since a new stent is rarely sold more than a year before it is replaced with a superior design.[33]

Innovation can be simplified by reducing the number of products or services developed and sold. When Steve Jobs returned to Apple in July of 1997, the company was selling so many computer models that, as he put it, "we couldn't even tell our friends which ones to buy." These included the 1400, 2400, 3400, 4400, 5400, 5500, 6500, 7300, 7600, 8600, 9600, the 20th Anniversary Mac, e-Mate, Newton, and Pippin. This long list not only confused Apple customers, it confused Apple developers, who wanted to know which products to work on and which to ignore.[34] By 1998, Apple was selling none of these products, and by 1999, Apple had only four computer models: a laptop and desktop for home and educational markets, and a laptop and desktop for business markets. This simplification was crucial to Apple's return to profitability.

Finally, a simple philosophy about what an innovation will be—and will not be—reduces unnecessary distraction and effort. If everyone follows a simple vision, it speeds development, focuses effort, and results in simpler products or services (which will be easier to build or implement). Jeff Hawkins, inventor of the Palm Pilot, also led the development of the hugely successful Palm V, telling the design team, "This product is all about style, it's all about elegance." He said, "I gave examples of products. I said—when the first [StarTac] phone came out, it sold for $1,600, and people were lining up to buy it. Why? Because it was new and it was elegant. So I said—I want to do the StarTac of PDAs." The team pressed Hawkins to add features like more software and a microphone. But he said, "No, no. Palm V is all about elegance and style and I won't entertain anything else." This simple vision, and Hawkins's persistence in putting it into action, made crystal clear to the team where to focus their creative efforts.[35]

## Innovation Means Living with Some Nasty Drawbacks

The terms *creativity, innovation,* and *fun* are often used in the same breath. But before you rush ahead to build or join an innovative company, I feel obliged to warn you about the hazards. Working in an innovative place can be annoying and frustrating, or worse. James Adams at Stanford and Barry Staw from the University of California assert that many people *say* they want a creative workplace, but few would be happy if they actually worked in one. Indeed, a few years ago the Intel Corporation removed "Fun" from the list of core values that employees wear on their badges. A cynic might say that Intel has never been a fun place, so at least they are no longer hypocritical about it. After all, Intel is well-known for encouraging conflict and internal competition. They even hold classes on how to use "constructive confrontation." Intel might be a bit nastier than absolutely necessary, but to build a company where innovation is a way of life, things need to be done that are unpleasant, or even downright frightening.

The 11 1/2 weird ideas here work, but that doesn't mean you will enjoy hiring people you don't like and who probably won't like you. It doesn't mean you will like being around people who are constantly fighting with you and one another. I don't know about you, but I get aggravated when I ask people who work for me to do something and they defy my request. For example, Dana Bookbinder of Corning's Sullivan Park R&D lab recently invented a new kind of plastic labware that is accelerating the drug discovery process at pharmaceutical companies. Bookbinder admits, however, that it took a while for people at Corning, especially his bosses, to get accustomed to him because "I have a very aggressive personality, a very assertive personality, and they didn't know what to do with me." Bookbinder said that in his nine years at Corning, he had only one worthwhile supervisor and that he does what he believes is right, not what he is told. It is to Corning's credit that they know how to manage (or to not try to manage) people like Bookbinder. Corning also rewards people like Bookbinder, honoring him with the prestigious Stookey Award in 2000 for outstanding exploratory research. But just because Corning knows how to deal with independent thinkers like Bookbinder does not mean that he is fun to manage.[36]

Think about the other weird ideas. If you like an orderly workplace, you won't be happy with the chaos that results when your organization is filled with people who have never been taught what they are supposed to do. There are some people who like working in a place where most things fail, are never finished, or reach dead ends. But not most people. When companies are too efficient, it is a warning sign that they are stifling innovation.

Beyond these annoying aspects of innovative places, you should also think hard about the risks that the evolutionary model implies for the average person or company with a new idea. The human tendency to be optimistic means that most of us believe we will be among the small percentage who succeed. But the most likely outcome is that you or your company will be among the many casualties required so that a few can survive and flourish. I return to James March one more time:

> Unfortunately, the gains for imagination are not free. The protections for imagination are indiscriminate. They shield bad ideas as well as good ones—and there are many more of the former than the latter. Most fantasies lead us astray, and most of the consequences of imagination for individuals and individual organizations are disastrous. Most deviants end up on the scrap pile of failed mutations, not as heroes of organizational transformation. . . . There is, as a result, much that can be viewed as unjust in a system that induces imagination among individuals and individual organizations in order to allow a larger system to choose among alternative experiments. By glorifying imagination, we entice the innocent into unwitting self-destruction (or if you prefer, altruism).[37]

Silicon Valley is renowned for the wealth it has produced. But most start-ups fail to produce fabulous wealth, even those funded by elite investors. Stories about the bursting of the Internet bubble can be misleading. There has always been a high failure rate among new companies during even the best of times. One experienced entrepreneur, who helped to start four failed start-ups and two successful start-ups, told me, "Most new companies are just the road kill in a system that makes venture capitalists rich." Some of these "alternative experiments" fail quickly and do limited harm. Kibu, an Internet site for teenage girls, was closed barely a year after it was founded. The experienced board of directors included Jim Clark, cofounder of Silicon Graphics and Netscape. They pulled the plug because they believed Kibu would never be profitable, so they returned over $10 million in remaining funds to the investors. And all of the displaced employees had new jobs within weeks.

Others aren't so lucky. Some companies and people burn through huge amounts of money, devour decades of members' lives, generate one promising idea after another, yet never succeed. Shaman Pharmaceuticals is such a case. CEO Lisa Conte started Shaman in 1989 to "send ethnobotanists into the jungle to seek out traditional healers and turn their ancient remedies into something you buy at a pharmacy with a prescription—curing first-world diseases, funneling royalties back to the third world, and making a bundle for Conte and her investors, which before long included big-time drug players like Eli Lilly."[38] Shaman's scientists collected leaves, bark, and twigs from over 2,600 plants and isolated the active ingredient in each, patented over 20 new compounds, and conducted clinical trials for drugs to treat diarrhea, fungus, and diabetes. Unfortunately, a decade later, Shaman still has no prescription drugs to sell and received a major setback when the U.S. Food and Drug Administration insisted on further clinical trials for its diarrhea drug. After a 500 to 1 reverse stock split in 1999, it switched to selling its diarrhea drug as a nutritional supplement rather than as a prescription drug, and whether the company will survive is very much in question.

I don't want to leave you with the impression that innovative companies are horrible places or that you are destined to lose all your money if you work in one. Many people love the mess and confusion. It is more satisfying to come up with new ideas than to repeat the same actions—and the same thoughts—again and again. It is exciting to work with people who are thrilled about some new idea. Even though many new ideas fail, these setbacks often occur where failure is tolerated, even rewarded. And there are large numbers of people who have become rich working in such places, even if the percentage is small. But you should know the hazards of innovation before devoting your days to it.

## Learn to Fail Faster, Not Less Often

If you believe this book, you will cringe when people talk about making innovation more efficient. It usually means they want to use the logic of routine work to manage innovative work. Once companies try to "reduce the number of screw-ups," innovation usually grinds to a halt. The key to more efficient innovation is failing faster, not less often. Consider what Audrey MacLean told me about failure. MacLean was CEO of Adaptive and is now a successful "angel" investor (she calls herself a "mentor capitalist") who has been featured in *Forbes* and *Red Herring* cover stories in recent years. She argues that one unrecognized reason people made so much money investing in Internet firms during the late 1990s was that failure was inexpensive. MacLean notes that it costs far less to try a new Web site than to develop computer hardware or a medical device, or to write a complex software program. The feedback from the market was so fast that "you could fail faster and cheaper than anything we had ever seen before. Most people focus on how much money was made on the upside, but don't talk about the fact that it was—and still is—so much cheaper than most businesses on the downside." MacLean warns, "None of this applies if you waste millions promoting a consumer Web site with no clue of how you are going to become profitable." But she adds, "Since it didn't take much time or money to put up a Web site, you could find out pretty quickly if it was going to fly or not. A lot of money was made very quickly when something worked, and not much money was lost on failed experiments."

It isn't easy to set things up so the plug can be pulled at the right time. The same confidence and persistence that increases the chances a risky idea will succeed is a double-edged sword. It can result in massive resistance to disbanding a company or project, even long after there is objective evidence it is time to quit. We have seen how stubborn innovators refuse to quit against long odds. There also may be historical or structural factors that make it hard to pull the plug. One of the most dramatic cases of commitment to a failing course of action was the decision to design and build the Shoreham Nuclear Power Plant by the Long Island Lighting Company. When this plant was first proposed in 1966, officials estimated it would cost about $75 million. Financial and safety concerns were raised at virtually every turn, and the plant was not completed until 1985. Shoreham was shut down in 1988 because of concerns about design and construction defects and ever-escalating costs, as well as a finding by a federal jury that company officials had deceived the State of New York in obtaining rate increases to build the plant. By the time the decision was made to shut the plant (which was never fully operational), over $5 billion had been spent.

Barry Staw and Jerry Ross have studied the problem of throwing good money after bad for over 25 years. Their study of the Shoreham case identifies forces that led to an "escalation syndrome"[39] This included public statements from top managers that the project would never be stopped and powerful coalitions inside and outside the company that stood to gain from building the plant. The rationalization that "too much had been invested to quit" led to decisions to waste even more money. Staw and Ross have developed guidelines for avoiding such situations. The most important one is that people who are responsible for starting some project or company, and who have made public statements saying they are committed to it and it is destined to succeed, should not be involved in deciding its fate. Projects need to be structured so that separate groups make decisions about starting and stopping. This is why most banks use one group to sell loans and a different group to decide whether to pull the plug on troubled loans.

Irrational persistence can also be reduced by eliminating or softening the costs of failure. If people believe that their reputations will be ruined by failure, they may rightly believe that pulling the plug means certain ruin and that—no matter how slim the chances—their only hope is to find some way to succeed. Three of the companies I've talked about here—AES, Hewlett-Packard, and SAS Institute—are well-known for such "soft landings." Staw and Ross also advise that "just knowing that one is under the sway of escalation can help." They suggest looking at situations from an outsider's perspective, routinely stopping and asking: "If I took the job for the first time today and found this project going on, would I support it or get rid of it?" This sort of question prompted Intel executives Gordon Moore and Andy Grove to get out of the unprofitable memory-chip business in 1985 and focus on microprocessors, a decision that made Intel billions. An even more aggressive way to avoid escalation situations is to sow the seeds for pulling the plug while a company, project, or product is still a success. Smart executives keep their people vigilant about ways that a current success can turn bad or be eclipsed by competitors. Cisco CEO John Chambers warns his people, "The companies that get into trouble are those that fall in love with 'religious technologies'. . . . The key to success is having a culture with the discipline to accept change and not fight the religious wars."[40]

### Open Is Good, Closed Is Bad

Being open to ideas from other people and places brings in variance and different perspectives, which can help your company avoid getting stuck in the past. And by being open to outsiders, ideas that are old to them, but new to you, can be borrowed or blended with what you already know to invent new management practices, services, and products. The value of openness is perhaps the main lesson from AnnaLee Saxenian's book *Regional Advantage,* which shows why Silicon Valley companies like Hewlett-Packard, Intel, Sun Microsystems, and Cisco have been so innovative, while once-great companies on Boston's Route 128 like DEC, Wang, and Data General declined and died. She shows how Silicon Valley thrives because engineers share ideas so openly, both to get help with technical problems and to show off how much they know.[41] This doesn't happen just inside companies, it happens between engineers from different companies. Not only do engineers routinely violate their intellectual property agreements, several CEOs have admitted to me that being a bit "leaky" in the right conversations is expected and desirable, because everyone understands that it makes innovation happen.

There are, of course, limits to how open a company can and should be about ideas. Concerns about protecting intellectual property are legitimate, and companies that are careful to guard their ideas can make a fortune, at least for a while. Kevin Rivette and David Kline show, for example, that many companies are sitting on unused patents that are worth millions.[42] IBM licensed its unused patents in 1990 and saw its royalties jump from $30 million a year to more than $1 billion in 1999, providing over one-ninth of its annual profits. Intellectual property constraints can also lead to innovation because, if one company owns a solution to some problem, it can spur people in other companies to invent an alternative solution.

Nonetheless, companies that are paranoid about their precious ideas being stolen can kill innovation because, when people from the company get a reputation for listening to other companies' ideas but not talking about their own, the lack of reciprocity may lead others to clam up. Or if people from such companies realize they can't engage in two-way exchanges, they may avoid talking with outsiders who can give them useful advice. Excessive secrecy appears to have played a role in the demise of Interval Research, a think tank started by Paul Allen, Microsoft cofounder and billionaire. As *The New Yorker* put it, "In March of 1992, Interval opened its doors, then promptly slammed them shut."[43] The dream behind Interval was that it would have the virtues of Xerox PARC, especially brilliant technologists who developed ideas that formed entire industries, and none of the drawbacks, such as developing great ideas that others profit from. Allen hired former Xerox PARC superstar David Liddle to run Interval. Liddle brought in a mix of well-known technologists, including the inventors of the laptop computer and inkjet printer, as well as behavioral scientists, artists and musicians, and brilliant young researchers from prestigious universities.44 The problem, according to Paul Saffo, director of the Institute for the Future, was that "they were plopped down in the middle of the greatest technology minds on the planet, in the middle of the biggest revolution of the century, and they never came out from behind their sandbags. . . . They hermetically sealed the place from Day One."45 Interval was closed on April 21, 2000, and even Bill Savoy, the executive who announced the closing to Interval's staff, admitted, "We probably should have brought in more outsiders earlier so we weren't breathing our own air."46

Among the most extreme and impressive illustrations of openness is the development of open source or free software. This includes Linux, currently the only serious challenge to Microsoft Windows. The main benefit of open source development is what is called Linus's Law, that "with more eyes, all bugs are shallow."47 As the development community grows, each new release grows more resilient and bug free because more people find and fix bugs. The open source community has developed a method of licensing that protects their openness. Open source software is protected by what they call "copylefting" work—not copyrighting it. Open source licenses that follow the copyleft principle add "distribution terms, which are a legal instrument that gives everyone the rights to use, modify, and redistribute the program's code or any program derived from it but only if the distribution terms are unchanged. Thus, the code and the freedoms become legally inseparable."48

These restrictions allow the code to stay open. Anyone has access to the source code and is free to modify it, but modifications must be returned to the code base. This causes odd situations in companies and other organizations like universities where a programmer improves some code that their employer wants to copyright and profit from, but the copyleft agreement makes that leverage impossible. An open source Web site points out: "When we explain to the employer that it is illegal to distribute the improved version except as free software, the employer usually decides to release it as free software rather than throw it away."49 There are philosophical reasons for developing free software, but much of the recent enthusiasm for the open source principle is pragmatic: By being open to diverse people and their ideas, the product keeps getting better and better.

## THE ATTITUDES OF INNOVATION

I hope that you use the weird ideas in this book to make your company more innovative. These ideas work. But after a decade of tinkering with them, I've realized that the exact methods used to innovate are less important than building a company where people have the right attitudes toward their work and each other. Psychologists tell us that emotions are the engine that propels human action. Feelings—not cold cognitions—drive people to turn good ideas and intentions into reality. So people who have the right attitudes will not only have an easier time implementing the weird ideas here, their worldview will also drive them to invent and use their own ideas about spurring innovation.

Every innovative company I know of is filled with people who are passionate about solving problems. When I talk to founder and chairman Jeff Hawkins and director of product design engineering Peter Skillman at Handspring about hand-held computers, they bounce up and down like my children do when they play with a wonderful new toy. I see the same spirit in Joey Reiman of BrightHouse, the "ideation company" that charges clients like Coca-Cola, Hardee's, and Georgia Pacific $500,000 to $1 million for a single idea. I can see Reiman in my mind's eye, roller skating around a circular stage in Berlin, bellowing to an audience from the advertising firm McCann-Erickson, "We do heartstorming, not brainstorming; creativity is much more about what people feel than what they think." The passion is more subtle in other innovative companies, but you can always find it.

Playfulness and curiosity are related attitudes of innovation. When Kay Zufall started cutting little shapes out of the wallpaper cleaner made at her brother-in-law's factory, she wasn't thinking about trying to develop a new product; she did it because she loves to tinker with ideas and things. Zufall is always trying to make things better and to have some fun along the way. I saw the same spirit in the IDEO engineers who grabbed my new digital camera (one of the first sold) and took it apart on the spot. They couldn't help themselves. They had never seen one before and *had* to see how it was put together. This persistent curiosity leads to odd moments, such as when a waiter asked some IDEO designers why they were taking the napkin holder apart. The answer—"because we wanted to look at how the springs work"—was not treated as credible. But it was true, and it is one of the main reasons IDEO has developed a renowned culture of innovation.

My last attitude of innovation is really a pair of attitudes: the ability to switch emotional gears between cynicism and belief, or between deep doubt and unshakable confidence. These emotions are the tag-team partners of the innovation process. If your company is dominated by only one, you are in trouble. Every innovative company we examined closely here makes use of this blend of emotions, from Disney, to 3M, to Handspring, to Sottsass Associates. People in these places believe that everything is wonderful, that all is possible when generating ideas, but they become cynics—or bring in some cynics—when deciding which to develop and which to stop. Once they pick an idea to develop and implement, belief rises again.

A blend of belief and cynicism can also help you get the most out of this book. As I said at the outset, when you think about my weird ideas, try to suspend disbelief, just for a while. Ask yourself: *What if these ideas are true?* How might I help organize or manage my company differently? How should I act differently to make myself more creative? Play with these ideas in your mind and experiment with them in your company. These weird ideas have firm grounding and have helped other companies develop useful new ideas, but they are not immutable truths. Some cynicism is needed to make the best use of them. Treat them like toys you might buy to mess around with: Try to break them, take apart the pieces to see how they work, try to improve them, and mix them with your other toys. You might develop some of your own counterintuitive ideas along the way. Ultimately, anything that brings in new knowledge, helps people see old things in new ways, or helps a company break from the past will do the trick.

# ACKNOWLEDGMENTS

The ideas in this book were born on a lovely September afternoon in 1993. Jim Adams, one of my most interesting and delightful colleagues, had dragged me to the Stanford Faculty Club. He bought me glasses of red wine (and Scotch for himself) while he tried to persuade me to teach in an executive program he was running on "Managing Innovation" for the Stanford Alumni Association. I had been resisting Jim's request during our hallway conversations, so he decided that drastic action was needed. I had been at Stanford for nine years and had just been promoted to full professor. The main reason that Stanford promoted me was that I had written dozens of articles for fellow academics about what and why things happen in organizations. I had given little thought to what executives, managers, engineers, and other people who faced actual problems might learn from my work. That is how most research universities operate, for better or worse. Most faculty are hired and promoted based on their ability to do research in a narrow academic specialty.

I believed I couldn't add much to what Jim Adams would teach these executives about creativity and innovation. After all, Jim wrote an engaging book on creativity called *Conceptual Blockbusting* that sold over 200,000 copies and another book that was just as useful called *The Care and Feeding of Ideas.* He had given many speeches to real managers, engineers, and scientists in real firms about ways to increase their creativity. Jim goaded, flattered, and insulted me as we drank. He insisted I had learned many things that managers needed to know from my years writing for, reading, and editing academic journals, and that I actually might enjoy talking to real human beings instead of my (often) pompous and hypercritical academic colleagues. He also reminded me that I had reached the point in my career where there was no risk to doing things that were actually useful: A tenured full professor at a wealthy university like Stanford probably has more job security than any professional on earth. I finally gave in, mostly because I wanted to stop him from hounding me. I said, "Okay, Jim, I'm going to try the most ridiculous topic I can imagine. Let me tell you some of the twisted ideas that I'm going to talk about." I scribbled a bunch of silly ideas on a napkin, peculiar things like "hire people who are wrong most of the time," "hire people who don't listen to you," "have an organization with no memory," and "be vague and boring when you talk about your work." I thought these absurd ideas would convince Jim to quit badgering me, but my plan backfired. I should have remembered that the greatest compliment that Jim can give a person, at least in his own mind, is that they are "really twisted," "way out there," or "weird as hell." So he got excited about these silly ideas and insisted that this was exactly what he wanted me to talk about to the executives in his program. I argued back that, while he thought these ideas were "cool," executives would find them ridiculous. Jim said I was wrong, that executives are like most people, always looking for useful new ideas and looking to have fun at work and in life. He argued that since I would have enormous fun teaching them these ideas, I should try them in his program right away. I gave in. I was sure that my odd ideas would annoy and bore these executives and that Jim would never again badger me about talking to any other managers, engineers, or executives. I could then go back to my quiet life, reading, writing for, and editing the obscure academic journals that I loved so much and that seemed so much safer.

I gave this talk to the executives in the "Managing Innovation" program in October of 1993. I called it something like "Weird Ideas About Enhancing Organizational Innovation" and proposed a dozen or so counterintuitive ideas about making organizations creative. I thought the executives would rebel against my twisted approach and tell me the ideas were absurd. They did argue with many of my ideas, but even when they did, they seemed to be thinking and learning about how to make their organizations more creative. In fact, the executives who argued with me most vehemently were also usually the most enthusiastic about the weird ideas and understood best what it takes to build a creative organization.

I have given descendants of that original talk more than a hundred times to several thousand executives at Stanford, the University of California at Berkeley, and various corporations. I have since given talks on dozens of other topics to executives, managers, and engineers in the subsequent years as well. The "weird ideas" seminar remains among my favorites, however, because audiences react so strongly to these odd ideas and the strange way that I frame them. Audiences *never* have a neutral reaction to this talk. They either hate it or they love it. Most love it, but it is not a good talk for an audience that takes itself too seriously.

I intended to write this book for many years, but life kept getting in the way. My wife, Marina Park, and I got distracted by having three charming and demanding children, Eve, Claire, and Tyler. I got sidetracked by writing other books, including *The Knowing-Doing Gap* (with Jeffrey Pfeffer). I wondered if I'd ever get around to working on this "weird ideas" book until, in early 1999, I had a series of eye operations that made it difficult for me to read or write for several weeks. But I could still talk! So I used this time to dictate the weird ideas talk that I'd been giving for years. The original dictated manuscript was pretty ragged. I deleted perhaps more than 75 percent of what I said, added another 150 pages or so, revised every sentence I kept, and massively reorganized the text. Yet, in reading this final version, I am struck—astounded is a better word—by how closely these ideas and (especially) the spirit in which I offer them resembles the talk I first sketched out on a napkin that September afternoon in 1993 when Jim Adams convinced me to give my very first talk to executives.

So, for starters, I thank (and blame) Jim Adams for starting the chain of events that led to this book. But he is not alone. I am lucky to be part of a delightful network of people at Stanford and beyond who have shaped these ideas and made it possible for me in hundreds of other ways to write this book. Beginning at Stanford, this book could not have been written without James March. More than anyone else, my ideas are borrowed from and inspired by his vast body of work. Beginning with his classic book (with Herbert Simon) *Organizations* in 1958, Jim has been one of the most productive and influential organizational researchers of all time, and though officially retired from Stanford, he is not done yet. Jim's ideas about exploration and exploitation were especially central to developing my weird ideas, but there are numerous other ways in which this book is shaped by his work, and by the delightful and challenging talks that we have had over the years.

   This book also could not have been written without the support of my colleagues in Stanford's Department of Management Science & Engineering, especially colleagues in the Center for Work, Technology and Organization (WTO) and the Stanford Technology Ventures Program.

Steve Barley, my codirector of WTO, has done hundreds of things that made it possible for me to finish this book, everything from raising funds, to going to dull meetings in my place, to cheering me up, to contributing ideas. Steve is one of my best friends and I am grateful for everything he does. My other two WTO faculty colleagues, Diane Bailey and Pam Hinds, have been equally supportive, and their drive and enthusiasm about their work inspires me to work harder at my own. Paula Wright, our administrative assistant, helped me with hundreds of chores along the way. The most wonderful thing about our center is that doctoral students are right across the hall from the faculty. These fine scholars and human beings include Mahesh Bhatia, Bart Balocki, Laura Castaneda, Adam Grant, Mark Mortensen, Kelley Porter, Keith Rollag, and Victor Seidel. Fabrizio Ferraro and Sally Fellenzer did wonderful work as research assistants. I've nagged all of them about ideas in the book, and I appreciate their patience. I want to give special thanks to Siobhan O'Mahony, who has, more than anyone else, helped me finish the book. Siobhan is relentless about digging up strange sources, editing, and making suggestions, and has made it all seem like a fun adventure.

My colleagues at the Stanford Technology Ventures Program (STVP) have been equally supportive. The charismatic and action-oriented founder and executive director of this program, Tom Byers, has built the most successful entrepreneurship program in any engineering school in the world. Tom Byers and STVP director Tina Seelig have not only given me encouragement, they have been generous in allocating funds to support this research.

My main home at Stanford is in the engineering school, but I also received support and a place to write from the Stanford Graduate School of Business. I have gleaned great ideas from colleagues there, including Deborah Gruenfeld, John Jost, Rod Kramer, Michael Morris, Maggie Neale, Lara Tiedens, and Katherine Klein. Charles O'Reilly has been especially helpful; he knows more about innovation than anyone at Stanford and has been remarkably generous with both his time and ideas. Jeffrey Pfeffer is my closest collaborator and friend at Stanford. I didn't know how to write a management book until we did *The Knowing-Doing Gap*; it was great chance to learn from the smartest person in my field. One of my main motivations for finishing this book is that I can now turn to a series of projects with Jeff, which is always delightful.

This work has also been shaped by colleagues outside of Stanford. Barry Staw of the University of California at Berkeley and I have had great conversations about creativity (and what is wrong with it) over the years. My wise and longtime friend Marjorie Williams of the Harvard Business School Press provided crucial advice when this manuscript was in an early and crude form. Gary Hamel and Liisa Valikangas from Strategos taught me about new lessons about the link between strategy and innovation. Jeff Miller, whom I've been racing sailboats with and against for 30 years, told me about his concept of "*vu ja de*," and let me steal it. David Owens of Vanderbilt University and I conducted research on status competitions in the product design process that shaped many of my ideas about innovation. Andrew Hargadon of the University of Florida deserves special thanks. Andy has let me join him now and then in developing his impressive stream of research on innovation. His diverse and imaginative ideas crop up in many places in this book.

The ideas in this book have also been shaped and illustrated by conversations and e-mail exchanges from many people who actually do and manage innovative work. These people include Corey Billington of Hewlett-Packard, John Seely Brown of Xerox PARC, Joe Davila of Homestead, Jeff Hawkins of Handspring, Peter Gaarn of Hewlett-Packard, Ginger Graham of Guidant, Mitchell Kapor of Accel, Justin Kitch of Homestead, Freada Klein of Klein Associates, John Reinertsen of McDonald's, Pete Servold of McDonald's, Mark Shieh, and Peter Skillman of Handspring. I thank the wise people at Reactivity, including Jeremy Henrickson, Carmela Krantz, Graham Miller, Bill Walker, Brian Roddy, and, especially, John Lilly, who read and commented on the book. I am grateful to everyone at IDEO Product Development for letting me hang around, notably Gwen Books, Brendan Boyle, Dennis Boyle, Tim Brown, Sean Corcorran, Cliff Jue, Tom Kelley, Chris Kurjan, Bill Moggridge, Whitney Mortimer, Larry Shubert, Craig Syverson, Scott Underwood, and Don Westwood for teaching me so much. David Kelley, IDEO's founder and chairman, as well as a Stanford engineering colleague, showed me more about how to build and tend to an innovative company than anyone else; he patiently answered my endless questions and let me snoop around his company. I still remember the first time I talked to David in 1994. He gave me the IDEO phone list and said, "Here, contact anyone you want." He probably didn't realize I would still be doing it seven years later!

My agent, Michael Carlisle, not only is skilled at his craft, his intensity and optimism is delightful. I appreciate the help and good advice from Michael and others at his company. Donald Lamm joined Michael as an able literary agent. Yet that job description  doesn't begin to capture all Don has done to help me with this book. He suggested the title, edited the proposal and manuscript, and most important of all, taught me about the odd but intriguing business of publishing. This book has been a great excuse to get to know Don, one of the wisest people I've ever met. I've been equally fortunate to work with Bruce Nichols, my editor at The Free Press. Bruce subtly and persistently pressed me to shape the manuscript in ways that made it better. He edits with what feels like a light touch, but he saved me from my worst weaknesses again and again. Bruce is the right editor for me; he cares deeply about quality, but he realizes that I am given to endless fiddling, so manuscripts must be declared complete and gently pried out of my grip if they are ever to be published.

Finally, I want to thank my family, especially my lovely Marina, my sweet and clear-thinking wife, for teaching me to write so long ago. When we first started living together in 1976, Marina was an English major and already skilled writer. I couldn't write a decent sentence; she showed me how to write well and to appreciate good writing. I also thank her for letting me take the time to finish this book. I have stolen much time from Marina and our three kids to finish this book. Eve, Claire, and Tyler deserve the greatest thanks of all. I love you and appreciate everything, especially the charming discussions about what is weird and what is not.

# NOTES

## CHAPTER 1

1. Teague, P., "Father of an Industry," *Design News,* March 6, 2000, www.manufacturing.net/magazine/dn/archives/2000/dn0306.00/feature2.html.
2. March, J. G., "Exploration and Exploitation in Organizational Learning," *Organization Science* 2 (1991): 71–87.
3. A similar distinction is made by many other people who write about innovation. See Sitkin, S., K. M. Sutcliffe, and D. G. Schroeder, "Distinguishing Control from Learning in Total Quality Management: A Learning Perspective," *Academy of Management Review* 19 (1993): 537–64; O'Reilly, C., "Corporations, Culture, and Commitment: Motivation and Social Control in Organizations," *California Management Review* 31 (1989): 24–38; Tushman, M. L., and C. O'Reilly, *Winning Through Innovation: A Practical Guide to Leading Organizational Change and Renewal* (Boston: Harvard Business School Press, 1997); Adams, J. L., *The Care and Feeding of Ideas: A Guide to Encouraging Creativity* (Reading, MA: Addison-Wesley, 1986); and Nemeth, C. J., and B. M. Staw, "The Tradeoffs of Social Control and Innovation in Groups and Organizations," in *Advances in Experimental Psychology,* ed. L. Berkowitz (New York: Academic Press, 1989), 175–310. Although there are some differences among these perspectives, the three fundamental principles presented here are primary ways to make the distinction between groups of people who are good at using old ideas versus generating, testing, and developing new ideas.
4. March, "Exploration and Exploitation."
5. Watson, J. L., "Transnationalism, Localization, and Fast Foods in East Asia," in *Golden Arches East: McDonald's in East Asia,* ed. J. L. Watson (Stanford, CA: Stanford University Press, 1997), 1–76.
6. See, for example, Deming, W. E., *Out of the Crisis* (Cambridge, MA: MIT Press/CAES, 1986); and Hackman, J. R., and R. Wageman, "Total Quality Management: Empirical, Conceptual and Practical Issues," *Administrative Science Quarterly* 40 (1995): 309–42.
7. Fedarko, K., "Russian Air Roulette: Service on Aeroflot Was Once Considered Just Riotously Bad. These Days, It's Getting Downright Dangerous," *Time,* April 18, 1994.
8. Nemeth and Staw, "Tradeoffs of Social Control and Innovation."
9. Gould, S. J., *Full House: The Spread of Excellence from Plato to Darwin* (New York: Harmony Books, 1996), 229–30.
10. See, for example, Hannan, M. T., and J. Freeman, *Organizational Ecology* (Cam-

bridge, MA: Harvard University Press, 1990); Campbell, D. T., "Variation and Selective Retention in Sociocultural Evolution," *General Systems* 16 (1969): 69–85; and McKelvey, B., *Organizational Systematics: Taxonomy, Evolution, Classification* (Berkeley: University of California Press, 1982).

11. Simonton, D. K., *Origins of Genius: Darwinian Perspectives on Creativity* (New York: Oxford University Press, 1999).

12. See, for example, Allen, T. J., *Managing the Flow of Technology* (Cambridge, MA: MIT Press, 1977); Allen, T. J., and D. Cohen, "Information Flow in Research and Development Laboratories," *Administrative Science Quarterly* 14 (1969): 12–19; DiMaggio, P., "Nadel's Paradox Revisited: Relational and Cultural Aspects of Organizational Structure," in *Networks and Organizations: Structure, Form, and Action,* ed. N. Nohria and R. G. Eccles (Boston: Harvard Business School Press, 1992); Hargadon, A., "Firms as Knowledge Brokers," *California Management Review* 40 (1998): 209–27; Hargadon, A., and R. I. Sutton, "Technology Brokering and Innovation in a Product Development Firm," *Administrative Science Quarterly* 42 (1997): 716–49; March, "Exploration and Exploitation"; and Nemeth and Staw, "Tradeoffs of Social Control and Innovation."

13. Millard, A., *Edison and the Business of Invention* (Baltimore: Johns Hopkins University Press, 1990), 15.

14. Anton, T., *Bold Science* (New York: Freeman, 2000), 48.

15. Surowiecki, J., "The Credit Card Kings," *The New Yorker,* November 27, 2000, 74.

16. Brendan Boyle, interview by Robert Sutton at Skyline Toys, Palo Alto, July 26, 1999.

17. The Furby, a sophisticated talking toy that responds to touching, movement, and voice commands, was one of the most successful new products sold during the 1998 Christmas season.

18. Zider, B., "How Venture Capital Works," *Harvard Business Review* (November-December 2000): 131–39.

19. Muio, A., "Great Ideas in Aisle 9," *Fast Company* (April 2000): 46.

20. Hackman and Wageman, "Total Quality Management."

21. Weick, K. E., "The Collapse of Sensemaking in Organizations: The Mann Gulch Disaster," *Administrative Science Quarterly* 38 (1993): 628–52.

22. Ibid., 633–34.

23. www.bemorecreative.com.

24. Schlender, B., "The Edison of the Internet," *Fortune,* February 15, 1999, 85.

25. This information about Ettore Sottsass and Sottsass Associates comes primarily from three sources: conversations with cofounder Marco Zanini in Milan Italy in April 2000; conversations with IDEO CEO David Kelley over the years, who visits Sottsass and Zanini every year and has recently had a house in Woodside, California, designed by Sottsass Associates; and Milco, C., *The Work of Ettore Sottsass and Associates* (New York: Universe Publishing, 1999). Also see www. Sottsass.com.

26. Sittenfeld, C., "This Old House Is a Home for Ideas," *Fast Company* (April 1999), www.fastcompany.com/online/26/brighthouse.html.

27. www.marketingadvantage.co.uk/Teabags.htm.

28. www.vdbfoods.co.uk/education/brook_adpg.htm.

29. Langer, E. J., "Minding Matters: The Consequences of Mindlessness-Mindfulness," in *Advances in Experimental Social Psychology,* ed. L. Berkowitz (New York: Academic Press, 1989): 137–73.

30. Teague, P., "Father of an Industry," *Design News,* March 6, 2000, www.manufacturing.net/magazine/dn/archives/2000/dn0306.00/feature2.html.

31. Buderi, R., *Engines of Tomorrow* (New York: Simon & Schuster, 2000).

32. From a speech William E. Coyne gave at Motorola University in Schaumburg, IL, July 11, 2000.

33. John Seely Brown, head of Xerox PARC from 1990 to 2000, in a conversation in Palo Alto, July 16, 2000.

34. Zajonc, R, "Emotions," in *The Handbook of Social Psychology,* ed. D. T. Gilbert, S. T. Fiske, and G. Lindzey (New York: McGraw-Hill, 1998), 591–634.

35. Ibid., 614.

36. Ibid.

**CHAPTER 2**

1. Miller, H., "Why Don't You Try to Write?" in *Creators on Creating,* ed. F. Barron, A. Montuori, and A. Barron (New York: Putnam, 1997), 27, 30.

2. Rabino, P., *Making PCR: A Story of Biotechnology* (Chicago: University of Chicago Press, 1996), 6–7.

3. I use the word *idea* here in the broadest possible way. A new live performance, a new way to clean ears, the Palm V computer, and the theory of relativity would, for example, all be creative ideas to people who find them new and valuable.

4. Lubow, A., "Mom & Me," *Inc. Online* (April 1999), 54, www.inc500.com/inc-magazine/archives/04990541.html.

5. My definition of creativity, which emphasizes its subjective aspects, is probably most closely related to that advanced by Teresa Amabile. See Amabile, T., *Creativity in Context* (Boulder, CO: Westview, 1996), 33. For other definitions of creativity, see Sternberg, R. J., *Handbook of Creativity* (Cambridge, MA: Cambridge University Press, 1999); and Adams, J. L., *Conceptual Blockbusting: A Guide to Better Ideas* (Reading, MA: Presus Books, 1986).

6. Research on such brokers includes Hargadon, A., and R. I. Sutton, "Building an Innovation Factory," *Harvard Business Review* (May–June 2000); Hargadon, A., "Firms as Knowledge Brokers," *California Management Review* 40 (1998): 209–27; and Hargadon, A., and R. I. Sutton, "Technology Brokering and Innovation in a Product Development Firm," *Administrative Science Quarterly* 42 (1997): 716–49.

7. The information about Edge Innovation comes from an interview conducted with Walt Conti, Ty Boyce, and other members of the *Willy* design team on February 16, 1995; from Patton, P. "Whale Tale," *I.D. Magazine* (November 1993), 56–91; from an interview with Edge investor David Kelley on November 2, 1999; and from their Web site www.edgeinnovations.com.

8. This information comes from the transcribed text of an interview that Gary Hamel had with Martin van Zwanenberg, which Hamel was kind enough to let me use in this book.

9. Information about the invention of Play-Doh comes from numerous conversations that Sally Fellzenger had with Kathryn and Robert Zufall; a letter from the Zufalls to Sally Fellzenger written in December 1998; "Popular Play-Doh Turns 30 This Year," *Baltimore Sun,* October 7, 1985, 1B, 3B; and www.yippeee.com and www.hasbro.com.

10. Barboza, D. "Living and Learning at Dishwasher U," *The New York Times,* September 12, 2000.

11. Kling, J., "From Hypertension, to Angina, to Viagra," *Modern Drug Discovery* (November/December, 1998): 1–38.

12. Villarosa, L., "Remedies for Hair Loss," *The New York Times on the Web,* October 20, 1998.

13. Reid, R., "*Architects of the Web: 1,000 Days that Built the Future of Business* (New York: Wiley, 1997), 113.

14. Ibid.

15. Billington, C., "The Language of Supply Chains," *Supply Chain Management Review* (Summer 2000): 86–92.

16. Corey Billington, interview by Robert Sutton, Palo Alto, October 26, 2000.

17. Singh, S., *Fermat's Enigma* (New York: Walker, 1997); and *The Proof* (1997), a film written and produced by John Lynch and directed by Simon Singh, executive producer, Paula S. Apsell (A BBC TV/WGBH Boston Co-Production).

18. Anton, T., *Bold Science* (New York: Freeman, 2000).

19. www.celera.com/corporate/about/press_releases/celera062600_2.html (downloaded on August 20, 2000).

20. Anton, *Bold Science*, 29.

### CHAPTER 3

1. Simonton, D. K., *Origins of Genius* (New York: Oxford University Press, 1999), 121.

2. March, J. G., "Exploration and Exploitation in Organizational Learning," *Organization Science* 2 (1991): 74.

3. Kahn, R., et al., *Organizational Stress: Studies in Role Conflict and Ambiguity* (New York: Wiley, 1964): 150–151.

4. MacFarquhar, L., "The Gilder Effect," *The New Yorker*, May 29, 2000, 103–11.

5. See March, "Exploration and Exploitation."

6. For a detailed review of this work, see Snyder, M., *Public Appearances, Private Realities: The Psychology of Self-Monitoring* (New York: Freeman, 1987).

7. Ibid., 14.

8. Gleick, J., *Genius: The Life and Science of Richard Feynman* (New York: Pantheon, 1992).

9. Feynman, R. P., *What Do You Care What Other People Think?* (New York: Norton, 1998).

10. Gleick, *Genius*, 316.

11. Feynman, *What Do You Care?* 117.

12. Gleick, *Genius*, 423.

13. Chatman, J. A., "Matching People and Organizations: Selection and Socialization in Public Accounting Firms," *Administrative Science Quarterly* 36 (1991): 459–84.

14. Brockner, J., *Self-Esteem at Work: Research, Theory, and Practice* (Lexington, MA: Lexington Books, 1998), 27.

15. Watson, J. D., *The Double Helix* (New York: Atheneum, 1968).

16. Ibid., 13.

17. Garbarini, V., and B. Cullman with B. Graustak, with special introduction by Dave Marsh, *Strawberry Fields Forever: John Lennon Remembered* (New York: Bantam, 1980), 99.

18. March. J. G., "The Future, Disposable Organizations, and the Rigidities of Imagination," in *The Pursuit of Organizational Intelligence,* ed. J. G. March (Malden, MA: Blackwell, 1999): 179–192.

19. Hiltzik, M., *Dealers of Lightning: Xerox PARC and the Dawn of the Computer Age* (New York: HarperBusiness, 1999).

20. Ibid., 127.

21. Ibid., 144.

22. For example, Smith, D. K., and R. C. Alexander, *Fumbling the Future: How Xerox*

*Invented, Then Ignored, the First Personal Computer* (New York: Morrow, 1988); Cringly, R. X., *Accidental Empires* (New York: HarperBusiness, 1992); "Xerox Won't Duplicate Past Errors," *Business Week,* September 29, 1997, 98; and *Triumph of the Nerds,* broadcast on PBS June 12, 1996.

23. Anton, T., *Bold Science* (New York: Freeman, 2000), 7.
24. Simonton, *Origins of Genius.*
25. Ibid., 121.
26. Waldroop, J., and T. Butler, *Maximum Success* (New York: Doubleday, 2000).
27. For example, Tony Attwood, the psychologist who wrote *Asperger's Syndrome: A Guide for Parents and Professionals* (Bristol, PA: Jessica Kingsley Publishers, 1998), recently described the close parallels between Einstein's behavior and the defining features of Asperger's syndrome (www.tonyattwood.com/issues.htmm, downloaded August 10, 2000).
28. Gleick, *Genius.*
29. Garbarini and Cullman, *Strawberry Fields Forever.*
30. Ibid., 46.
31. Ibid., 47.
32. Giuliano, G., *The Beatles: A Celebration* (New York: St. Martin's Press, 1986), 203.

### CHAPTER 4

1. For reviews, see Cialdini, R. B., *Influence: The Psychology of Persuasion,* chap. 5 (New York: Quill, 1993); Williams, K. Y., and C. A. O'Reilly, "Demography and Diversity in Organizations; A Review of 40 Years of Research," in *Research in Organizational Behavior,* vol. 20, ed. B. M. Staw and L. L. Cummings (Stamford, CT: JAI Press, 1998), 77–140; Pfeffer, J., "Organizational Demography," in *Research in Organizational Behavior,* vol. 5, ed. L. L. Cummings and B. M. Staw (Greenwich, CT: JAI Press, 1983), 299–357; and Pfeffer, J., *New Directions for Organization Theory: Problems and Prospects,* chap. 4 (New York: Oxford University Press, 1997).
2. Kanter, R. M., *Men and Women of the Corporation* (New York: Basic Books, 1977).
3. Ibid., 48.
4. Ibid.
5. Leiber, R. "Feat of Clay," *Fast Company* (April 2000): 230–44.
6. Young, J., *Steve Jobs: The Journey Is the Reward* (New York: Scott, Foresman, 1988).
7. Ibid., 137.
8. Cialdini, R. B., *Influence: The Psychology of Persuasion* (New York: Quill, 1993), 173–74.

### CHAPTER 5

1. Justin Kitch, interview by Robert Sutton and Jeffrey Pfeffer at Homestead.com, Menlo Park, California, January 13, 2000.
2. These quotes and related information are from a conversation I had with David Kelley on July 22, 1999.
3. Ibid.
4. These quotes and related information are from several conversations I had with Tom Kelley during July 1999 at IDEO.
5. Meindl, J. R., S. B. Ehrlich, and J. M. Dukerich, "The Romance of Leadership," *Administrative Science Quarterly* 30 (1985): 78–102; and Meindl, J. R., "On Leadership: An Alternative to Conventional Wisdom," in *Research in Organizational Behavior,* vol. 12, ed. B. M. Staw and L. L. Cummings (Greenwich, CT: JAI Press, 1990), 159–204.

6. Hiltzik, M., *Dealers of Lightning* (New York: HarperBusiness, 1999), 232.
7. Ibid., 234.
8. Ibid.

### CHAPTER 6

1. For reviews of the research on the reliability and validity of the selection interview, see Arvey, R. P., and J. E. Campion, "The Employment Interview: A Summary and Review of Recent Research," *Personal Psychology* 35 (1982): 281–322; Eder, R. W., and G. R. Ferris, *The Employment Interview: Theory, Research, and Practice* (Newbury Park, CA: Sage, 1989); and Borman, W. C., M. A. Hanson, and J. W. Hedge, "Personnel Selection," *Annual Review of Psychology* 48 (1997): 299–337. For the most part, authors who review this literature conclude that, as it is usually done, the selection interview is of little value in distinguishing between which employees will perform well or poorly, and even those few authors who argue that the typical interview is a useful selection tool concede that it is not an especially powerful one.
2. Svenson, O. "Are We All Risky and More Skillful Than Our Fellow Drivers?" *Acta Psychologia* 47 (1981): 143–48.
3. Cringely, R. X., *Accidental Empires* (New York: HarperBusiness, 1996), 11.
4. Charlton, J., *The Executive's Quotation Book* (New York: St. Martin's Press, 1983): 74.
5. Anderson, C. W., "The Relation Between Speaking Times and Decision in the Employment Interview," *Journal of Applied Psychology* 44 (1960):267–68.
6. For writings on wisdom, see Sternberg, R. J., *Wisdom: Its Nature, Origins, and Development* (Cambridge, UK: Cambridge University Press, 1990); especially, see Meacham, J. A., "The Loss of Wisdom," in *Wisdom,* 181–211; and Meacham, J. A., "Wisdom and the Context of Knowledge: Knowing What One Doesn't Know," in *On the Development of Developmental Psychology,* ed. D. Huhn and J. A. Meacham (Basel, Switzerland: Krager, 1983), 111–34.

### CHAPTER 7

1. Kotter, J. P., and J. L. Heskett, *Corporate Culture and Performance* (New York: Free Press, 1992), 1.
2. Coyne, W., "3M: "Vision Is the Engine That Drives Our Enterprise," in *Innovation: Breakthrough Thinking at 3M, DuPont, GE, Pfizer, and Rubbermaid,* ed. R. M. Kanter, J. Kao, and F. Wiersema (New York: HarperBusiness, 1997), 51.
3. For example, see Ash, M. K., *Mary Kay on People Management* (New York, Warner Books, 1984); "The Men's Wearhouse: Success in a Declining Industry," Case #HR-5 (Palo Alto, CA: Graduate School of Business, Stanford University, 1997); and O'Reilly III, C. A., and J. Pfeffer, *Hidden Value* (Boston: Harvard Business School Press, 2000).
4. See, for example, O'Reilly, C., "Corporations, Culture, and Commitment: Motivation and Social Control in Organizations," *California Management Review* 31 (1989): 24–38.
5. Chatman, J. A., "Matching People and Organizations: Selection and Socialization in Public Accounting Firms," *Administrative Science Quarterly* 36 (1991): 459–84.
6. See New United Motors Manufacturing, Inc. (NUMMI), Case #HR-11 (Palo Alto, CA: Graduate School of Business, Stanford University, 1998).
7. Ibid., 2.
8. Ibid., 3.

9. March, J. G., "Exploration and Exploitation in Organizational Learning," *Organization Science* 2 (1991): 71–87.

10. Bowen, D. E., G. E. Ledford Jr., and B. R. Nathan, "Hiring for the Organization, not the Job," *Academy of Management Executive* 5 (1991): 35–51.

11. Ibid., 35.

12. Sitkin, S., "Learning Through Failure: A Strategy of Small Loses," in *Research in Organizational Behavior,* vol. 14, ed. B. M. Staw and L. L. Cummings (Greenwich, CT: JAI Press, 1992), 231–66.

13. This information comes from a series of 12 interviews conducted by Stephen Barley, Jeffrey Martin, and Robert Sutton at this firm in January and February of 1999; from archived information given to us by members of the corporation; and from a story published in an industry magazine. I can't provide any more information about this corporation because the interviews were conducted with the understanding that we would protect the identity of the corporation.

14. Deutsch, C. H., "Software That Can Make a Grown Company Cry," *The New York Times,* November 8, 1998.

15. Pfeffer, J. and G. R. Salancik, *The External Control of Organizations: A Resource Dependence Perspective* (New York: Harper & Row, 1978).

16. Kirkpatrick, D., "IBM: From Big Blue Dinosaur to E-Business Animal," *Fortune,* April 26, 1999.

17. Burrows, P., and P. Elstrom, "HP's Carly Fiorina: The Boss," *Business Week,* August 2, 1999.

18. Carly Fiorina, "Art of Reninvention in the New Economy," speech given in Chicago, April 17, 2000; text available at www.hp.com/ghp/ceo/speeches/reinvent.html.

19. Steve Jobs, speech given at DeAnza College's Flint Center, Cupertino, California, May 6, 1998.

20. "Blurb Buddies," *Fast Company* (December 1998): 54.

21. http://disney.go.com/Disney World/DisneyInstitute/ProfessionalPrograms/Disney_Difference/index.html.

22. Pfeffer, J., and R. I. Sutton, *The Knowing-Doing Gap: How Smart Companies Turn Knowledge into Action* (Boston: Harvard Business School Press, 1999).

23. Cummings, A., and G. R. Oldham, "Enhancing Creativity: Managing Work Contexts for the High Potential Employee," *California Management Review* 40 (1997): 22–38.

24. Kirton, M. J., *Adaptors and Innovators* (London: Routledge, 1989); Kirton, M. J., "Adaptors and Innovators: A Description and Measure," *Journal of Applied Psychology* 61 (1976): 622–29; and Keller, R. T., "Predictors of the Performance of Project Groups in R&D Organizations," *Academy of Management Journal* 29 (1986): 715–26.

25. Sutton, R. I., K. M. Eisenhardt, and J. V. Jucker, "Managing Organizational Decline: Lessons from Atari," *Organizational Dynamics* 14 (1986): 17–29.

26. Interview by Pamela Epstein and Robert Sutton, Stanford University, August 1, 1984.

27. Indrema presentation, Bay Area Linux Users Group, San Francisco, September 19, 2000.

28. Coyne, "3M," 43–63.

29. Packard, D., *The HP Way: How Bill Hewlett and I Built Our Company* (New York: HarperBusiness, 1995), 108.

30. Maas, P., *The Terrible Hours: The Man Behind the Greatest Submarine Rescue in History* (New York: HarperCollins, 1999).

31. Ibid., 65.

32. Ibid., 106.

33. Coyne, "3M," 50.

34. Leiber, R., "Feat of Clay," *Fast Company* (April 2000):230–44.
35. Ibid. p., 244.
36. Fishman, C., "Creative Tension," *Fast Company* (November 2000) p. 372.
37. O'Mahony, S., unpublished Interview with an anonymous San Francisco Bay Area Linux programmer, July 2000.
38. Seabrook, J., "Rocking in Shangri-la," *The New Yorker,* October 10, 1994, 66.
39. Ibid., 68.
40. Reid, R., *Architects of the Web: 1,000 Days that Built the Future of Business* (New York: Wiley, 1997), 121.
41. Ibid., 122.

## CHAPTER 8

1. Hirshberg, J., *The Creative Priority* (New York: HarperBusiness, 1998), 30.
2. Lowery, N., and D. W. Johnson, "Effects of Controversy on Epistemic Curiosity, Achievement, and Attitudes," *Journal of Social Psychology* 115 (1981): 31–43.
3. Charlton, J., *The Executive Quotation Book* (New York: St. Martin's Press, 1983), 30.
4. For writing and research on brainstorming and related idea generation methods, see Adams, J. L., *The Care and Feeding of Ideas: A Guide to Encouraging Creativity* (Reading, MA: Addison-Wesley, 1986); Osborn, A. F., *Applied Imagination,* 3d ed. (New York: Scribner's, 1963); Sutton, R. I., and A. Hargadon, "Brainstorming Groups in Context: Effectiveness in a Product Design Firm," *Administrative Science Quarterly* 41 (1996): 685–718; and Van de Ven, A. H., and A. L. Delbeq, "The Effectiveness of Nominal, Delphi, and Interacting Group Decision-making Processes," *Academy of Management Journal* 17 (1974): 605–21.
5. I first heard Peter Skillman make this point in an interview that I did with him in April of 1995, when he was working at IDEO Product Development. I spoke to him recently about brainstorming at Handspring, his current employer, and he reported that he continues to use the same techniques.
6. Jehn, K. A., "A Multi-method Examination of the Benefits and Detriments of Intragroup Conflicts," *Administrative Science Quarterly* 40 (1995): 271.
7. Eisenhardt, K., J. L. Kahwajy, and L. J. Bourgeois III, "How Management Teams Can Have a Good Fight," *Harvard Business Review* (July-August 1997): 82.
8. Hiltzik, M., *Dealers of Lightning* (New York: HarperBusiness, 1999).
9. Ibid., 16–17.
10. Ibid., 145.
11. Ibid., 147.
12. Ibid., 17.
13. Kurtzberg, T. R., "Group Conflict and Creativity" (Ph.D. diss., Kellogg School of Management, Northwestern University, 2000).
14. See, for example, Watson, D., and L. A. Clark, "Negative Affectivity: The Disposition to Experience Aversive Emotional States," *Psychological Bulletin* 96 (1984): 465–90; and Staw, B. M., and J. Ross, "Stability in the Midst of Change: A Dispositional Approach to Job Attitudes," *Journal of Applied Psychology* 70 (1985): 469–80.
15. Staw, B. M., N. E. Bell, and J. A. Clausen, "The Dispositional Approach to Job Attitudes: A Lifetime Longitudinal Test," *Administrative Science Quarterly* 31 (1986): 56–77.
16. McGhee, P. E., and J. H. Goldstein, *Handbook of Humor Research: Basic Issues,* Vol. 1 (New York: Springer-Verlag, 1991; and McGhee, P. E., and J. H. Goldstein, *Handbook of Humor Research: Applied Studies,* Vol. 2 (New York: Springer-Verlag, 1991).

17. See Sutton, R. I., and A. L. Callahan, "The Stigma of Bankruptcy: Spoiled Organizational Image and Its Management," *Academy of Management Journal* 30 (1987): 6. For example, one joke was, "My definition of waste is a busload of lawyers going off a cliff that has two empty seats."

18. Eisenhardt, K., J. L. Kahwajy, and L. J. Bourgeois III, "How Management Teams Can Have a Good Fight," *Harvard Business Review* (July-August 1997): 77–85.

19. Ibid., 81.

20. Zajonc, R. B., "Emotion and Facial Efference: An Ignored Theory Reclaimed," *Science* 228 (April 1985): 15–21; and Zajonc, R. B., S. T. Murphy, and M. Inglehart, "Feeling and Facial Efference: Implications of the Vascular Theory of Emotion," *Psychological Review* 96 (1989): 395–416.

21. Anderson, C. A., "Temperature and Aggression: Ubiquitous Effects of Heat on the Occurrence of Human Violence," *Psychological Bulletin* 106 (1989): 74–96; Baron, R., *Human Aggression* (New York: Plenum, 1977); and Griffitt, W., "Environmental Effects on Interpersonal Affective Behavior: Ambient-Effective Temperature and Attraction," *Journal of Personality and Social Psychology* 15 (1970): 240–44.

22. Isen, A. M., K. A. Daubman, and G. P. Nowicki, "Positive Affect Facilitates Creative Problem Solving," *Journal of Personality and Social Psychology* 52 (1987): 1122–31; and Isen, A. M., M. M. Johnson, E. Mertz, and G. F. Robinson, "The Influence of Positive Affect on the Unusualness of Word Associations," *Journal of Personality and Social Psychology* 48 (1985): 1413–26.

23. Isen, A. M., and R. A. Baron, "Positive Affect as a Factor in Organizational Behavior," in *Research in Organizational Behavior,* vol. 13, ed. L. L. Cummings and B. M. Staw (Greenwich, CT: JAI Press, 1991): 21.

24. See Seligman, M. E. P., *Helplessness* (San Francisco: Freeman, 1975); Abramson, L. Y., M. E. P. Seligman, and J. D. Teasdale, "Learned Helplessness in Humans: Critique and Reformulation," *Journal of Abnormal Psychology* 87 (1987): 32–48; and Seligman, M. E. P., and P. Schulman, "Explanatory Style as a Predictor of Productivity and Quitting Among Life Insurance Sales Agents," *Journal of Personality and Social Psychology* 50 (1986): 832–38.

25. See Taylor, S. E., *Positive Illusions* (New York: Basic Books, 1989); and Taylor, S. E., and J. D. Brown, "Illusion and Well-being: A Social Psychological Perspective on Mental Health," *Psychological Bulletin* 103 (1988): 193–210.

26. Isen, A. M., and N. Geva, "The Influence of Positive Affect on Acceptable Level of Risk: The Person with a Large Canoe Has a Large Worry," *Organization Behavior and Human Decision Processes* 39 (1987): 145–54; and Isen, A. M., and R. Patrick, "The Influence of Positive Affect on Risk Taking: When the Chips Are Down," *Organization Behavior and Human Performance* 31 (1983): 194–202.

27. Roberts, D. R., "The Influence of Emotional State on Decision-Making Under Risk" (Ph.D. diss., Palo Alto, CA: Graduate School of Business, Stanford University, 1993).

28. Hatfield, E., J. T. Cacioppo, and R. L. Rapson, *Emotional Contagion* (Cambridge, UK: Cambridge University Press, 1994); and M. J. Colligan, J. W. Pennebaker, and L. R. Murphy, *Mass Psychogenic Illness: A Social Psychological Analysis* (Hillsdale, NJ: Erlbaum, 1982).

**CHAPTER 9**

1. Kriegal, R., and D. Brandt, *Sacred Cows Make the Best Burgers* (New York: Warner Books, 1996), 97.

2. Seabrook, J., "Rocking in Shangri-la," *The New Yorker* (October 10, 1994), 73.

3. Simonton, D. K., "Creativity as Heroic: Risk, Failure, and Acclaim," in *Creative Action in Organizations,* ed. C. M. Ford and D. A. Gioia (Thousand Oaks, CA: Sage, 1995), 88.

4. Peters, T., *Thriving on Chaos* (New York: Harper & Row, 1987).

5. Pfeffer, J., and R. I. Sutton, *The Knowing-Doing Gap: How Smart Companies Turn Knowledge into Action* (Boston: Harvard Business School Press, 2000), 131.

6. Power, C., "Why So Many Flops?" *Business Week,* August 16, 1993.

7. Peters, *Thriving on Chaos,* 315.

8. Seabrook, "Rocking in Shangri-la."

9. Sitkin, S., "Learning Through Failure: The Strategy of Small Loses," in *Research in Organizational Behavior,* vol. 14, ed. B. M. Staw and L. L. Cummings (Greenwich, CT: JAI Press, 1992), 253.

10. Bennis, W., and Nanus, *Leaders: Strategies for Taking Charge* (New York: HarperBusiness, 1997), 70.

11. Lohr, S., "Belluzo to Microsoft: Ex-CEO of SGI Will Head Software Giant's Net Operations," *San Jose Mercury News,* August 25, 1999, 2C. This story was from the *New York Times* news service.

12. Bosk, C., *Forgive and Remember: Managing Medical Failure* (Chicago: University of Chicago Press, 1979), 178.

13. David, S., "Crank It Up," *Wired,* August 8, 2000, 184–97.

14. Hastings, D. F., "Lincoln Electric's Harsh Lessons from International Expansion," *Harvard Business Review* (May-June 1999) 178.

15. Simonton, "Creativity as Heroic."

16. Ibid., 88.

17. Pfeffer, J., and R. I. Sutton, "The Smart Talk Trap," *Harvard Business Review* (May-June 1999):135–42.

18. I am unable to reveal identifying information about this firm. In fact, a few incidental facts have been changed to further protect the identity of the company and team members.

19. Peacock, E., "Monica Mazzei," *Wallpaper* (July 2000): 31.

20. Anonymous, *Bringing Balance: Yin-Yang for Helios,* unpublished case report (Palo Alto, CA: Department of Industrial Engineering and Engineering Management, Stanford University, 1998).

## CHAPTER 10

1. March. J. G., "The Future, Disposable Organizations, and the Rigidities of Imagination." Presented at the annual meetings of The Academy of Management in Vancouver, B.C., August, 1995: 5.

2. Koppell, T., *Powering the Future* (New York: Wiley, 1999), 263.

3. Merton, R. K. "The Self-fulfilling Prophecy," *Antioch Review,* 1948, vol. 8: 193–210.

4. Speech by CEO Jorma Ollila of Nokia. Stanford Business School. March 6, 2001.

5. de Santillana, G., *Crime of Galileo* (Chicago: University of Chicago Press, 1978).

6. Howard, F., *Wilbur and Orville: A Biography of the Wright Brothers* (New York: Dover, 1998).

7. Cerf, C., and V. Navasky, *The Experts Speak: The Definitive Compendium of Authoritative Misinformation* (New York: Villard, 1998), 228.

8. Ibid., 330.

9. March. J. G., "Wild Ideas: The Catechism of Heresy," in *The Pursuit of Organizational Intelligence,* 226.

10. Rutan, B. *Breakthroughs: When and Why They Happen.* Speech given at the Innovative Thinking Conference, Scottsdale, Arizona. February 8th, 2001.
11. Talbot, M, "The Placebo Prescription," *The New York Times Magazine,* January 9, 2000.
12. Ibid., 27.
13. See Rosenthal, R., and D. B. Rubin, "Interpersonal Expectancy Effects: The First 345 Studies," *Behavioral and Brain Sciences* 3 (1978): 377–86; Rosenthal, R., and L. Jacobson, *Pygmalion in the Classroom: Teacher Expectations and Pupils' Intellectual Development* (New York: Holt, Rinehart & Winston, 1968); Livingston, J. S., "Pygmalion in Management," *Harvard Business Review* 47 (1969): 81–89; and Eden, D., "Self-Fulfilling Prophecy as a Management Tool: Harnessing Pygmalion," *Academy of Management Review* 9 (1984): 64–73; Eden, D., *Pygmalion in Management: Productivity as a Self-Fulfilling Prophecy* (Lexington, MA: Lexington Books, 1990).
14. Eden, D., and A. B. Shani, "Pygmalion Goes to Boot Camp: Expectancy, Leadership and Trainee Performance," *Journal of Applied Psychology* 67 (1982): 194–99.
15. Rubin, H., "Art of Darkness," *Fast Company* (October 1998): 132.
16. Koppell, *Powering the Future.*
17. Ibid., 185.
18. Maas, P., *The Terrible Hours: The Man Behind the Greatest Submarine Rescue in History* (New York: HarperCollins, 1999).
19. Weingartner, F., *Motorola: A Journey Through Time and Technology* (Schaumburg, IL: Motorola University Press, 1994).
20. Barboza, D., "Iridium, Bankrupt, Is Planning a Fiery Ending for Its 88 Satellites," *The New York Times,* August 11, 2000, C1, C5.
21. Freedman, D. H., "This Is Rocket Science," *Inc.* (July 2000): 75–88.
22. Ibid., 76.
23. Ibid., 82.
24. Nyberg, D., *The Varnished Truth* (Chicago: University of Chicago Press, 1993); and Bok, S., *Secrets: On the Ethics of Concealment and Revelation* (New York: Pantheon, 1984).

**CHAPTER 11**

1. Anton, T., *Bold Science* (New York: Freeman, 2000), 62.
2. Branson, R., *Losing My Virginity* (New York: Times Business, 1998), 153.
3. Ibid., 154.
4. Ibid., 156.
5. See www.homestead.com.
6. Justin Kitch, interview by Robert Sutton and Jeffrey Pfeffer at Homestead.com, Menlo Park, California, January 13, 2000.
7. Jensen, A., "Why the Best Technology for Escaping from a Submarine Is No Technology," *American Heritage of Invention and Technology* (Summer 1968): 44–49.
8. Osborn, A. F., *Applied Imagination,* 3d ed. (New York: Scribner's, 1963).
9. Ibid., 155.
10. Ibid., 156.
11. McGrath, J. E., *Groups: Interaction and Performance* (Englewood Cliffs, NJ: Prentice-Hall, 1984); and Offner, A. K., T. J. Kramer, and J. P. Winter, "The Effects of Facilitation, Recording, and Pauses on Group Brainstorming," *Small Group Research* 27 (1996): 283–98.
12. Sutton, R. I., and A. Hargadon, "Brainstorming Groups in Context: Effectiveness in a Product Design Firm," *Administrative Science Quarterly* 41 (1996): 685–718.

13. Vorhaus, J., *Creativity Rules: A Writers Handbook* (Los Angeles: Silman-James Press, 2000).

14. Ibid., 14.

15. Ibid., 15.

16. Pfeffer, J., and R. I. Sutton, *The Knowing-Doing Gap: How Smart Companies Turn Knowledge into Action* (Boston: Harvard Business School Press, 2000).

17. Behrens, S., "We'll Look Back on This Old Barney: An Early Input-Output Gizmo You Could Hug," *Current Online,* January 19, 1998, www.current.org/tech /tech801b.html.

18. Ibid.

19. Wherry, R., "Dumb and Dumber," *Forbes,* January 10, 2000, www.forbes.com/forbes /00/0110/6501056a.htm.

20. Ibid.

21. Stern, J., and M. Stern, *Pet Rocks: Encyclopedia of POP Culture* (New York: Harper-Perennial, 1992). Also see the Pet Rock page at www.virtualpet.com/vp/farm /petrock /petrock.htm.

22. Langer, E. J., "Minding Matters: The Consequences of Mindlessness-Mindfulness," in *Advances in Experimental Social Psychology,* ed. L. Berkowitz (New York: Academic Press, 1989), 137–73.

23. Ibid., 139.

24. Zajonc, R. A., "Emotions," in *Handbook of Social Psychology,* ed. D. T. Gilbert, S. T. Fiske, and G. Lindsey (New York: Oxford University Press, 1998), 591–634.

25. Schweiger, D. M., W. R. Sandberg, and P. L. Rechner, "Experiential Effects of Dialectical Inquiry, Devil's Advocacy, and Consensus Approaches to Strategic Decision Making," *Academy of Management Journal* 32 (1989): 745–72.

26. Janis, I. L., *Crucial Decisions: Leadership in Policymaking and Crisis Management* (New York: Free Press, 1989), 279.

27. Freiberg, K. and J. Freiberg, *Nuts: Southwest Airlines' Crazy Recipe for Business and Personal Success* (New York: Doubleday, 1998).

28. Anton, T., *Bold Science* (New York: Freeman, 2000).

29. Ibid., 62.

30. McGhee, P. E., and J. H. Goldstein, *Handbook of Humor Research: Basic Issues,* vol. 1 (New York: Springer-Verlag, 1991); and McGhee, P. E., and J. H. Goldstein, *Handbook of Humor Research: Applied Studies,* vol. 2 (New York: Springer-Verlag, 1991).

31. MacKenzie, G., *Orbiting the Giant Hairball: A Corporate Fool's Guide to Surviving With Grace* (New York: Viking, 1996).

32. Ibid., 122.

**CHAPTER 12**

1. Sitkin, S., K. M. Sutcliffe, and D. G. Schroeder, "Distinguishing Control from Learning in Total Quality Management: A Learning Perspective," *Academy of Management Review* 19 (1993): 537–64.

2. From a speech that William E. Coyne gave at Motorola University in Schaumburg, IL, July 11, 2000.

3. Asakura, R., *Revolutionaries at Sony* (New York: McGraw-Hill, 2000), 42.

4. Zajonc, R., "Social Facilitation," *Science* 149 (July 1965): 269–74.

5. Mullen, B., C. Johnson, and E. Salas, "Productivity Loss in Brainstorming Groups: A Meta-analytic Integration," *Basic and Applied Psychology* 12 (1991):2–23. See, for example, McLaughlin, J. B., and D. Reisman, "The Shady Side of Sunshine," *Teachers*

*College Record* 87 (1986):472–94. Sutton, R. I., and D. C. Galunic, "Consequences of Public Scrutiny for Leaders and Their Organizations," in *Research in Organizational Behavior*, vol. 18, ed. (Greenwich, CT: JAI Press, 1996): 201–50.

6. Kidder, T., *The Soul of a New Machine* (New York: Avon Books, 1981).

7. Nonaka, I., "Toward Middle-Up-Down Management: Accelerating Information Creation," *Sloan Management Review* (spring 1988): 9–18.

8. Kawasaki, G., *The Macintosh Way* (New York: Harper Collins, 1989), 16.

9. Rhodes, R., *The Making of the Atomic Bomb* (New York: Simon & Schuster. 1987; and Gleick, J., *Genius: The Life and Science of Richard Feynman* (New York: Pantheon, 1992), 160.

10. Hill, R. C., "When the Going Gets Tough: A Baldrige Award Winner on the Line," *Academy of Management Executive* 7 (1993): 75–79.

11. Ibid., 79.

12. McCracken, G., *Plenitude: Culture by Commotion* (Toronto: Periph.Fluide, 1997).

13. Ibid., 69.

14. Wetlaufer, S., "Common Sense and Conflict: An Interview with Disney's Michael Eisner," *Harvard Business Review* (January-February 2000): 119.

15. Metcalfe, B., "Invention Is a Flower, Innovation Is a Weed," *MIT Technology Review* (November/December 1999): 54–57.

16. Ibid., 57.

17. Balu, R., "Listen (No, Listen Carefully,)" *Fast Company* (May 2000): 307.

18. *@Issue Magazine*, vol. 6, no. 2. Fall, 2000: 16–23.

19. Druckerman, P., "How to Project Power Around the World," *Wall Street Journal*, November 13, 2000, A23, A26.

20. Amabile, T. M., "Unleashing Creativity," presentation at the Strategos Institute Revolutionaries' Conference, San Jose, California, June 13, 2000.

21. Amablie, T. M., "How to Kill Creativity," *Harvard Business Review* (September-October 1998):77–87.

22. Thuraisingham, C., and C. O'Reilly, *Homestead.com*, teaching case, Palo Alto, CA: Graduate School of Business, Stanford University, 2000.

23. From a speech by Tom Koogle delivered to Stanford's Mayfield Fellows in Woodside, California, July 30, 2000.

24. Herrigel, E., *Zen in the Art of Archery* (New York: Random House, 1981).

25. Schrage, M., "What's That Bad Odor at the Innovation Skunk Works?" *Fortune*, December 6, 1999.

26. Mintzberg, H. "The Manager's Job: Folklore and Fact," *Harvard Business Review* (1990) July–August: 49–61.

27. Gleick, Genius, 382.

28. Lazarus, R. S., "The Costs and Benefits of Denial," in *Stress and Coping: An Anthology*, ed. A. Monat and R. S. Lazarus. (New York: Columbia University Press, 1985), 154–73.

29. Personal communication from Herbert Simon to Mark Fichman, December 12, 2000. This point is also made in Simon, H. "Information Can Be Managed," *Think* 33(3), (1967): 8–12.

30. Kidder, T. *The Soul of a New Machine,* 60.

31. Schrage, M., *Serious Play* (Boston: Harvard Business School Press, 1999), 88.

32. Hertsgaard, M., *On Bended Knee: The Press and the Reagan Presidency* (New York: Schocken Books, 1989).

33. Galunic, C. D., "The Evolution of Intracorporate Domains: Divisional Charter Losses

in High Technology, Multidivisional Corporations," (Ph.D. diss. Palo Alto, CA: Stanford University, School of Engineering, 1994).

34. Eisenberg, E. M., "Ambiguity as a Strategy in Organizational Communication," *Communication Monographs* 51 (1984): 227–42.

35. Reid, R., *Architects of the Web: 1,000 Days that Built the Future of Business* (New York: Wiley, 1997), 125.

**CHAPTER 13**

1. Polanyi, M., "The Potential of Adsorption: Authority in Science has Its Uses and Its Dangers," *Science* 141 (1963): 1012.
2. Watson, J. L., "China's Big Mac Attack," *Foreign Affairs,* May-June 2000,
3. Tilin, A., "Supreme O," *Wired,* December 19, 1999, 178.
4. Gleick, J., *Genius: The Life and Science of Richard Feynman* (New York: Pantheon, 1992), 324.
5. Ibid., 387.
6. Goodall, J., *In the Shadow of Man* (New York: Houghton Mifflin, 1988), 6.
7. Dyson, J., *Against the Odds* (London: Orion Business Books, 1997), 264–65.
8. Asakura, R., *Revolutionaries at Sony* (New York: McGraw-Hill, 2000), 229.
9. Gundling, E., *The 3M Way to Innovation: Balancing People and Profit* (New York: Kodansha, 2000).
10. Koppell, T., *Powering the Future* (New York: Wiley, 1999), 15.
11. Salter, C., "Life in the Fast Lane," *Fast Company* (October 1998): 78.
12. Millard, A., *Edison and the Business of Innovation* (Baltimore: Johns Hopkins University Press, 1990), 9.

**CHAPTER 14**

1. Anton, T., *Bold Science* (New York: Freeman, 2000), 12.
2. Grove, A., *Only the Paranoid Survive* (New York: Doubleday, 1996), 89.
3. Coutu, D. L., "Creating the Most Frightening Company on Earth: An Interview with Andy Law of St. Luke's," *Harvard Business Review* (September-October 2000): 146.
4. Langer, E. J., "Minding Matters: The Consequences of Mindlessness-Mindfulness," in *Advances in Experimental Social Psychology,* ed. L. Berkowitz (New York: Academic Press, 1989), 137–73.
5. Asakura, R., *Revolutionaries at Sony* (New York: McGraw-Hill, 2000), 17.
6. March, J. G., "Three Lectures on Efficiency and Adaptiveness in Organizations," Swedish School of Economics, Helsinki, Finland, 1994, 53.
7. Tushman, M. L., and C. O'Reilly III, *Winning Through Innovation* (Boston: Harvard Business School Press, 1997); and Christensen, C., *The Innovator's Dilemma* (Boston: Harvard Business School Press, 1998).
8. Tushman, M. L., P. C. Andersen, and C. O'Reilly III, "Technology Cycles, Innovation Streams, and Ambidextrous Organizations: Organizational Renewal Through Innovation Streams and Strategic Change," in *Managing Strategic Innovation and Change,* ed. M. L. Tushman and P. C. Andersen (New York: Oxford University Press, 1996).
9. Pfeffer, J., and R. I. Sutton, *The Knowing-Doing Gap: How Smart Companies Turn Knowledge into Action* (Boston: Harvard Business School Press, 2000).
10. Interview with Gary High, director of Human Resource Development, People Systems, Saturn Corporation, Detroit, Michigan, March 25, 1998.
11. Burrows, P., and P. Elstrom "HP's Carly Fiorina: The Boss," *Business Week,* August 2, 1999.

12. Hamel, G., *Leading the Revolution* (Boston: Harvard Business School Press, 2000).

13. Alinsky, S., *Rules for Radicals* (New York: Vintage Books, 1989).

14. Hamel, G., "Waking Up IBM," *Harvard Business Review* (July–August 2000): 5–11.

15. Ibid., 9.

16. This material comes from an interview with Annette Kyle on September 17, 1998. For a more complete description of Kyle's revolution, see Pfeffer and Sutton, *The Knowing-Doing Gap*.

17. MacFarquhar, L., "The Gilder Effect," *The New Yorker*, May 29, 2000, 103–111.

18. LaBarre, P., "The Company Without Limits," *Fast Company* (September 1999): 160–70.

19. See "Human Resources at the AES Corporation: The Case of the Missing Department," Case #SHR-3 (Palo Alto, CA: Graduate School of Business, Stanford University, 1997); and O'Reilly III, C. A., and J. Pfeffer, *Hidden Value* (Boston: Harvard Business School Press, 2000).

20. "Human Resources at AES," 15.

21. Katz, R., "The Effects of Group Longevity on Project Communication and Performance," *Administrative Science Quarterly* 27 (1982): 81–104; and Katz, R., and T. J. Allen, "Investigating the Not-Invented-Here Syndrome: A Look at Performance, Tenure, and Communication Patterns of 50 R&D Project Groups," *R&D Management* 12 (1982): 7–19.

22. Gersick, C., and J. G. and J. R. Hackman, "Habitual Routines in Task-Performing Groups," *Organizational Behavior and Human Decision Processes* 47 (1990): 65–97.

23. LaBarre, P., "This Organization Is Disorganization," *Fast Company* (June 1996): 77–80.

24. Ibid., 80.

25. Ibid.

26. Wilson, T. D., and J. W. Schooler, "Thinking Too Much: Introspection Can Reduce the Quality of Preferences and Decisions," *Journal of Personality and Social Psychology* 60 (1991): 181.

27. Slowiczek, H., and P. M. Peters, *Discovery, Chance, and the Scientific Method*, www.accessexcellence.com, October 1, 2000.

28. Chang, K., "Chemistry Nobel Recognizes Work in Plastics," *The New York Times*, November 11, 2000, A23.

29. Weick, K., "The Collapse of Sensemaking in Organizations: The Mann Gulch Disaster," *Administrative Science Quarterly* 38 (1993): 628–52.

30. Ibid., 641–42.

31. Ibid., 642.

32. Haslam, S. A. et al., "Inspecting the Emperor's Clothes: Evidence that Randomly Selected Leaders Can Enhance Group Performance," *Group Dynamics: Theory, Process and Research* 2 (1998): 168–84.

33. Malkiel, B. G., *A Random Walk Down Wall Street*, 7th ed. (New York: Norton, 2000).

34. Ibid., 1.

35. Weick, K. E., and R. L. Daft, "The Effectiveness of Interpretation Systems," in *Organizational Effectiveness: A Comparison of Multiple Models*, ed. K. S. Cameron and D. A. Whetten (New York: Academic Press, 1983), 74.

36. Bennis, W., *Why Leaders Can't Lead* (San Francisco: Jossey-Bass), 21.

37. Matlin, M., and D. Stang, *The Pollyanna Principle* (Cambridge, MA: Schenkman, 1978).

38. Anonymous, "Business: Rebuilding the Garage," *The Economist*, July 15, 2000, 59–60.

39. www.hp.com/ghp/features/invent/gene.pdf.

40. Surowiecki, J., "The Billion-Dollar Blade," *The New Yorker*, June 15, 1998, 43–49.
41. Ibid. p. 46.

**CHAPTER 15**

1. This experiment was described to me in a telephone interview I conducted with Freada Klein on October 12, 2000.
2. Fishman, C., "Creative Tension," *Fast Company* (November 2000): 358–88.
3. From a speech that William E. Coyne gave at Motorola University in Schaumburg, IL, July 11. 2000.
4. MacKenzie, G., *Orbiting the Giant Hairball* (New York: Viking, 1998), 63.
5. Ibid., 64.
6. Pfeffer, J., R. B. Cialdini, B. Hanna, and K. Knopoff, "Faith in Supervision and Self-Enhancement Bias: Two Psychological Reasons why Managers Don't Empower Workers, *Basic and Applied Psychology* 20 (1998): 313–21.
7. Shields, D., "The Good Father," *The New York Times Magazine*, April 23, 2000, 58–61.
8. Ibid., 60.
9. Ibid.
10. Hargadon, A., and Y. Douglas, "When Innovations Meet Institutions: Edison and the Design of the Electric Light," working paper, Warrington College of Business Administration, September 2000. University of Florida Gainesville
11. Ibid., 19.
12. Metcalfe, B., "Invention Is a Flower, Innovation Is a Weed," *MIT Technology Review* (November/December 1999): 56.
13. See, for example, Burgelman, R. A., "A Process Model of Internal Corporate Venturing in the Diversified Firm," *Administrative Science Quarterly* 28 (1983): 223–44.
14. Ngueyen, P. D., "A Faster Plan," *Red Herring* (May 2000): 138–46.
15. Cialdini, R. B., *Influence: The New Psychology of Modern Persuasion* (New York: Quill, 1984).
16. Rock, A., "Strategy vs. Tactics from a Venture Capitalist," *Harvard Business Review* (November–December 1987).
17. Elsbach, K. D., and R. M. Kramer, "Assessing Images of Others' Creativity: Impression Formation in the Hollywood Pitch," working paper, Palo Alto, CA: Graduate School of Business, Stanford University, (1999).
18. Ngueyen, "A Faster Plan," 144.
19. Sobel, D., *Longitude: The True Story of a Lone Genius Who Solved the Greatest Scientific Problem of His Time* (New York: Penguin, 1996), 8.
20. www.rog.nmm.ac.uk/museum/harrison/longprob.html, the Royal Observatory, Greenwich, England (downloaded December 21, 2000).
21. Surowiecki, J., "The Billion-Dollar Blade," *The New Yorker*, June 15, 1998, 43–49.
22. Dahle, C., "The Agenda–Social Justice," *Fast Company* (April 1999): 166–82.
23. Platt, L., "Magic Johnson Builds an Empire," *The New York Times Magazine*, December 10, 2000, 118–21.
24. Chapman, C., "Designed to Work," *Fast Company* (April 2000): 259–68.
25. Ibid., 256.
26. Ibid., 268.
27. MacFarquhar, L., "Looking for Trouble," *The New Yorker*, December 6, 1999.
28. Ibid., 80.
29. Ibid., 78.
30. Dow Jones Online News, Monday, June 26, 2000.

31. Some identifying features of this firm and process are changed to protect their anonymity, but the crucial facts: that the process contained multiple stages, was too complex, and that no product had ever made it through this gauntlet, are true.

32. Slater, R. *Jack Welch and the GE Way* (New York: McGraw-Hill, 1999), 135.

33. From an interview by Jeffrey Pfeffer and Robert Sutton with Peter McInnes and Vidya Nayak in Santa Clara, California, on December 9, 1999, and an e-mail message from Ginger Graham on December 29, 2000.

34. Steve Jobs, from a speech given at DeAnza College's Flint Center, Cupertino, California, on May 6, 1998.

35. From an interview Robert Sutton conducted with Jeff Hawkins on August 2, 2000.

36. Fishman, C., "Creative Tension," *Fast Company* (November 2000): 358–88.

37. March, J. G., "The Future, Disposable Organizations, and the Rigidities of Imagination." Presented at the annual meetings of The Academy of Management in Vancouver, B.C., August, 1995: 4–5.

38. Ybarra, M. J., "Medicine Woman: It's a Jungle Out there," *SV: The San Jose Mercury News Sunday Magazine,* July 25, 1999, 11.

39. Ross, J. and B. M. Staw, "Organizational Escalation and Exit: Lessons from the Shoreham Nuclear Power Plant," *Academy of Management Journal 36* (1993): 701–732.

40 Bunnell, D. *Making the Cisco Connection* (New York: Wiley, 2000), 75.

41. Saxenian, A., *Regional Advantage: Culture and Competition in Silicon Valley and Route 128* (Cambridge: Harvard University Press, 1996).

42. Rivette, K., and D. Kline, *Rembrandt's in the Attic* (Boston: Harvard Business School Press, 1999).

43. Heilman, J., "The Next Big Idea," *The New Yorker,* February 23 and March 2, 1998.

44. O'Brien, T., "The Think Tank that Tanked," *Silicon Valley Magazine* (September 2000): 3.

45. Ibid.

46. Ibid.

47. Raymond, E. S., *The Cathedral & the Bazaar, Musings on Linux and Open Source by an Accidental Revolutionary* (O'Reilly: Sebastopol, CA, 1999), 27.

48. www.gnu.org/copyleft/copyleft.html.

49. Ibid.

# INDEX